SOCIAL POLICY
Institutional Context
of Social Development
and Human Services

Demetrius Iatridis
Boston College

Brooks/Cole Publishing Company
Pacific Grove, California

I**T**P™ The trademark ITP is used under license.

To Mary, Anna, Tanya, Stavros, and Makis

A CLAIREMONT BOOK

Brooks/Cole Publishing Company
A Division of Wadsworth, Inc.

Printed in the United States of America
10 9 8 7 6 5 4 3 2 1

Library of Congress Cataloging-in-Publication Data

Iatridis, Demetrius S.
   Social policy : institutional context of social development and
   human services / Demetrius Iatridis.
       p.   cm.
   Includes bibliographical references and index.
   ISBN 0-534-19212-2
   1. Social policy.   2. Economic policy.   3. Welfare state.
   I. Title.
   HN28.I26   1994
   361.6′1—dc20   93-24327
                                                                      CIP

Sponsoring Editor: *Claire Verduin*
Marketing Representative: *John Moroney*
Editorial Associate: *Gay C. Bond*
Production Editor: *Laurel Jackson*
Manuscript Editor: *Meg Korones*
Permissions Editor: *Karen Wootten*
Interior and Cover Design: *Sharon L. Kinghan*
Art Coordinator: *Susan Haberkorn*
Interior Illustration: *LM Graphics*
Indexer: *Do Mi Stauber*
Typesetting: *Bookends Typesetting*
Printing and Binding: *Malloy Lithographing, Inc.*

Contents

Preface

The focus of this book is on understanding and assessing public social policy. By introducing students and practitioners to the societal context of policy planning, I emphasize how the institutional forces of society—ideological, political, social, economic, and cultural—combine to influence policy making.

In this book, readers are introduced to the societal context of worldwide social policy. As citizens of a worldwide community, we rely increasingly on a global viewpoint and approach social policy from different cultural and ideological perspectives.

Because of this, I emphasize several controversial, ideological issues of social policy: the distributive role of government, the growth of the welfare state, social justice and equality, individual and collective freedom and democracy, materialism and altruism, the morality of the free market versus the managed economy, the persistence of unemployment and poverty, the boundaries of well-being, and the empowerment of individuals and communities. Who is responsible for determining the quality of life or for providing solutions? Who should bear the costs and reap the benefits of societal development? What justifies governmental action or inaction? The worldwide controversies surrounding these issues highlight the nature of social policy and the dilemmas inherent in selecting alternative solutions to major societal problems.

Although both the public and private sectors are central to society's well-being and are symbiotic, I focus on the concerns of the public sector. Governmental action—or inaction—provides more regular, decisive parameters of a country's social policy because it reflects the crucial character of the social contract between the modern state and its citizens.

Although several excellent books on social policy are available, most do not focus on an institutional, worldwide approach. For example, many authors concentrate on social welfare programs, poverty data, and the characteristics of the poor; others focus on current or past social policies; some are concerned with the historical evolution of social services; and still others approach the issues from an administrative or organizational perspective. In this book, I neither describe nor prescribe social services and social welfare programs. Instead, the focus is on broad concepts of social policy as a vehicle for providing citizenship rights to all people. A model of social, economic, and cultural forces on policy formulation is presented, together with analyses of alternative social policy solutions.

This book is designed for graduate courses in social policy, policy analysis, and the welfare state, courses offered primarily in schools of social work. However, it might also be appropriate to use this book in other programs.

To emphasize the importance of social policy in preventing and solving modern societal problems, I begin each chapter with several quotations from newspapers and other mass media. This will help the reader to connect theoretical policy concepts with actual social conditions and to understand that social problems are indeed controversial.

Part One of this book is concerned with the nature, scope, and practice of social policy. It includes a model that demonstrates the institutional context of social policy making. This model is used in Part Two to analyze the influence of policy theory on practice and the relationships between ideology, political power, the free market, the welfare state, well-being, and poverty.

Each chapter draws on concepts from different disciplines to show the multidimensional aspects of social policy. The systems approach used here provides the elasticity needed to connect social institutions. Recognizing these connections helps one realize that knowing a single aspect of social policy requires understanding its relation to the whole.

Books like this represent a shared enterprise. As George Seferis, poet and Nobel prizewinner, suggests, "Our words are the children of many peoples." I owe a great debt to all the scholars on whose work I rely concerning many of the policy issues central to this book. Their ideas, experience, and research have proven invaluable.

I am also grateful to my students, colleagues, and critics for their contributions. My students, who have articulated the need for a book like this, have been tolerant and patient. They have also made valuable suggestions about material in several versions of the manuscript. I greatly appreciate their ideas for alternative approaches to teaching social policy.

My thanks to the reviewers who read earlier versions or parts of the manuscript and suggested countless improvements. They include James F. Flanagan, Providence College; Alejandro Garcia, Syracuse University; Leon Ginsberg, University of South Carolina; June Hopps, Boston College; Thaddeus P. Mathis, Temple University; David F. Metzger, Indiana University; S. M. Miller, Boston University; John Morrison, Aurora University; Diane Lyden Murphy, Syracuse University; and Donald Schon, Massachusetts Institute of Technology. However, I bear full responsibility for any errors or limitations that may be found in this book.

Kevin James of Boston College's secretarial department and Scott Kinder of the College's computer design department generously helped with word processor complications and computer design of the figures.

I am especially grateful to my family and friends for their endless support and understanding. This book could not have been completed without their encouragement and tolerance.

Demetrius Iatridis

Social Policy in a Global Perspective: Frameworks of Analysis

Social policy has two related characteristics. First, social policies do not exist in a vacuum. Rather, they result from the institutional transformation of socioeconomic systems. Second, social policy is macro; it concerns preventing and solving major societal problems. To understand any part of social policy, we must understand the whole: the transactions between people and their environment, and the sociocultural context of social policy.

Social policies do not exist in a vacuum. They result from the socioeconomic environment and its ideological, political, economic, cultural, legal, and technological forces. Unless we understand the sociocultural and economic context of social policy, we cannot assess how to solve or prevent societal problems.

Social workers recognize that policies differ among societies because they result from and reflect the institutional environment of each society: its values, norms, conflicts, ambivalences, and laws; its power structure, economic organization, social stratification, and types of government and family; and its racial and ethnic landscape. Democratic societies establish social policies that encourage democratic behavior, and dictatorial societies establish social policies that promote oppressive behavior.

It is important to understand the influence of major institutions and the cultural milieu on social policies. Why do governments foster or reject certain policies? Why do policymakers (including the U.S. Supreme Court—a major instrument of national social policy making) reject or incorporate competing ideologies and conflicting interests of social classes or population groups? For example, what is the context of the U.S. Supreme Court's 5–4 abortion decision in 1992? It reaffirmed a woman's constitutional right to abortion before fetal viability, but it also authorized state regulation of that right. It did not overturn *Roe* v. *Wade,* yet it authorized states to restrict abortion rights.

Social workers also recognize that social policy influences human behavior, the relations among people, and society's functions. The Supreme Court's 1992 decision concerning abortion places American women into two classes: those who live in the "right" states or have money to travel and can therefore easily obtain abortions; and those who cannot—the young, the poor, and those living in rural areas. Social workers know that as a result of parental notification laws, the parents of a teenager seeking an abortion might impose severe restrictions or punishments rather than discourage abortion.

1

Social policy is macro. Understanding the macro-level dimension of social policies requires analyzing the whole and viewing social problems in the context of interactions between people and the environment. For example, the disadvantaged fare worse now than they did a generation ago, partly because governmental policies today are less helpful to them. At the same time that good jobs are disappearing, the government has reduced aid to those hurt by the changing economy. During the Reagan years, government programs designed for the economically disadvantaged shrank by $51 billion; the Bush administration continued the policy of cutting aid for the disadvantaged. President Clinton, however, has indicated that his administration will increase social services, particularly health care.

Hunger also illustrates the macro approach to social policy. International development officials relate famine to poor methods of food production and distribution; misguided trade policies; and bad sanitation, roads, schools, and health care. These officials also attribute the problem of hunger to the absence of political reform, liberalization, or stability; the lack of a free and vigorous press; the stifling of political expression; the lack of entitlements for cash or relief for the unemployable; and the need for a substantial infusion of long-term capital investment.

Ending the calamity of hunger requires much more than generous donations of humanitarian aid. The recent famines in Ethiopia and Somalia are good examples. Today, famine can occur even when the overall supply of food is sufficient to feed everyone in the United States or on the entire planet. Hunger is both a social and a natural event. Food prices rise because demand increases faster than supply, the population may be barred from buying even when plenty of food is stored, and political instability or discrimination may prevent the distribution of food.

The macro characteristics of social policy require the use of effective approaches and analytic tools. These are frequently derived from the complementarity of macro and micro views and from the perspectives of social economy, class analysis, globalization, and comparative ideological analysis.

THE COMPLEMENTARITY
OF MICRO AND MACRO LEVELS

Micro, or clinical, approaches concern work with individuals, families, and small groups. Macro, or policy-planning, approaches concern work with organizations, communities, institutions, or societies. Social policy planners view micro and macro approaches, the people-environment fit, as interlocking elements of social work practice. Although antithetical in some respects, micro and macro approaches are complementary, and both are necessary in social policy planning. In social work practice, macroanalysis strengthens microanalysis, and a micro perspective enriches that of macro approaches. For example, clinical social workers use macroanalysis to understand clients' behavior and the environmental forces that influence it. Workers must also understand the macro forces in society in order to introduce changes that prevent behavioral dysfunction and to accelerate growth and development of individuals and groups. Although their focus is on individual and group behavior, clinical social workers are necessarily concerned with social changes that will meet socially recognized needs. As a profession, social work is committed to change in the context of a person-environment model. In other words, we are committed to transforming social conditions and institutional arrangements (including racism, sexism, and ageism) that do not meet societal needs and that undermine individual and social development.

In this context, social work practice is both therapeutic and reformist, aiming at both adjustment of individuals and transformation of social conditions. Social workers know that helping clients adjust to malfunctioning environments is not enough; we should also aim to transform dysfunctional conditions and institutions in society. Micro approaches alone, without their macro counterparts, are likely to obscure the broad societal problems (hunger, power imbalance, discrimination, economic mismanagement, and social underdevelopment) that influence the lives of social work clients.

On the other hand, social workers view clinical (micro) theory and approaches as central in formulating social policies. If social policies are to promote individual and societal well-being, they must flow from theories of human development and social functioning. Effective theories are crucial because social policy aims to prevent dysfunction and promote the growth and development of individuals, families, groups, and communities. Social policy practice links the macro and micro concerns of social work.

SOCIAL ECONOMY

The broad perspective of *social economy* is an effective tool of macrolevel analysis. Social economy, or political economy, analyzes the relations of people to the economy and highlights the fundamental institutional forces and conflicts inherent in social policy.[1] But while political economy focuses on understanding the state and power, social economy transcends these boundaries and encompasses the broader relations of the economy to individuals and to society.

For example, both famine and the empowerment of individuals and communities are related not only to the power of the state, but also to societal values, the behavior of individuals and communities, and the psychology of deprivation. Social economy provides a macro perspective of society and its political and socioeconomic context. It helps us understand the links between the individual and society, between the environment and social work clients.

CLASS ANALYSIS

Class analysis (whether Weberian or Marxist) is another comprehensive, useful way to assess public social policy and its fundamental controversial issues.[2] Class determines who gets what and who is treated fairly. As suggested by Titmuss and others, class is the degree of ability to have command over resources through time.[3] Social scientists have long debated the relevant approaches or dimensions in the study of social policy; each approach (class analysis, socioeconomic stratification, pluralism, the life cycle) has its protagonists and critics. I believe class analysis allows for an approach

that encompasses macro concepts that highlight the institutional concerns and conflicts of social policy. Class analysis can help us assess fundamental issues like social
justice and equality, income and taxation, unemployment, education, housing, AIDS,
homelessness, social security, and the legal system.

For example, social phenomena based on power, such as poverty and deprivation, can best be understood by analyzing those who have and those who do not:
ethnic and racial groups, men and women, or the lower, middle, and upper classes.
A higher rank in the hierarchy or greater control over the productive processes of
society increase access to scarce and valued resources.

GLOBAL PICTURE OF SOCIAL POLICY

Social workers—as citizens of a worldwide community, members of a helping profession, and participants in an international labor market—must understand and assess
clients' needs and social policy approaches in different cultural and ideological systems.
Since the avalanche of changes in telecommunication and transportation in the 1980s
and 1990s has brought the world together, social workers function in an interdependent global context. Our lives are now influenced directly by economic, social, and
political development or crises in other countries; major institutions, including corporations, banks, and labor markets, recognize no national boundaries. Because social,
economic, and political crises are now more globalized than ever before, social workers
must be aware of the need to understand and assess social policy today in the context
of fundamental, worldwide public conflicts.

A global perspective that transcends nationalistic and ethnocentric limitations
helps us understand the significance of alternative solutions to perennial problems
of social policy. Different ideological systems solve social problems in different ways.
The emergence of federations of nations, including the European Community, North
America, the countries of the Pacific Rim, and Latin America, make global approaches
and understanding crucial.

IDEOLOGICAL ANALYSIS

Comparative social policy analysis must include the ideological base of social policies.
"Neutral social policy" is an oxymoron, and so is "neutral analysis." Ideology[4]
permeates social institutions and plays a central role in social policy making; it is a
tightly knit system of beliefs organized around a few central values, such as capitalism,
socialism, communism, nationalism, freedom, fairness, or family. Ideological analysis
provides a theoretical foundation for social workers to review and assess the ideological
base of social policy.

Comparative social policy analysis demonstrates the basic nature of social policy
and its fundamental role in society, the characteristic forms that social policy takes,
the fundamental relationship between social policy and the institutional environment,
and the crucial implications of major social policy alternatives. By observing many
individuals, social workers better understand patterns of human behavior; by observing

a wide spectrum of social policy forms in major ideological systems, analysts can understand the social policy in a given community or country. Comparative social policy analysis highlights the common elements and cohesiveness of social policy, its goals and objectives, the common institutional factors at work, the implications of alternative social policies, and the underlying reasons for different social policies.

For example, by contrasting social policy associated with major socialist and capitalist perspectives, we can understand better the fundamental values of social justice, democracy, freedom, the management of the state and the economy, fairness, and empowerment. My intent in this text is not to endorse either socialism or capitalism; this is the responsibility of each social worker.

In this text I use the terms *socialist* and *capitalist* to represent the entire continuum of ideologies, from radical to conservative. Both the socialist and the capitalist perspectives consist of clusters of different but similar orientations. American capitalism differs from capitalism in Sweden, Denmark, or France; there are also many models of socialism. The socialist-capitalist continuum represents many different radical and conservative perspectives on issues like governmental control of the economy, centralization or decentralization of decision making, delivery of human services, private and state ownership, and power concentration. The left pole of the continuum represents radical perspectives; the right pole, conservative views; and the middle of the continuum, moderate orientations. For example, the United States—with a relatively noninterventionist government and a limited welfare state—is at the right side of the continuum, whereas Sweden—a country with relatively strong governmental guidance of the economy and a strong welfare state—is located near the center. Communism and socialism are represented by the left side of the continuum.

I use the socialist and capitalist perspectives to illuminate issues of social policy that go beyond political parties and transcend contemporary political developments in various countries. The collapse of central command planning and communist parties in Central and Eastern Europe, the incorporation of East and West Germany, the emergence of the European Economic Community, and the crisis of values in the United States and other capitalist countries have intensified the need to explore new social policy alternatives. Social policy analysts recognize that patterns of freedom, democracy, social justice, fairness, and empowerment for human development are inherent in the very nature of social policy and are crucial in selecting alternative social policies.

OBJECTIVITY AND BIAS

Researchers try to be objective in assessing normative concepts inherent in social policy, but the task is difficult, if not impossible. Social workers' professional training, ways of thinking, and value commitments influence their approaches to practice. Both capitalist and socialist perspectives suffer these limitations.

Socialism tends to suppress political freedom and human rights and fosters a one-party monopoly, despotic centralization, and elitism. Capitalism on the other hand, tends to generate perennial poverty amid affluence and endemic powerlessness amid a monopolistic concentration of power.

Although I contrast socialist and capitalist perspectives, my intent is to underline the cohesive role of ideology and the unity of ideology in social policy. This book aims to promote synthesis, not dichotomy, and to enhance the understanding of merging ideologies that some commentators see evolving.⁵

But, while avoiding polarization and enhancing synthesis, I do not pretend to be neutral when discussing social policy issues. Rather, I wish to make it clear that I believe in the following:

- The universal right to economic, social, cultural, and political freedom
- The universal right to vital community resources for survival, empowerment, and social development
- Distributive social justice and equity favoring the less powerful
- Governmental responsibility for well-being and citizenship rights
- Active participation of citizens in determining both their future and the use of scarce resources
- Self-determination and self-government

While these are my values, I encourage students and readers to formulate their own perspectives and conclusions. One challenging and rewarding aspect of social policy is the intellectually rich debate about the meaning of life and its quality for all citizens in modern society. I earnestly hope that students and readers will challenge their own perspectives and open new visions in their work.

NOTES

1. Although the term *political economy,* which comes to mind in these cases, describes the institution of the state and its power in relation to the economy and society, the term *social economy* encompasses all the relations of the economy in the context of society. Transcending the boundaries of power and the state as political institutions, social economy, in my view, expresses more completely the total human reality.
2. In ordinary usage, *class* is variously defined in terms of income, wealth, occupation, status, lifestyle, and family background. This is appropriate in public social policy perspectives because it emphasizes the way in which society links social justice and unequal work situations with wealth, income, power, and status. Although Marx analyzed class in relation to the ownership of capital and the means of production, others define class in various economic terms. Still others suggest that class is not mainly economic.
3. Although this ability may be affected by other variables, such as age and gender, these dimensions can also be included in the dimension of class. See R. M. Titmuss, *Problems of Social Policy* (London: Her Majesty's Stationery Office, 1950); *Social Policy, An Introduction* (London: Allen & Unwin, 1974); and *The Gift Relationship: From Blood to Social Policy* (London: Allen & Unwin, 1970).
4. One of the most debated concepts in social sciences, ideology can be defined as beliefs, attitudes, and opinions that form a tightly or a loosely related set. Popularized by L. Althusser, the term *ideological state apparatus* refers to one means by which the domination of one class is secured. It functions by incorporating all classes in society within a dominant ideology. Religious and educational institutions, the media of communication, the family, trade unions, and political parties are examples of this apparatus. See the following works: L. Althusser, *For Marx* (London: Allen Lane, The Penguin Press, 1969); L. Althusser,

Lenin and Philosophy and Other Essays (London: New Left Bank, 1971); A. Callinicos, *Althusser's Marxism* (London: Pluto Press, 1976); and E. P. Thompson, *The Poverty of Theory* (London: Merlin, 1978).

5. It has been suggested by supporters of the social-convergence theory that, given the logic of industrialization, all societies will tend to be secular, urban, mobile, and democratic. An industrial global society will be based on a new form of consensus; this may reduce major ideological differences. The social-convergence theory claims that all societies converge to a common point because effective industrialization requires certain characteristics, such as the social and technical division of labor, separation of the family from the workplace, a mobile work force, and some form of rational economic planning. It is far from clear, however, whether all societies must assume a common form of industrialization or whether considerable industrial variation is compatible with a common industrial base. The convergence thesis, typical of the optimistic analysis of industrial society that was common in the early 1960s, is linked both with the "end of ideology" theory and with development theory, which regards Western society as the only appropriate model of rapid economic progress.

APPROACHES TO SOCIAL POLICY

My goal in Part One is to explore the nature and scope of social policy—that is, to provide a frame of reference for understanding its implications for social work practice. Chapter 1 focuses on the institutional nature and boundaries of social policy as a field; it includes a discussion of the fundamental assumptions of social policy and a model of its institutional environment. Chapter 2 explains the process of analyzing and planning social policies.

Social policy has many definitions: broad or narrow, comprehensive or partial, public or private, exclusionary or inclusive of population groups or societal functions, and oriented toward either theory or practice. No definition is accepted in all professions or countries. In market (capitalist) countries, social policy usually targets selected population groups, problems, or functions of society. Social policy tends to be decentralized to regional and local authorities, eclectic in goals and programs, and associated mainly with social welfare, the poor, and the disadvantaged. In contrast, nonmarket (socialist) social policy is centralized at the national bureaucratic level and usually provides universal coverage.

Leaders of different countries and the general public perceive the nature and scope of social policy in different ways. American commentators find the debate over definitions of social policy and social welfare useful and informative, but unpopular, and the debate does not ordinarily yield special insights into the subject. Therefore, I analyze social policy selectively to highlight its fundamental approaches and basic principles. Without some frame of reference, it is difficult to gain even a general understanding of the nature of social policy.

CHAPTER 1

Social Policy
as a Field

"Unlike 70 nations worldwide, the United States does not provide medical care and financial assistance to all pregnant women; unlike 61 nations worldwide, it does not insure or provide basic medical care to all workers and their dependents; unlike 63 nations, it does not provide a family allowance to workers and their children; and unlike 17 industrialized nations, it does not have paid maternity/paternity-leave programs."[1]

"Since 1980 the People's Republic of China has strongly urged parents in urban areas to have only one child,[2] while Greece provides a cash benefit for each additional child to all families, regardless of income or residence."[3]

"American policy permits women to be paid less than men for the same job. The average weekly earnings of women are 52–82% of men's earnings."[4]

"Sweden's government-spending rate is 39.1% of the country's gross national product (GNP), while the U.S. rate is 21% of the U.S. GNP."[5]

"The United States has more income inequality than do most European countries.[6] In the past two decades, especially during the 1980s, the rich in the United States became much wealthier, while the poor grew even more desperate as their real income deteriorated at an even faster rate."[7]

"In Brazil 50–60% of all income is captured by the highest 10% of all households, while only 2% of all income goes to the poorest 20% of all households. In the United States the top 20% of all households receives 39.9% of all income, while the lowest 20% receives only 5.3% of income."[8]

"The White House and Congress may intervene again in the crisis of the savings and loan associations. The $164 billion rescue operation by the federal government is faltering; $300–$400 billion may be needed to save the industry."[9]

" 'This White House prefers its tax police to get after the bottom- and middle-income taxpayers, not the rich,' said the commissioner of the U.S. Internal Revenue Service."[10]

"Children in [the United States] are more likely to live in poverty, live with one parent, or be killed than are children in other industrialized nations: Australia, Canada,

France, Germany, Hungary, the former Soviet Union, and the United Kingdom.[11] Young American males are five times more likely to be murdered as are those in other developed countries."[12]

THE SOCIETAL CONTEXT OF SOCIAL POLICY

These quotations from daily newspapers indicate that governments tolerate some social conditions and ignore others and that conditions tolerated in some countries are not accepted in others. How does social policy relate to social conditions and to how governments view social problems?

Social policy concerns basic questions about the well-being of individuals, groups, and communities. Why do governments not establish policies to prevent or change undesirable social conditions and thus improve societal well-being? Why do some countries have more income inequality than others? Why do only some governments provide protection from societal ills and establish programs to prevent them? Why do some countries encourage population growth while others either discourage it or have no comprehensive demographic or family planning policies? Why has the U.S. government of the early 1990s been willing and able to subsidize the banking industry while curtailing programs for families?

The Institutional Framework

Analysis of society's institutions can help answer these complex questions. Institutions such as the government, the economic market, the educational system, religions, and the family constitute the context of social policy. They reflect a country's ideology, social practices, organizational system, laws, and technology. The parameters of public social policy are the relationships that exist among culture, technology, the state, production, distribution, the family, the size and distribution of incomes and power among social classes and population groups, and the scale and nature of public and private consumption. These institutions and relationships determine social policy and explain why governments address or ignore certain social problems.

The term *institution* refers to social practices that are built around a distinct set of transgenerational values. These values are usually considered important and are sanctioned and maintained by social norms.[13] Different schools of thought treat the concept of institution in different ways. Functionalists see institutions as fulfilling the needs of individuals or societies; phenomenologists concentrate on the way in which people create or adapt institutions rather than merely respond to them.

Although it is relatively stable, the institutional structure of society evolves and changes. This process affects social practices and both integrates and creates conflict among social roles. As institutions change, they mold the behavior of individuals, groups, and communities. Old institutions adapt and evolve, and new institutions emerge to meet new needs. In preindustrial societies, for example, the family was the main institution, with various educational, religious, political, and economic obligations. At that time, several modern institutional domains, such as the economy and medicine, were still undifferentiated.

This is not the case, however, in today's more complex and specialized industrialized societies. Modern institutions have become highly differentiated from each other, and new institutions have developed. For instance, economic and legal institutions in industrialized societies are separate and autonomous from political institutions. The economy has emerged as a new and dominant social institution; economic principles of self-interest, profit, and efficiency are now more important than other ideological, legal, and social practices. Economic capital has emerged as the basic sociopolitical power in modern society.

Existing institutions continue to change. However, three major types of institutions are conventionally identified. *Political institutions,* including the U.S. Congress, political parties, and the electoral system, regulate the use of and access to power. *Economic institutions* like the market produce and distribute goods and services. *Social institutions,* including the family, the educational system, and religions, produce patterns of human relations. Each category of institutions can be further divided. For example, social institutions include (1) stratification institutions, which determine the distribution of positions and resources; (2) kinship institutions, which deal with marriage, the family, and socialization of the young; and (3) cultural institutions, which are concerned with religious, scientific, and artistic activities.

The Field of Social Policy

The major institutions of society constitute the complex context of social policies. Social policy emanates from society's institutional structure, which can be better understood as a system[14] of interdependent political, economic, and social institutions[15] that interact with social practices. The structure of society's institutions incorporates basic ideology and reflects and influences a country's dominant goals, values, attitudes, intellectual tradition, conflicts, areas of consensus, technological capabilities, distributive justice, and cultural patterns. In this context, the institutions of society converge and compete for resources in reproducing society's basic profile; they also promote the well-being of its citizens. *Well-being* denotes the general welfare of society as a whole, including all social classes, geopolitical groups, age groups, and ethnic or racial groups.

Basic Social Policy Issues

In reproducing society's basic profile, institutions address three fundamental issues of basic concern to the field of social policy:

- *The desired society:* What kind of society, community, or organization is sought? Which forces constitute the major dimensions of the ideal, desired society? What kind of social relations should be achieved?
- *Organization of resources:* How should institutional forces be structured, and how should physical and human resources be used? What should be their role, rank, and relation to each other and society as a whole?
- *Distribution:* What share of the produced goods and services should be allocated to individuals, groups, and social classes? How should power and services be distributed? What are the appropriate premises (need, merit, contribution to the production process, and so forth) for distributive justice?

Social policy is concerned with how societies formulate, determine, resolve, implement, and evaluate these three interrelated issues.[16]

For example, in analyzing the socioeconomics of the 1980s and 1990s, one might ask the following questions:

1. What kind of society is desired in the context of neoconservatism? Neoconservatives visualize, among other things, an unfettered economic market, a competitive society, and individualism.
2. How do neoconservatives use societal resources to achieve their desired society and human relations? Neoconservatives want the private-voluntary sector to service the welfare needs of the population. A minimal welfare state will emphasize individual responsibility; government will not intervene in the economic market, which will be the main mechanism for the distribution of income and wealth.
3. How do neoconservatives wish to distribute goods and services among individuals and social classes? Neoconservatives believe that unequal distribution of income, wealth, and power is inevitable, desirable, and determined by the marginal productivity of each individual in the workplace.

These three issues are interdependent. For example, if neoconservatives desire a competitive society with a dominant private sector, they probably will not establish social policies that favor a strong, public-sector welfare state or opt for noncompetitive mechanisms of income distribution. The kind of society sought determines how society's resources are organized. In turn, the distribution of well-being is associated with the kind of ideal society sought and its institutional organization.

Many believe that social policy should be concerned with the development of all citizens and the creation of a more just and integrated social order. In this context, social policy[17] should explain how and why communities, institutions, and organizations develop[18] and should prescribe action to improve living conditions through widespread, active participation of people. While social policy is planned in many settings, typically social-policy planners analyze why society has produced certain results. They explore how social conditions or organizations may be deliberately altered to produce more favorable results. They also evaluate the ramifications of interventions for the society as a whole and for specific social classes, population groups, regions, and institutions.

Underlying social policy planning efforts are ideological, technological, and organizational expectations of individuals, society, human nature, government, social changes, and social relations. Historically, societies accomplish social policy through five broad approaches: tradition (cultural process), command (political process), economic logic (market process), active participation of citizens in determining their lifestyles (social process), or a combination of these approaches (the approach in advanced industrial countries).

Different as they are, these approaches provide norms for societal functioning. Their framework defines the specific nature of social policy and its goals. With these approaches policy planners can identify and analyze social conditions, define and evaluate problems, and propose intervention.[19] (See Chapter 2.)

Modern societies need complex, interdependent social policy solutions to national problems that arise from ideology, technology, organization, scarcity, production,

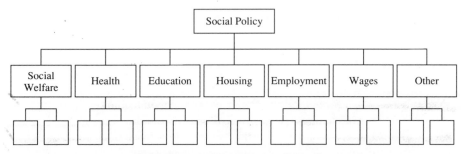

FIGURE 1-1   Subunits of social policy

and distribution, as well as from well-being and developmental needs. In the process, social policy must resolve conflicts between individualism and collectivism, between desired and feasible conditions, and among competing needs in a pluralist society. For example, should policy prioritize the needs of children or those of senior citizens? The interests of the working class or those of the wealthy? Should it promote goals of individuals or those of society? Should it emphasize collaboration or competition, materialism or altruism?

Subunits of Social Policy

Social policy as a field has acquired several specializations, or subunits, that are specific functional areas of social policy planning. Social welfare policy is concerned with public transfers of income and related social services. In the 1950s, Wilensky and Lebeaux referred to social policies that satisfy temporary, urgent economic needs as "residual social welfare"; the broader array of societal provisions was called "institutional social welfare."[20] Health policy concerns allocation of health and medical resources. Housing policy emphasizes planning and producing neighborhoods with adequate community facilities, good environmental conditions, and strong social infrastructure. In urban policy, the focus is on the human settlement and its infrastructure. Family planning, demographic planning, and other functional areas are also subunits of social policy planning (see Figure 1-1).

Each subunit can be further divided into components identified by policy functions, purpose, sponsors, recipient populations, or administrative level. For example, social welfare includes public, private, preventive, and curative social insurance and income security schemes. Policies can be international, national, regional, or local; they can include administrative, legislative, and judicial measures.

Although subunits focus on specific functions, the field of social policy is concerned with the constitution and development of society as a whole, with the solution of its human and physical development problems, and with individual well-being. Although it focuses on the macro level, social policy derives much from the social sciences concerned with individual, group, and community behavior. The field emphasizes cooperation and shared responsibility among society's institutions and its structural elements, the entire population, and the individual. Social policy is a collective instrument for altering basic social relations and the profile of society and for improving the living conditions and lifestyles of all population groups, social classes, and individuals. As such, it concerns all social workers and permeates the entire practice of social work.

Ideological Perspectives and Values in Social Policy

Social policy is planned from the perspective of an ideology, theory, or set of values that affects social classes and population groups differentially. Therefore, values are major dimensions of social policy that convey legitimacy, public commitment, and loyalties and help structure the behavior of individuals, groups, and communities.

Of course, social workers should try to keep their personal values and commitments separate from their scholarly and professional work. Objectivity is a goal worth striving for in practice. Social policy is a valuable tool in conflict resolution, but its normative components must be recognized.

In a broader sense, capitalist policies and programs differ from socialist ones. American public social policy promotes *capitalism* and economic individualism; it tries to minimize intrusions by the government into economic activities and individual lifestyles. The ideologies of pragmatism[21] and positivism[22] also contribute to American social policy and influence public opinion on the role of the welfare state. In contrast, people in Sweden or France, though within the capitalist framework, tolerate more extensive governmental direction of socioeconomic activities. In socialist nations like the People's Republic of China, Vietnam, Zambia, or Cuba, social policy is grounded in the central government's control of the market economy.

Both capitalism and socialism are phenomena of values, consciousness, and preference as well as systems of economic production and distribution, societal structure, political power, and governance. Values and ideology affect the response to fundamental issues of social policy such as the role of government; governmental management of the economic market; tolerance of income and power inequality; the scope of the welfare state, including citizenship;[23] rejection or acceptance of poverty in the midst of affluence; collective or individual responsibility for societal ills; and friction between private-market and welfare-state policy.

Capitalist values and ideals lead to capitalist institutional arrangements, priorities, and distributions. For example, capitalist views emphasize private-sector responsibility for developing human resources; a limited state; a systemic division of labor; extensive private ownership of the means of production; a private-market economy that distributes income, wealth, power, and services; limited redistribution of income and power; limited, categorical public social programs;[24] a corrective public social policy focusing mainly on the poor; individual responsibility for social welfare; civil rights favoring the individual; and a pluralist, multiparty political system.

Fascist values favor social organization in which key economic, social, and political decisions are made jointly by corporate groups and the dictatorial state. In the fascist state, the political community includes a number of corporate groups, with individuals represented politically via their membership in these groups rather than by individual elections. Individuals have influence only through their membership in corporate bodies. Fascist perspectives[25] establish suppressive institutional arrangements and favor the powerful, nationalism, and racial supremacy.

Socialist values and ideology[26] include the goals of democratic centralism;[27] a centrally managed economy driven mainly by state socioeconomic planning; a less-stratified society; state ownership of the means of production and distribution to guarantee employment and to equalize income; and a one-party, totalitarian political system. Socialist values establish public institutions for the development of societal resources; practically unlimited state authority; minimal class divisions; public owner-ship of the means of production; no private-sector market economy; equitable distribu-tion of income, wealth, power, and resources; comprehensive, universal[28] social pro-grams; collective and state responsibility for social welfare; collective civil rights; and an elitist, dictatorial one-party political system.

Socialist countries use the term *social policy* rather than *welfare state.*[29] Their citizens receive more social services as a right than do citizens of capitalist coun-tries. All socialist state policy is frequently referred to as "social policy," aiming to benefit all citizens through centrally planned, nationwide socioeconomic develop-ment programs.[30]

Conservative and Liberal Capitalist Social Policy

There are several versions of capitalism (and of socialism). Each version of capitalism emphasizes different values and priorities. For example, social policies in capitalist Sweden, Denmark, and Norway differ considerably from those in the United States.

Since World War II, distinctly different social conditions and public social policies have prevailed in the United States under conservative and liberal governments. In the 1980s and 1990s, *conservative* presidents Ronald Reagan and George Bush estab-lished neoconservative policies, as did prime ministers Margaret Thatcher and John Major in the United Kingdom. Under the pretext of revitalizing sluggish economies, these leaders slashed budgets of public social programs, reduced taxes for industrial establishments and high-income households, increased poverty and income inequality by favoring the affluent and powerful, and weakened environmental and consumer policies to protect corporations and the private market.[31] In effect, they implemented conservative capitalist ideological goals, giving capitalist economic principles priority over the goals of fairness and distributive social justice.[32]

In some respects, neoconservative (or neoliberal) policies represent a revival of President Calvin Coolidge's guidelines. When Coolidge took office in the 1920s, he offered an economic proposal that historian Charles Beard described as "transparent in its simplicity": taxes were to be reduced, not on goods consumed by the masses, but on the incomes of the wealthiest. The idea was to leave more money in the hands of the rich for investment so that the poor might obtain better jobs. Coolidge also proposed less interference with business and corporations through administrative orders and through the prosecution of trusts before the courts.[33]

Very different social conditions materialized when liberal capitalist principles prevailed in the United States under the administrations of presidents Franklin Delano Roosevelt, John F. Kennedy, and Lyndon B. Johnson; in the United Kingdom under the Labour party; and in Sweden and Denmark under welfare capitalism.[34] Liberal capitalist governments enacted social policies emphasizing the active participa-tion of citizens in deciding their own future, greater governmental guidance of the private-market economy, more extensive universal social programs to protect the powerless, planned redistribution of income and services favoring lower-income groups, and increased governmental responsibility for the socioeconomic development of a wider spectrum of the population.

Unequal distribution of income and power is strongly associated with conservative capitalist, institutional arrangements. Equality in income distribution increases with liberal policies and institutional arrangements.

Radicals in capitalist countries propose even more egalitarian policy interventions in the private-market economy. They urge more extensive, universal social development programs.[35]

Complementarity and Friction in Social Policy

The values and ideologies in a society can complement or conflict with one another. For example, materialistic values can conflict with altruism; economic policy can conflict with political goals. Social workers and legislators are aware of the complementarity and conflict among social policies, organizations, and institutions—particularly between economic and social policies.

Complementarity and integration of social policies and institutions can be so pronounced that it becomes difficult to separate economic from social policy. Although many current social problems are economic, there are no purely "economic" solutions. Economic growth, development, inflation, productivity, public expenditures, and the like are sociopolitical phenomena rooted in society's institutions and attitudes. The reverse is also true. Social policy reformers should consider the context of economic institutions because political and social policies have economic consequences and are framed from prevailing economic assumptions.

The complementarity of social and economic policies was evident in the United States for several decades after World War II. The prevailing liberal ideological commitments, including freedom, full employment, reconstruction and development, democracy, equality, and distributive social justice, fostered acceptance of the welfare state and citizenship as compatible with the private-market economy.[36] The liberal commitments, made mostly during World War II, were deeply rooted in public demands and political promises for a better, more just postwar world. However, they were also associated with efforts to justify the bitter struggle against fascism.

The increasing state intervention in economic management and public social welfare services after World War II were also an institutional adaptation to advanced industrialism. "Logic-of-industrialization" theorists asserted that institutional integration, harmony, and symbiosis were necessary between the economy of advanced industrialism and the provisions of the welfare state. A mixed economy and the welfare state converged to balance economic growth with social development, freedom with security, and enterprise with stability.[37] Strong public support, political solidarity, and the industrialized context combined to expand and consolidate the welfare state after World War II.[38]

But friction can also occur between economic and social institutions. The three postwar decades of relative harmony between private-market economic imperatives and the welfare state were followed by friction between economic and social goals.

This has been reflected in the West by conflicting conservative and liberal capitalist public social policies. Conservative capitalists believe that egalitarian social policies conflict with the market economy, private property, and class privilege.[39]

Even in the early 1960s, Marshall in the United Kingdom suggested that the principle of citizenship conflicts with capitalism and class inequality.[40] In the 1990s, the attack of capitalist democracy on the welfare state has been based on the notion of a conflict between equality and democracy (political values) on one hand, and class and inequality (economic values) on the other hand.

Although it is too early to predict future developments in Central and Eastern European countries that replace central planning with a private-market economy, evidence indicates that these countries already have similar conflicts—particularly about inflation, poverty, guaranteed employment, and citizenship rights.[41]

As Lockwood and others have suggested, conflict occurs when institutions are not in harmony with each other.[42] Economic institutions may pursue policies that conflict with the needs of political or social institutions. According to several authors, including Simmel and Coser, institutional conflicts may center on control over resources or assume the form of class-based power struggles.[43] Dahrendorf views the distribution of power and authority, rather than of capital, as the central conflict in all social institutions.[44] This contrasts with Marx's dichotomous model of social conflict, which divides society into two basic classes, capital and labor.

In Dahrendorf's view, government participates in class struggles but usually favors the ruling class; coercion, in the form of law or other social institutions, maintains and justifies the value system of society, its status quo, and its distribution of power and well-being. Social changes result from conflict between groups with antithetical interests.

Some theories, including functionalism,[45] do not account adequately for social conflict, social change, or other forms of instability. In functionalism, social activities are derived from consensus and aimed at stability. However, policy making relates to conflict resolution, particularly in the allocation of resources and in distributive justice. The relationship between the economy and the welfare state in the United States shows this.

Mediating Conflict

Social policy can mediate economic and social conflict. According to several commentators, including Dye, public policy can regulate conflict and enhance complementarity within society; affect the distribution of goods, services, benefits, and rewards; organize bureaucracy; and regulate behavior.[46] Several authors, such as Easton and Lasswell, have defined public policy as "the authoritative allocation of values for the whole society"[47] or as "a projected program of goods, values, and practices."[48] Heclo supported similar views.[49]

The Unity of Social and Economic Policy

The interdependence of economic and social policies necessitates a unified socio-economic approach to minimize conflict and enhance outcomes. Some commentators, however, separate economic issues from social policy. Although the two domains inevitably merge, these authors ignore the economic components of social policy. They view the free economic market as characterized by quid pro quo (which excludes the distribution of free, unilateral welfare benefits) but say that social policy operates differently. Hence, they isolate social and economic institutions.

Can we distinguish social policy from economic issues? In Scandinavia and the European Economic Community, labor market policy, unemployment wages, and the provision of jobs are unified rather than being separated into social or economic policy. In contrast, some writers in the United Kingdom and the United States think these matters are economic and are separate from social policy concerns. Similarly, education, housing, and health care are not universally regarded as components of social policy.

The mingling of market and non-market principles and processes[50] makes it difficult for any study of contemporary social policy to ignore the tax system that redistributes income, the way in which the economy is tuned, the role of inflation and interest rates, and the income and employment policies that are pursued. All of these have important, direct social policy implications and especially affect the powerless and the disadvantaged.

Economic policy is also influenced by social policy, psychosocial behavior, and the state of a culture. For example, the idea that parents with small children should compete in the labor market and the concept of minimum wages change the nature of the labor force and the functioning of economic rewards. Approaching socioeconomic issues together is more realistic and effective rather than ignoring their interdependence.

A SOCIAL POLICY MODEL AND IMPLICATIONS

Overview of the Model

This model depicts the nature of social policy as a field. To understand the societal context and nature of social policies, we must grasp how the institutional forces of society—ideological, political, social, economic, and cultural—combine to influence policy making and social conditions. The model presented in Figure 1-2 is a tool to help readers visualize the institutional nature of social policies that address social conditions and the development of individual, group, and community well-being.

Social policies that emanate from a specific institution are indicated by arrows. The arrows also show social policy direction and influence. For example, the arrows indicate that institutional social policy (A) influences the form of social policies in (B). In turn, these influence social conditions in (C). Through feedback, (C) influences policies in (A). This cyclical process of social policy continues until the desired results are achieved.

Using the model, social workers examine how ideological, political, and social variables combine to influence social policy. The model also shows how social policy relates to ideological input and how this affects the well-being of society.

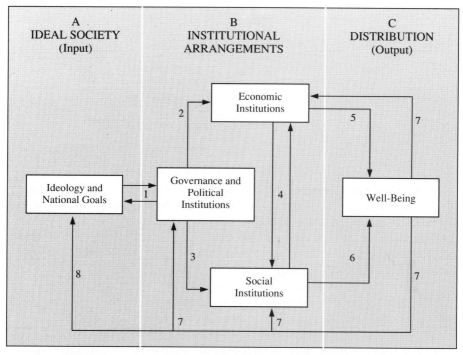

FIGURE 1-2   A model of the institutional context of social policy

Section A contains the input to the model; that is, the ideology that describes what kind of society is desired. Section B and arrows 2 through 6 represent the organizational structure, resources, and political, economic, and social institutions. Section C shows the model's output, the condition of well-being. Feedback arrows 5 through 8 show the distribution of goods and services and the influence of output conditions on reformulating social policies.

A, B, and C are interdependent and cyclically related; A influences B, which affects C, which in turn influences A. (The relationships in Figure 1-2 are summarized in Figure 1-3.)

Implications of the Model

There is no fixed or permanent input or output in this model. Because of its circular form, one cannot identify a beginning or an end. Ideology is presented as the model's input to emphasize the normative base of social policies. Because of the circular nature of feedback, the input of the model can be ideology, economic institutions, social institutions, well-being, or the political system.

As a tool, the model calls for analysis of the relations among major institutions. It does not imply a specific sequence in the exploration of institutional relations or a fixed input and output. For example, Figure 1-4 indicates a different sequential order of analyzing relations, and different output or input flows than those presented

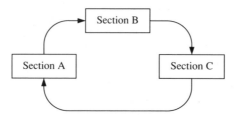

FIGURE 1-3   The circular structure of the model

in Figure 1-2. These and other alternatives depend in practice upon the way a policy issue is formulated or a social policy intervention is planned and carried out.

In practice the circle of input, output, and feedback is usually repeated several times until the desired results are achieved. The completion of each cycle permits more analysis in the next cycle and achieves more desired results. This is similar to other social planning efforts and societal processes. For example, the socialization of individuals involves repeated, systemic feedback.[51]

Applying the Model:
The Socioeconomic Crisis of the 1980s and 1990s

The model provides guidelines for the practice of social policy. It can be applied in different practice situations and in all areas of the social policy field. For example, the model can be applied to the socioeconomic crisis of the 1980s and 1990s and its policy implications for social programs and social services.

The socioeconomic crisis of the 1980s and 1990s in the United States originated in the neoconservative ideology that prevailed in the early 1980s and its social policies. Neoconservatives called for less government, an unfettered economic market, budget cuts in social programs, less taxation of the rich, high budget deficits, and more emphasis on individualism (Figure 1-2, section A, arrow 1). These values provided the rationale for the political, economic, and social policies of the Reagan and Bush administrations (Figure 1-2, section B, arrows 2 through 4).

The ideological and political will of neoconservative administrations generated federal economic and social policies that were less interventionist and that reduced taxes for the rich, increased military spending, and reduced social welfare. These policies reduced living standards and affected the well-being of many Americans (Figure 1-2, section C). The feedback (Figure 1-2, arrows 7 and 8) from decreased well-being and increased inequality of income affected the political climate, the 1992 presidential election, and the status of neoconservatism. The increases in poverty, hunger, illiteracy, infant mortality, crime, and substance abuse, along with growing inequality of income, wealth, and power,[52] caused the reevaluation of neoconservative socioeconomic policies and brought about efforts to change the ideological input. The deterioration of income and social conditions for most Americans generated pressure for more effective socioeconomic policies and raised questions about neoconservative ideology.

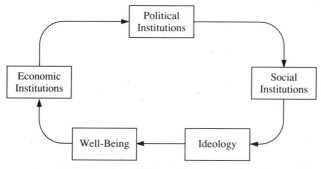

FIGURE 1-4   Different input and output

DEBATES ABOUT THE NATURE OF SOCIAL POLICY

Overview

Social workers who explore social policy are confronted with some basic dilemmas. First, the lack of a widely accepted definition of social policy can be puzzling. For example, the social policy framework reflected in the model and the views developed in the previous section are not supported by all commentators or schools of thought. Second, some authors who use the term *social policy* do not define it precisely. Those who define it do so with various assumptions, concepts, and orientations. For example, some commentators prefer broad perspectives of social policy like the model presented here; others view social policy in a narrow perspective that equates social policy with measures for the poor. Some authors focus on social policy as a field and emphasize its philosophical nature; others see social policy as a technical process of solving problems. Finally, *social policy* is sometimes used as a synonym for other terms, such as *public social welfare, social planning,* or *policy analysis.*

In contrast to *foreign policy* or *defense policy*—terms that are clear to most people—the term *social policy* connotes different ideas and activities in different countries. Even in a nation that regularly uses the term, *social policy* does not always mean the same thing or refer to precisely the same set of phenomena. The same can be said of such terms as *social security, public social welfare,* and *welfare state.* The words *policy* and *public* are less controversial than the word *social.* As Dye and others have suggested, *policy* denotes a set of principles to guide and justify action, whereas *public policy* denotes government action.[53] The controversy lies in the precise meaning of *social.*

This chapter concerns the nature of social policy, its values, and philosophy. Chapter 2 explores the practice of social policy: analysis, implementation, and social action. Although some authors focus on either the field or the process of social policy, the two are complementary. The philosophy, ideology, and values that define the field of social policy also guide the process. However, recent literature in the United States reflects a progressive shift of emphasis from the theoretical to the practical.

The Comprehensive (Societal) Perspective

An increasing number of authors emphasize the societal scope of social policy. Their approach reflects a comprehensive view of social policy. This broad view encompasses institutional organization, policy, and programs, as well as society's concern for the well-being and development of all citizens and communities. Gil's framework for analysis and development of social policy suggests that social policy consists of "rules for the ways of life."[54] Jones states that social policy represents attempts "to interfere in, and by some criteria, to improve or correct a given social order."[55] Some writers, including Pinker, Furniss, and Tilton, have pointed out that Western social policy is designed as much to reward effort, achievement, and loyalty among society's members as to compensate individuals for social disadvantages.[56]

A central point is whether social policy is geared mainly to promoting the interests of society as a whole or the welfare of individuals.[57] For example, Titmuss believed that social policy is primarily a means of promoting individual welfare.[58] In contrast, several authors, including Cahnman and Schmitt, Girod and De Laubier, and Jones, as well as those who hold modern German *Sozialpolitik* orientations, have suggested that the predominant concern of social policy is to promote the long-term interests of society.[59] Although these views are not antithetical in the context of the model, the first places a strong emphasis on the poor and powerless, and the second on the responsibility of society.

Earlier references to the comprehensive nature of social policy include those by Rein. Moving progressively toward broader social policy approaches, he suggested that the social purposes and consequences of agricultural, economic, labor, fiscal, physical development, and social welfare policies "form the subject matter of social policy." Rein perceived social policy "as planning for social externalities" and for the egalitarian distribution of social benefits.[60] Schottland joined this group when he advocated that public social policy is concerned with laws, policies, and government practices that "affect the social relationships of individuals and their relationship to the society of which they are a part."[61]

Boulding wrote that social policy centers "in these institutions that create integration and discourage alienation."[62] Tropman recognized by implication that social policy is related to the entire social system and therefore has a much broader nature than social welfare programs.[63] In the context of public social planning, Austin said that social policy and programs are designed "to make social order more consistent with particular social values" and to achieve equality and social justice in society.[64] The comprehensive view is also reflected in socialist policy, which places high priority on establishing universal programs.

Even authors with narrow perspectives on social welfare policy and programs recognize broader social policy concerns. For example, while discussing social welfare policy, Jansson directed attention not only to social welfare problems but to broader institutional problems "that affect the implementation of specific policies."[65] Although their focus was social welfare policy, Gilbert and Specht discussed broad "dimensions of choice" and their merits, recognizing that "social policy is often used to designate a more extensive range of activities" than social welfare.[66] Titmuss considered direct services and cash benefit payments as the "iceberg phenomena of social welfare" and called fiscal and occupational welfare the "submerged parts of the iceberg of social policy."[67]

Narrow (Social Welfare) Perspectives

Critics of the comprehensive view consider broad definitions of social policy too general. Authors like Marshall equate social policy with governmental programs (cash or in-kind benefits) consisting primarily of social insurance, public assistance, health, and housing services.[68] Following this British tradition, several American writers equate social policy with social welfare programs and services—the dominant view in the United States.[69] Titmuss suggested that the ingredient of social policy is social welfare (or social services), including income maintenance and public health.[70] Morris used the term *social welfare policy* as a synonym for *social policy.* When he referred to the need for a broader "societal approach," he implied that both public and private social "welfare" activities should be considered.[71] Tropman associated social policy with social welfare in his "three social policy elements": social policy is collective, social policy focuses on social relationships, and social policy is concerned with the disadvantaged.[72]

Narrow perspectives are associated with fragmented, ad hoc, categorical social welfare programs and social services that target selected groups and dysfunctions. Although they meet those needs that are beyond the individual's capacity to deal with, their theoretical base does not illuminate the underlying common dynamics of societal problems.[73]

Which social policy perspective is most appropriate in social work practice? Which model is most effective? Social workers should choose their own theoretical framework of social policy according to their own assumptions about our profession and its values and to their own view of the nature of society. Comprehensive and narrow views and the perception of social and economic domains are associated with the rapidly changing role of social policy in the fundamental societal transformations in advanced industrial countries. Although these perceptions do not necessarily have to mesh, they are not as incompatible with one another as they seem to be.

The crucial issue is not whether social policy should promote societal or individual needs and interests or whether the field of social policy should emphasize a philosophical or a practice orientation, a social or economic approach, or a scientific ("neutral") or normative base. Important as these distinctions are, the fundamental issue is the role of social policy in the concerted development of a society and all its members; in the prevention and treatment of dysfunctions; and in the promotion of a humane, open, and more equitable social order—a commitment that is central to several professions, including social work. The pursuit of this goal can be enhanced by contributions from all these approaches within a holistic institutional framework.

NOTES

1. *S.O.S. America! A Children's Defense Budget* (Washington, DC: Children's Defense Fund, 1990), p. 3.

2. Peng Zhiliang, "Necessary, Voluntary—and Effective," *China Reconstructs* 25(5) (May 1986):13.

3. Greek Parliament, Act 1153 of 1972, *The Advisory Committee and Its Accomplishments*, Chair A. P. Voyadgis, March/April 1972, 686–711. For details, see D. Iatridis, *Social Planning and Policy Alternatives in Greece* (Athens, Greece: National Centre of Social Research, 1980), 214–217.

4. M. F. Fox and C. H. Biber, *Women at Work* (Palo Alto, CA: Mayfield, 1981), 34.

5. D. Braun, *The Rich Get Richer* (Chicago: Nelson-Hall, 1991), 70.

6. Ibid., 7–8.

7. Ibid., ix.

8. *World Development Report* (Washington, DC: World Bank, 1988), 223–273; and Braun, *Rich Get Richer*, 73–74.

9. J. Knight and J. G. Brenner, "Savings and Loans Lose $19 Billion; Worst Year," *Washington Post*, March 27, 1990, 1; and N. Nasg, "Losses at Savings and Loans," *New York Times*, March 27, 1990, 1, D6.

10. D. Nyhan, "Let's Sic the General on the Tax Cheats," *Boston Sunday Globe*, March 24, 1991, A21.

11. U.S. Bureau of the Census, *Report for the House Select Committee on Children, Youth, and Families* (1990), cited in *Educational Week* (March 28, 1990): 7. This report states that the health and economic status of children in the United States frequently are lower than those of children in other industrialized countries.

12. Ibid., 7.

13. N. Abercrombie et. al., *Dictionary of Sociology* (New York: Penguin, 1964), 110.

14. Although systems theory was the dominant paradigm in social sciences in the 1950s and 1960s and was widely influential in the study of political processes, industrialization, development, and modernization, the theory has also been criticized, particularly the aspects associated with Parsons' social system and voluntaristic theory of action. In the 1970s, Marxist theory, with its focus on change and conflict, was seen as the major alternative to systems theory. Further possibilities for the development of systems theory have been explored by Habermas. As used in this text, the concept of social system is not tied to any particular concept of social sciences, but is basic to all paradigms. See T. Parsons, *The Social System* (New York: Free Press, 1951); T. Parsons, *The System of Modern Societies* (Englewood Cliffs, NJ: Prentice-Hall); J. Habermas, *Theory and Practice* (London: Heinemann Educational Books, 1973); and J. Habermas, *Towards a Rational Society* (London: Heinemann Educational Books, 1971).

15. *System* refers to any set of interrelated components, such as the social system, the solar system, or the school system. A system's environment is the larger system of which it is a subsystem. The boundaries of the system distinguish it from the environment. *Input* is the effect of the environment on a system. *Output* is the effect of the system on the environment. *Feedback* is the mutual causality among variables to effect equilibrium. Input, output, and arrangements that process input and create output usually constitute the three major components of systems.

16. Although the three issues refer here to society as a unit, they may also refer to a community, to a large organization, or to a large group as units that engage in policy making.

17. D. Iatridis, "A Societal Framework for Planning Interventions," *Proceedings, Annual Conference of the Engandiner Kollegium*, September 1971, Saint Moritz, Switzerland, 99–112.

18. Emphasizing the macro level, the levels of public social policy practice include society, communities, institutions, and organizations. The societal level is fundamental in that it tends to constrain mezzo- and micro-application levels.

19. Similar professional elements appear in the literature on social policy planning and social work. Social policy planning uses philosophical concepts to guide identification of and solutions to social problems. Several authors refer to values, facts, and action as components of social policy. See W. N. Dunn, *Public Policy Analysis* (Englewood Cliffs, NJ: Prentice-Hall), 36.

20. H. L. Wilensky and C. N. Lebeaux, *Industrial Society and Social Welfare* (New York: Russell Sage Foundation, 1958), 134–140.

21. Pragmatism, which is similar to British empiricism, emphasizes the practical consequences of concepts or actions. No concept or action has meaning unless it can be applied. Pragmatism denotes strongly that a belief or theory is true if it "works" or "pays." Concepts or actions have no intrinsic value other than what is derived from practical consequences.

22. Adherents of positivism insist that science can deal only with observable entities that are known directly through experience. The doctrine has been criticized in social science literature by realists who argue that causal explanation proceeds by identifying the underlying mechanisms, perhaps unobservable, that connect phenomena; by social scientists who argue that if positivism is accepted, then social sciences cannot be science at all; and by others who argue that positivism stops at producing quantified facts and does not include genuine interpretations. Radicals have also argued that positivism in the social sciences, as an example of technical rationality, requires control of societies.

23. The concept of citizenship as a status that provides access to rights and powers is associated with the view that the state's provision of a basic minimum of economic security and social services is an essential ingredient of the status of the citizen in modern society. See T. H. Marshall, *Sociology at the Cross Roads and Other Essays* (London: Heinemann, 1963). While civic rights include freedom of speech and equality before the law, and political rights include the right to vote and to organize politically, socioeconomic rights include economic welfare and social security. In contrast to preindustrial society, in which rights were confined to a narrow elite, industrial societies have extended socioeconomic rights (which include trade unionism, collective bargaining, and the growth of the welfare state) to all population groups.

24. In categorical approaches, social policies and programs are conceived as responses to the specific social needs or problems of specific population groups. Such policies tend to be fragmented, ad hoc, and unrelated to the social policy system as a whole, obscuring deeper cause-and-effect relationships. For example, in the United States the federal government makes available to states categorical grants—funds that must be spent for narrowly specified services.

25. The term *fascism* is often applied to corporatist political systems, including Italian fascism, German Nazism, and the Spanish Falange. Fascism is an authoritarian, nationalistic, illiberal political movement embracing totalitarianism, violence, distrust of democratic politics, a commitment to the single-party state, and faith in charismatic leaders. While there are a number of theories which seek to explain fascism, several authors, including Poulantzas, use social class analysis to argue that fascism is a result of a deep economic and ideological crisis of the dominant capitalist class. The fascist state replaces democratic, parliamentary politics in response to the crises of capitalist society, which is threatened by the organized working class. See N. Poulantzas, *Political Power and Social Classes* (London: New Left Books, 1973); N. Poulantzas, *State, Power, Socialism* (London: New Left Books, 1978); N. Poulantzas, *Fascism and Dictatorship* (London: New Left Books, 1974); B. Moore, *The Social Origins of Dictatorship and Democracy* (London: Alley Lane, Penguin Press, 1968); and S. J. Woolf, ed., *The Nature of Fascism* (New York: Random House, 1968).

26. The term *socialism* is used here in a general sense to include communism rather than to denote a technical, transitional phase leading to communism.

27. The Soviet state before 1991 was organized and functioned on the principle of democratic centralism, namely, the electiveness of all bodies of state authority from the lowest to the highest, their accountability to the people, and the obligation of lower bodies to observe the decisions of higher ones (Chapter 1, Article 3 of the Soviet Constitution). Conceived by Lenin, democratic centralism is responsible for the Communist Party's functioning much like a military establishment. Orders go down the chain of command and are rigorously enforced. Discussions and debates at various Party meetings remain strictly within the limits prescribed from above. Decisions are never questioned once they have been made. See Vadim Medish, *The Soviet Union,* 3rd ed. (Englewood Cliffs, NJ: Prentice-Hall, 1987), 86. In August, 1991, radical changes began to alter the structure of the Soviet state and its oppressive institutions.

28. Universal approaches incorporate a comprehensive conception of social policy that recognizes that the dynamic source of all social problems is rooted in the fabric of society as a whole. Thus, programs are based on the universal needs of the population for development. Universalism tends to be associated with progressive social policy reforms and egalitarianism. See V. George and P. Wilding, *The Impact of Social Policy* (Boston: Routledge & Kegan Paul, 1984), 64, 66.

29. The term *welfare state* usually refers in the West to a state that assumes responsibility for the welfare of its citizens in the context of a private-market economy and a plural polity. The term denotes the idea of collective responsibility for welfare, including its appropriate institutions, such as social welfare services. See Chapter 6 of this text for a detailed discussion of the welfare state. See also R. Mishra, "Social Analysis and the Welfare State: Retrospect and Prospects," in E. Oyen, ed., *Comparing Welfare States and Their Future* (Brookfield, VT: Gower, 1986), 31.

30. Z. Ferge, "The Crisis and the Welfare State in Eastern Europe with a Focus on Hungary," *European Economic Review* 31 (1987): 212–219; Z. Ferge, "The Fourth Road: The Future for Hungarian Social Policy," in B. Deacon and J. Szalai, eds., *Social Policy in the New Eastern Europe* (Brookfield, VT: Avebury, 1990); Z. Ferge, *A Society in the Making* (New York: Penguin, 1979); Z. Ferge, "The Changing Hungarian Social Policy," in Oyen, *Comparing Welfare States and Their Future;* and I. Jeffries, *A Guide to the Socialist Economies* (New York and London: Routledge & Kegan Paul, 1990).

31. For the aftermath of President Reagan's social policies, see H. Johnson, *Sleepwalking through History: America in the Reagan Years* (New York: Norton, 1991); Braun, *The Rich Get Richer;* P. J. Day, "The New Poor in America: Isolationism in an International Political Economy," *Social Work* 34:3 (1989): 227–233; I. V. Sawhill, ed., *Challenge to Leadership: Economic and Social Issues for the Next Decade* (Washington, DC: Urban Institute, 1988); C. F. Stone and I. V. Sawhill, *Economic Policy in the Reagan Years* (Washington, DC: Urban Institute, 1984); M. Abramovitz, "The Privatization of the Welfare State: A Review," *Social Work* 31:4 (1986): 257–264; T. Joe and C. Rogers, *By the Few, for the Few: The Reagan Welfare Legacy* (Lexington, MA: Lexington Books, 1985).

32. See D. Iatridis, "Neoconservatism Reviewed," *Social Work* 28:2 (1983): 101–107; and D. Iatridis, "Social Deficit: Neoconservatism's Policy of Social Underdevelopment," *Social Work* 33:1 (1988): 11–15.

33. C. A. Beard and M. R. Beard, *The Rise of American Civilization,* vol. 2 (New York: Macmillan, 1930): 701.

34. W. I. Trattner, *From Poor Law to Welfare State,* 4th ed. (New York: Free Press, 1989), Chapters 13 and 14. *Welfare capitalism* refers to the system that, although capitalist, uses a great deal of redistribution and welfare transfers to achieve greater equality.

35. For radical social work, see M. Simpkin, "Radical Social Work: Lessons for the 1990s" in P. Carter et al, eds., *Social Work and Social Welfare Yearbook* 1 (Philadelphia: Open University Press, 1989): 159–173; J. H. Galper, *The Politics of Social Services* (Englewood Cliffs, NJ: Prentice-Hall, 1975); J. H. Galper, *Social Work Practice: A Radical Perspective* (Englewood Cliffs, NJ: Prentice-Hall, 1980); J. Wineman, *The Politics of Human Services: A Radical Alternative to the Welfare State* (Boston: South End Press, 1984). See also *Catalyst: A Socialist Journal of the Social Services,* published quarterly by the Institute for Social Service Alternatives, New York.

36. See Trattner, *From Poor Law to Welfare State.*

37. Mishra, "Social Analysis and the Welfare State," 20–32.

38. See George and Wilding, *The Impact of Social Policy,* 26; and G. Room, *The Sociology of Welfare* (London: Martin Robertson, 1979), 63.

39. Mishra, "Social Analysis and the Welfare State," 20–32.

40. Marshall, *Sociology at the Cross Roads,* 87.

41. P. Passell, "Socialist Eggs, Market Omelet," *New York Times,* April 11, 1990, D2; J. Kaufman, "Economic Shambles in the East Divides the United Germany," *Boston Globe,* March 6, 1991, 13; J. Kuron, J. Kis, V. Precan, and V. Bulovsky, "The Crumbling of the Soviet Bloc," *Journal of Democracy* 1 (1990): 71–90; *New York Times* editorials; "Blindly into Capitalism," *Herald Tribune,* October 1, 1990, 6; and Associated Press, "In East Germany, a Protest of Capitalism," *The Boston Globe,* November 5, 1990, 8.

42. D. Lockwood, "Some Remarks on 'The Social System,'" *British Journal of Sociology* 7 (1956): 134–146.

43. G. Simmel, *Conflict and the Web of Group Affiliation* (New York: Free Press, 1955); L. A. Coser, *The Function of Social Conflict* (New York: Free Press, 1956); and L. A. Coser, "Conflict: Social Aspects" in D. L. Sills, ed., *International Encyclopedia of Social Science,* vol. 3 (New York: Free Press, 1962): 232–236. For the conflict perspective, see G. Lenski, *Power and Privilege* (New York: McGraw-Hill, 1966); A. G. Frank, "Functionalism, Dialectics, and Synthetics," *Science and Society,* Spring 1966; K. Marx and F. Engels, "The Forces of Social Change," in T. B. Bottomore and M. Rubel, eds., *Karl Marx: Selected Readings in Sociology and Social Philosophy* (Harmondsworth: Penguin Books, 1961); P. L. Van Den Berghe, "Dialectic and Functionalism: Toward Theoretical Synthesis," *American Sociological Review* 28 (1963): 695–705; R. Dahrendorf, "Toward a Theory of Social Conflict," *The Journal of Conflict Resolutions II* (1958): 170–183.

44. R. Dahrendorf, *Class and Class Conflict in an Industrial Society* (London: Routledge & Kegan Paul, 1959).

45. Functionalism focuses on the structure of the social system in relation to its functions and emphasizes society's permanent aspects and the mechanisms of stabilization rather than change. See T. Parsons, "Some Considerations on the Theory of Social Change," *Rural Sociology* 26 (1961): 219–239.

46. T. H. Dye, *Understanding Public Policy,* 6th ed. (Englewood Cliffs, NJ: Prentice-Hall, 1987): 2, 3.

47. D. Easton, *The Political System* (New York: Knopf, 1953), 129.

48. H. D. Lasswell and A. Kaplan, *Power and Society* (New Haven, CT: Yale University Press, 1970), 71.

49. H. Heclo, "Policy Analysis," *British Journal of Political Science* 2 (1972), 85.

50. M. Hill and G. Bramley, *Analyzing Social Policy* (New York: Blackwell, 1966), 5.

51. *Socialization* is the process through which people learn to conform to social norms; this makes possible an enduring society and the transmission of its culture between generations. The individual internalizes social norms and tries to act according to the expectations

of others. See Chapter 2 for a discussion of the need to repeat the social-policy process until the desired results materialize.

52. J. Yenkin, "30 Million Americans Go Hungry," *Boston Globe,* September 10, 1992, 3; *Boston Globe* editorial, "Deepening Poverty in America," *Boston Globe,* September 7, 1992, 14; D. L. Cohen, "Despite Widespread Income Growth, Study Finds Increase in Child Poverty," *Education Week,* August 5, 1992, 24; "More Poverty for All," *New York Times,* September 6, 1992, 2; "Gap Between Rich and Poor Widens," *Boston Globe,* August 28, 1992, 15; D. Iatridis, "Neoconservatism Reviewed," *Social Work* 28 (March/April 1983): 101–107; D. Iatridis, "New Social Deficit: Neoconservatism's Policy of Social Underdevelopment," *Social Work* 33 (January/February 1988): 11–18; M. Marriott, "On Meaner Streets, The Violent Are More So," *New York Times,* September 13, 1992, 6 E.

53. Dye, *Understanding Public Policy,* 3; and W. N. Dunn, *Public Policy Analysis.*

54. D. Gil, *Unravelling Social Policy* (Rochester, VT: Schenkman, 1990), 13.

55. C. Jones, *Patterns of Social Policy: An Introduction to Comparative Analysis* (London: Tavistock, 1986), 16.

56. R. Pinker, *The Idea of Welfare* (London: Heinemann Educational Books, 1979), 224; N. Furniss and T. Tilton, *The Case of the Welfare State: From Social Security to Social Equality* (Bloomington, IN: Indiana University Press, 1979), Chapter 1.

57. Jones, *Patterns of Social Policy,* 13.

58. R. Titmuss refers to individual needs that are beyond the individual's capacity to resolve without outside help. This view is articulated in his major publications, including R. M. Titmuss, *Problems of Social Policy* (London: Her Majesty's Stationery Office, 1950); *Essays on the Welfare State* (London: Allen & Unwin, 1958), 39–42; *Commitment to Welfare* (London: Allen & Unwin, 1968); *The Gift of Relationship: From Human Blood to Social Policy* (London: Allen & Unwin, 1970); and *Social Policy: An Introduction* (London: Allen & Unwin, 1974).

59. W. J. Cahnman and C. M. Schmitt, "The Concept of Social Policy (*Sozialpolitik*)," *Journal of Social Policy* 8(1); 47–59; R. Girod and P. De Laubier, eds., *L'Etude de la Politique Sociale* (Berne: Commission Nationale Suisse pour l'UNESCO, 1974); C. Jones, "Teaching Social Policy: Some European Perspectives," *Journal of Social Policy* 8 Part 4 (1979): 509–526; and Jones, *Patterns of Social Policy,* 14.

60. M. Rein, *Social Policy: Issues of Choice and Change* (New York: Random House, 1990), 4, 5.

61. National Association of Social Workers, *Goals of Public Social Policy* (New York: National Association of Social Workers, 1963).

62. K. Boulding, "Boundaries of Social Policy," *Social Work* 12:1 (1967): 3–11.

63. J. E. Tropman et al., *Strategic Perspectives on Social Policy* (New York: Pergamon Press, 1976), xiii.

64. D. M. Austin, "Social Planning in the Public Sector," *Encyclopedia of Social Work,* 620–625.

65. B. Jansson, *Social Welfare Policy* (Belmont, CA: Wadsworth, 1990), 18.

66. N. Gilbert and H. Specht, *Dimensions of Social Welfare Policy* (Englewood Cliffs, NJ: Prentice-Hall, 1974), 3.

67. Titmuss, *Commitment to Welfare,* 192.

68. T. H. Marshall, *Social Policy* (London: Hutchinson University Press, 1965), 7.

69. The *Encyclopedia of Social Work,* 18th ed. (Silver Spring, MD: National Association of Social Workers, 1987) has no separate section on social policy as such. By implication, the subject of social policy is subsumed in the articles on "Social Welfare," "Policy Analysis," and "Social Planning."

70. Titmuss, *Commitment to Welfare.*

71. R. Morris, "Social Welfare Policy: Trends and Issues," *Encyclopedia of Social Work*, 664.

72. J. E. Tropman, "Policy Analysis: Methods and Techniques," *Encyclopedia of Social Work*, 268–283.

73. This view is close to the Titmuss tradition in the United Kingdom and the prevailing view in most capitalist countries today, including the United States. See Titmuss, *Commitment to Welfare*.

CHAPTER 2

Social Policy as an Intervention Process: The Practice Component

"Australia and the United States have the highest percentage of children living in poverty: 17%."[1]

"The United States has become the first society in which the poorest group in the population is children."[2]

"In other developed countries, at least 99% of poor families with children receive governmental assistance; in the United States, only 73% receive aid."[3]

"Among the industrialized countries in the study, only the [former] Soviet Union, which has 25 deaths per 1,000 live births, has an infant-mortality rate that exceeds the U.S. rate of 10 deaths per 1,000 live births."[4]

"Cuba, a third-world country, has an infant mortality rate of 10.6 deaths per 1,000 live births—reduced from 46.7 per 1,000 in 1969."[5]

"In 1988, the United States ranked 19th worldwide in infant mortality—trailing Singapore, Hong Kong, Spain, and Ireland."[6]

"In 1988, the United States ranked 21st worldwide in the mortality rate for children younger than 5, trailing East Germany, Singapore, New Zealand, and Japan."[7]

"In 1986, the United States ranked 19th in the number of school-age children per teacher, trailing Libya, East Germany, Lebanon, and Cuba."[8]

"One in ten U.S. teenagers aged 15–19 becomes pregnant, the highest teenage pregnancy rate recorded in industrialized nations."[9]

"37 million Americans have no health insurance, including 12 million children under 18 and 9 million women of childbearing age."[10]

"Approximately 3 million Americans are homeless;[11] 30% of them are mentally ill,[12] and 30–40% of them are families with children."[13]

"750 million to 1 billion people worldwide, 1 out of every 5, are chronically hungry. Every day, 35,000 people worldwide die from hunger and hunger-related diseases. Three-quarters of those who die are children under age 5. In the United States, an estimated 20 million people suffer from hunger.[14] Another study reports that 5.5 million people under age 12 are hungry in the United States."[15]

THE SOCIETAL CONTEXT OF PRACTICE

The social conditions highlighted in these quotations relate to the practice of social policy. Hunger, poverty, or poor health in advanced industrial countries reflect inadequate management of social policy and social change. Has social policy emerged as a method in social work practice? Are there adequate standards, knowledge, attitudes, skills, and training of social policy practitioners? What is the state of professional practice in social policy?

This chapter is not about how to practice social policy. Rather, it describes how to think clearly about social policy practice, how to understand its management, and how to approach it.[16]

MANAGING THE INTERVENTION-CHANGE PROCESS

Since World War II, policy planners have learned much about the characteristics of the intervention-change process in the context of practice. It is now possible to talk about the management of policy interventions for change in more systematic, effective, and professional ways than ever before. The following guidelines may lead to a more empowering view of the intervention-change process in social policy.

Policy Problems: In the Eye of the Beholder

Policy problems are subjective; they result from norms, values, and priorities. Therefore, planners must remember that policy problems are not objective entities whose existence may be established by determining what social conditions prevail or what the facts are. In this sense, problems are subjective—that is, they are in the eye of the beholder.

Governmental statistics that show increasing unemployment may constitute a problem for certain people but not for others. Certainly an unemployed person perceives unemployment as a problem, but employers who see unemployment as an opportunity to renew their labor force at a lower cost and to increase their profits may consider it an opportunity, not a problem.

Typically, only some social conditions are universally perceived as problems. Social conditions are considered problematic when they reflect unrealized values or priorities, have a significant impact on society, or involve a controversy.[17]

Different people may attribute the same problem to different causes. Some see unemployment as an economic problem whose potential resolution lies in restructuring the supply and demand for goods and services, creating jobs, and reducing the labor force. Others see it as a psychological, social, or administrative problem that may be resolved by creating work incentives for individuals who are predisposed to leisure.

Policy planners are aware that identifying, structuring, and explaining problems is subjective and that how people structure a problem determines how they will explain and attempt to resolve it. Those who structure a social problem control the answers; the way a problem is defined and explained influences the way it is likely to be solved.

The Systems Approach

Social conditions and problems are not independent entities, they are parts of whole systems. It is difficult to change policy without changing most parts of a system. Fragmented, piecemeal reform rarely results in significant benefits. Because change in one part of a system affects all other parts, policy planners use holistic approaches that view the targeted organization, community, or institution in its entirety, including its links to the environment.

Although policy planners recognize that the quality of the whole differs from the quantitative sum of its parts, they also know how difficult it is to consider the myriad interdependencies that exist.[18] A complete, correct assessment of social policy interventions can reflect many interdependencies among social conditions or phenomena, including demographic, cultural, sociological, political, economic, and educational conditions, and a host of spatial, physical, ecological, and other factors.

All these areas are affected by social policy interventions. Interventions can include changes in income; distribution of wealth, services, and power; characteristics of the labor force; patterns of employment, unemployment, and underemployment; migration; social mobility or isolation; the structure and cohesion of families and neighborhoods; and the standards of health and well-being.

Sound Theories: The Foundation of Practice

Social policy planners view practice as activity embedded in social work theory. To understand policy practice, we need to grasp the relationships between knowledge and action, between theory and practice, and between assumptions about the nature of realities and what makes professional practice possible and effective.

Appropriate theoretical frameworks must guide social policy practice. These frameworks, or relationships between and among ideas, help policy planners conceptualize problems and the issues involved. Theories help policy planners collect and analyze information and recommend action. Theory, particularly about the socio-economic environment, organizational behavior, the intervention process, and administration, also helps policy planners implement policy recommendations and organize interventions.

To intervene effectively in a system, policy planners make assumptions about its nature, how it operates, and how it can change. Competing theories about social organization, human behavior, the clients of social work, and the nature of change suggest different approaches and units of analysis.

For example, the competing theories of consensus and conflict pose contrasting views of social organization and how order is established and preserved in society. Consensus theory posits that every society has a fundamental agreement about social values and norms. In this view, society is a persisting, well-integrated configuration of elements resting on the consensus of citizens—a moral community sharing certain values. Policy planners who subscribe to this theory for understanding social problems are likely to focus on functions served rather than on the consequences of events and to assume that social change is a gradual, adjustive process that leaves the core of the system unchanged.

In contrast, conflict theory presents coercion as the basis of social order, with class conflict crucial to understanding societal functions. In this view, society hosts various power struggles, every society has constraints imposed on some of its members by others, and cohesiveness is achieved by coercion and enforced constraints. Policy planners who select this theory for analysis generally focus on who benefits from the established social relations; they assume that only central, systemic social change can modify the core of the system.

Empirical evidence partially supports both the conflict and the consensus views. Therefore, some policy planners select a combination of both theories in a complementary, rather than an antithetical, approach.

Policy planners also make assumptions about the nature of human behavior. Social work practice has used mainly Freudian psychoanalytic theory to explain observations of clients, individual problems, irrational behavior, and resistance to change. Despite the limitations of psychoanalytic concepts and the schools of thought that developed around them, these concepts have influenced social work practice. Particularly important have been the idea that human behavior is purposeful and determined and the assumption that some determinants of human behavior are unconscious or unrecognized by clients.[19]

Ideological perspectives[19] that affect social policy are also based on assumptions about human nature. Supporters of capitalism, including economists Friedman and Gilder,[20] assume that consumers' economic preferences are present from birth. In this view, human beings are by nature acquisitive, materialistic, selfish, competitive, and individualistic, and they calculate rationally every purchase or economic activity. In contrast, socialists assume that human beings are altruistic, collectivistic, and collaborative.

In the context of social sciences, the behavior of individuals, groups, and communities is shaped by the society in which we live and is not just biologically determined. Hence, no human beings are "naturally" inferior; and human "nature" is partly a function of the interactions between individuals and their environment.

Assumptions about human nature and behavior are associated historically with distributive justice, the prevailing power structure, and the economic relationships of production, distribution, and consumption. For example, Aristotle assumed that slavery was natural and that women were naturally inferior. He accepted these ideas uncritically because society and its power structure at that time were organized to reflect these concepts. In the Middle Ages, it was thought that serfdom naturally reflected human nature and behavior: the serfs were happy working for the landlord because that was their nature, and the landlord was happy directing, judging, and even executing serfs because that was the landlord's nature. Saint Thomas Aquinas contended that some prices are natural and that it is sinful to buy or sell at more or less than these prices. In the Middle Ages, usury was considered unnatural—a religious sin punishable by imprisonment in England.

It is no coincidence that because of these past dominant views of human nature, slavery and serfdom were supported. It is also no surprise that capitalism supports the free market, economic individualism, private enterprise, limited welfare transfers, and minimal governmental intervention, or that socialism supports collectivism, public enterprises, governmental control of market functions, and the welfare state. Assumptions about social organization and human behavior tend to justify a society's institutional arrangements and public social policy.

In putting theory into practice, social policy planners connect reflection and action. Policy planners differ in the kinds of reflective activity through which they apply theory to practice and analyze their interaction with clients. Schon, Argyris and Schon, and Forester have focused attention on reflection in practice. These and other commentators highlight practice dilemmas, including causal accounts of the practitioner's actions and the role of reflection in practice.[21]

Effects of Change

Simply being told to follow a different policy because it is desirable is seldom enough to help people, organizations, or communities understand the reasons for change. Planners recognize that affective aspects of change cannot be ignored if change efforts are to be successful. Successful implementation requires that participants understand the reasons for change and the implications of new policies.

Because change is highly personal, participants typically are concerned about how the change will affect them. Participants often wonder whether they are up to the task, whether the new policy will require more work, and how they will be seen by their peers. By seeking to understand these concerns and to design strategies to address them, policy planners ease tensions and pave the way for successful implementation.

The Utility of the Long View

In spite of intense political and economic pressure for policy reform, change takes time. It is counterproductive to push people, organizations, and communities faster than change can be assimilated. Most important, the intervention must be presented as a clear, compelling vision for the future, and improvement in social conditions must be significant and continuous. To this end, planners take measures to maintain the reform, reward successes and contributions, and keep the momentum for change and innovation.

The Nature of Social Change and Predictions of the Future

Social policy planners come to terms with competing concepts about the nature of and reasons for change and permanency and about trajectories of future events. These concepts have been debated since ancient Greece. The diametrically opposed views of two pre-Socratic philosophers and epistemologists, Parmenides and Heraclitus, are at the root of contemporary debates.

Parmenides argued that only the permanent, the eternal, the stable, and the unchanging are real and that all change is illusory, transitory, imperfect, and unreal.[22] Heraclitus saw reality as a flowing river, apparently the same, but actually ever-changing.[23] To him, all was constant flux and change; he dismissed the permanent and stable as unreal, as evidence of human imperfection, and as a distortion of the truth. These two thinkers remain important because each began a major, persistent theme in Western intellectual theory. Parmenides has had emulators in Christian theology, in romantic idealism, and in 20th-century mathematical logic. Heraclitus's followers include the medieval nominalists, the 19th-century evolutionary philosophers, and today's existentialists. Einstein's notion that energy equals mass times the square of velocity of light ($E = mc^2$) illustrates contemporary Heracliteanism applied to the physical world. Change is continuous, caused by an exchange of energy. The only continuity is change; descriptions of facts are extracted from continuous change.

In the context of contemporary social conditions and social policy practice, the notion of continuous change (social Heracliteanism) is important. For example, descriptions of social conditions are a snapshot of a continuous process of change. Individuals, families, groups, organizations, and communities—the clients of social work—are integral parts of broader, ever-changing systems, organized by information exchange and information processing. Theoretical perspectives that guide social policy interventions depict social systems as analogous to a flowing river, apparently the same but ever-changing. Most important, the repercussions of environmental interventions spread to affect all systems, merging in complex ways with the effects persisting from previous actions while altering the basis of the next action.

In the Heraclitean context, change is constant in social policy practice. Clients are dynamic systems whose relationships are constrained or supported by a wide range of societal resources. No social system is static. The causes and effects of the system's problems are complex, multidimensional, and reciprocal.

Policy planners recognize, therefore, that their approach to practice must account for change, choice, and conflict. In this context, social Heracliteanism helps planners shift from a deterministic view of organizations, communities, and social institutions as stable, machinelike systems to the probabilistic understanding that social systems evolve. Interventions in complex cybernetic systems require richly varied frameworks, approaches, knowledge, techniques, and tools.

Models and Modeling as Tools

To understand complex problems in practice, policy planners construct *models*, which are generalized descriptions or simplified pictures (graphic, verbal, or mathematical). A model does not represent an ideal to be emulated; rather, it clarifies problems and guides effective interventions. Poverty, well-being, and other societal problems are complex and difficult to grasp without modeling their structure and functions.

The process of modeling helps planners abstract and relate the essential components of the problem under investigation.[24] Construction of a model begins conceptually with efforts to understand the central forces that created the problem and continue to sustain it. As soon as planners understand these forces, they can develop a formal model. Models that simulate complex phenomena can be effective tools in social policy practice: They can promote experimentation and quantification, particularly when experimentation with social phenomena is difficult or impossible.

Models can facilitate analysis by identifying leverage points and can help social workers assess primary and secondary effects of proposed interventions.[25]

For example, social workers can model unemployment and population as two distinct, interacting systems, each consisting of its own feedback loop (see Figure 2-1). Population is affected by births, deaths, and migration, while the size of the labor force and the migration of workers to other areas in search of jobs affect unemployment. Population, influenced by the birth and death rates, changes the size of the labor force, which in turn has an impact on the unemployment rate. Unemployment increases migration as workers search for employment.

Planners use models based on systems dynamics to study complex and sometimes counterintuitive socioeconomic phenomena, such as regional economic development, urban decay, narcotic addiction, the generation and transfer of technology, criminal justice, environmental pollution, and public policy.[26]

Limitations of the Intervention-Change Process

In considering the feasibility of an intervention and its results, policy planners recognize that only some social conditions and problems can be reversed, regardless of effort and resources. Constraints, limitations, timing, and complexity may defy solution.

For example, the human environment poses many constraints on the rate and direction of changes. Nothing grows indefinitely; nothing exists in an infinite supply.[27] Policy planners are also aware of the enormous complexity of the human environment.[28] This complexity takes two forms. Static (or structural) complexity involves the sheer magnitude of economic, social, political, ideological, and spatial factors. Dynamic (or behavioral) complexity includes the ways in which these structural factors interact over time and how these interactions produce the overall system behavior (growth, stagnation, oscillation, or decay). Policy planners recognize the limitations of intervening in complex, probabilistic systems; changes can cause unpredictable repercussions.

INTERVENTION ROLES AND TYPES

In social policy planning, social workers assume varied roles and practice different types of policy. The most important types include laissez-faire, rational, normative, and advocacy policy.

Laissez-Faire

This type of policy requires almost no planned intervention or tasks other than the decision not to intervene. The major task of the practitioner is to do little or nothing. Laissez-faire policy practitioners expect that in due time the forces inherent in a system will become active, and problems will wither away. Exemplified by the neoconservative (or neoliberal) administrations of U.S. presidents Ronald Reagan and George Bush, this type of policy planning assumes that a problem can best be solved without

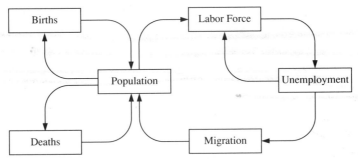

FIGURE 2-1   Feedback of demographic forces in unemployment

policy intervention because the forces of the unfettered economic market (or other institutions and organizations) will resolve it. The fewer planned interventions, the better for the functioning of the system.

Critics of this policy, including liberals, supporters of controlled and guided economic markets, and socialists, maintain that laissez-faire policy planning tends to prolong dysfunctions and increase their cost. The critics also say that laissez-faire policies benefit the status quo and the ruling class, deemphasize preventive or developmental efforts, and perpetuate inequalities or powerlessness.

In social work policy practice, practitioners decide whether or not to intervene after careful, critical analyses of the problem, the client system, possible effects on the environment, and professional commitments.

Rational Policy Planning

This type of social policy intervention is based mainly on logic and scientific reasoning. Rational policy planning dominates several professions and disciplines, particularly in policy analysis tasks. Its supporters emphasize the important benefits derived from objective procedures and from quantifying and measuring concepts. Normative, subjective judgments are excluded and the planner assumes scientific, technical roles.

Critics of this type of policy maintain that although rational, technical planning is useful, it is ineffective in selecting the goals of policy interventions (goals are normative in nature). Thus rational planning is limited to the selection of means; it can only indicate the most effective ways to achieve given goals. Like a good road map, rational planning can suggest the best way to get somewhere but cannot indicate where one should go. Critics argue that participants in rational planning usually accept given goals uncritically. By definition, goal setting constitutes a normative judgment. In accepting "objective" goals without evaluating them, policy planners can unintentionally promote undesirable results.

Critics also point out that participants in rational planning exclude considerations of justice, equality, and ethics. However, strictly technocratic principles can be irrelevant or inappropriate in situations requiring social justice and ethical goals.

Social workers in policy practice use rational planning and technical tools, but in a normative context guided by the values and commitments of social work.

Normative Policy Planning

In contrast, participants in normative planning accept and use value concepts and principles without rejecting necessarily rational and objective procedures. Supporters claim that selecting appropriate goals is crucial in social policy planned to generate change and reform. Far from being undesirable, values are beneficial and complement technological procedures. Normative policy planners say that the term *rational planning* is an oxymoron because empiricism, the basis of rational policy planning, is itself a normative concept and a value preference.

Critics of normative planning maintain that the subjectivity introduced by normative procedures deprives policy making of objectivity. According to this view, policy planners should accept the goals of society or the client system rather than allow normative elements (externalities) to "contaminate" the process of policy planning.

Policy planning in social work is based on both scientific and normative contexts, tasks, and procedures.

Advocacy Policy Planning

Based on the deliberate promotion of specific goals and interests of clients, advocacy planning is used to empower specific groups, including the poor, children, women, the elderly, communities, organizations, minority groups, or consumers. In the context of professional values and commitments, policy planners support and promote the goals of client groups and design policy interventions that secure or protect client groups' rights, entitlements, or interests. Advocacy policy planners make action-oriented recommendations to protect clients; they may emphasize clients' legal rights, rights that flow from due process, social justice considerations, or unjustified policies of organizations and communities.

Supporters claim that race, sex, and social-class advocacy promotes social justice, reverses negative effects of social structures and norms that discriminate, redresses social problems, and empowers the powerless. Critics point out that every effort to organize a group for social action or to protect certain rights can stimulate counter-efforts or movements to neutralize the effort. They argue that advocacy can generate major conflicts or can favor groups that have more resources and power.

Policy social workers are committed to advocacy and social action. The civil rights movement and the War on Poverty are two examples of how social workers and others can use advocacy planning. The goal of advocacy was legitimized by the National Association of Social Workers (NASW) both in its statement on advocacy and in the NASW Code of Ethics.[29]

Subtypes of Policy Planning

Various subtypes of policy planning represent differences in the nature of clients and problems or emphasis on special techniques and tools. These subtypes include the following:

- *Comprehensive or synoptic policy planning,* which is characterized by efforts to include all variables involved in problems and their solution

- *Strategic policy planning,* in which planners select one or a few variables to maximize specific results
- *Contingency policy planning,* characterized by its emphasis on flexibility in the face of unexpected developments
- *Incremental policy planning,* which is an attempt to repeat the previous year's plans with only small changes each year; it is practiced in bureaucratic settings where restricted resources must be distributed competitively
- *Organizational policy planning,* characterized by the view of policy as an organizational output revealing organizational motives
- *Bureaucratic policy planning,* in which policy is viewed as a political outcome of power, bargaining processes, and incrementalism
- *Scanning or mix policy planning,* a combination of several policy types.[30]

MAJOR PRACTICE TASKS: THE SOCIAL POLICY PROCESS

Social Problems and Issues

Social policy planners are invariably concerned with social problems and the issues they represent. For example, inadequate care for children involves health care financing, access to health care services, lack of primary health care at the neighborhood level, inappropriate home environments, child abuse and neglect, and services for special needs. Inadequate national health care and insurance involves discrimination, social justice, cost of and access to health care services, methods of funding national insurance, collaboration of health providers (physicians, hospitals, private insurance companies), and the organization and coordination of health care delivery at all levels.

Family planning is another example of a social problem that involves several issues. The Family Planning in the U.S. proposal, introduced as a social policy document to U.S. congressional policymakers, described the status of family planning; addressed the issues involved, including those of unwanted fertility in the U.S.; and recommended legislative frameworks to address the problem.[31]

Intervention Levels and Activities

Policy planners formulate action-oriented proposals designed to prevent or resolve social problems, issues, or conditions that undermine well-being or development. In the process, they engage in varied administrative, legislative, judicial, and social action tasks to promote change at the local, state, regional, national, or international level. International policy considerations come into play in the form of global standards and comparative social policy. For example, the World Health Organization has recommended standards and strategies for health care by the year 2000. The debate about national health insurance in the United States involves consideration of what other countries do and what they have accomplished.

At all intervention and governmental levels, it is crucial to understand the legislative and decision-making processes and their relation to other governmental units. For example, social policy planners must know what congressional committees and executive departments of government are involved in a policy area, what regulatory measures and decision-making processes are in play, and how they influence other levels of government.

Values, Ideology, and Ethics

Social policy practice is a value-laden process in which many decisions are driven by numerous and sometimes conflicting values and ideologies. The values of clients who use the policy recommendations and the values of social work help define and resolve social problems. The very concept of a social problem implies an unrealized value. For example, the problem of unemployment denotes the unrealized value of employment. The problem of hunger denotes an unrealized value of adequate nutrition.

Throughout the policy process and interaction with clients, social workers in policy practice apply the ethics of social work. For example, they promote planned changes for reform, distributive justice, equality, and empowerment. They also secure the active participation of clients (individuals, groups, and communities) in democratic processes that promote self-determination and actualization.

Stages of Social Policy Practice

Social policy planners use diverse theories and approaches and assume varied roles in different social problems or types of practice. However, they perform common tasks to organize and guide their efforts in two stages of policy practice: policy analysis and implementation planning.

Policy Analysis

During the policy analysis stage, policy planners try to define the social problem, identify key policy issues, analyze the history of policy issues and efforts to resolve the problem, identify key players and decision-making bodies, model the decision-making process, synthesize the information, and make recommendations. The following steps are involved:

- Gathering information about the social problem, social conditions, or opportunity for development
- Establishing a frame of reference to conceptualize and define the nature of the problem and the issues involved
- Designing a methodology
- Choosing and conducting technical analyses to study factors that may cause the social problem
- Developing conclusions, reasoned policy arguments, and plans; recommending intervention if indicated; and predicting outcomes
- Communicating recommendations to clients or users (policy makers, groups, organizations, communities, or decision makers)

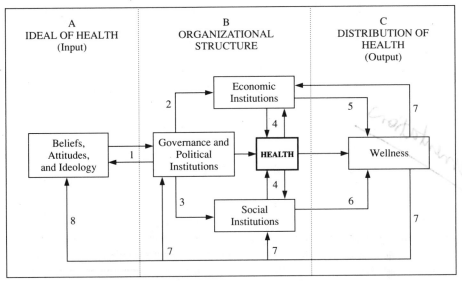

FIGURE 2-2   The institutional context of health care policy

Understanding the socioeconomic environment of the social problem and the client is crucial in policy analysis. To this end, policy planners use varied guidelines or models. For example, the model of social policy described in the previous chapter (Figure 1-2) is also useful in this context. Adjusted to the social problem of inadequate health care, the model guides the analysis of the socioeconomic environment of health (Figure 2-2).

Typical tasks in policy analysis can be grouped into four related phases: analysis of problems and interventions, formulation of action-oriented policy recommendations, communication of these recommendations to clients, and feedback. Figure 2-3 (on page 44) shows the four phases of policy analysis.

Depending on the discussion of recommendations and the reactions of clients, policy planners might have to collect more data, identify more policy alternatives, and consider new or different variables, values, or issues. In so doing, they may repeat tasks (A, B, and C of Figure 2-3) several times until either desired results are achieved or the analysis is discontinued. With each new cycle, the intensity and depth of analysis increase.

The policy analysis stage constitutes a cognitive undertaking to provide information and recommendations to clients so they can determine whether and how to act. This stage refers to a varied group of tasks focused on helping clients (usually policy makers) solve social problems. In social work, practitioners of policy analysis explicitly include values, respond to clients, incorporate both the future and the past, and attempt to resolve multidimensional social problems. Policy analysis has an empirical orientation; it begins with social problems and includes attempts to induce concepts and causal theories. Thus, the policy analysis stage represents an undertaking by which policies are adopted and their effects are assessed.

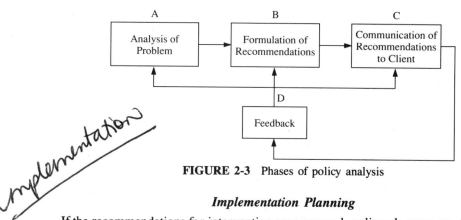

FIGURE 2-3   Phases of policy analysis

implementation

Implementation Planning

If the recommendations for intervention are approved, policy planners can then plan the implementation. During this stage (Figure 2-4) policy planners organize the implementation, implement and monitor the project, evaluate outcomes, and adjust tasks through feedback flows. The following tasks are involved:

- Designing projects to implement the recommended policies
- Securing and organizing human and material resources
- Communicating to those responsible the organization of projects and explaining the purpose, scope, and procedures of the intervention, including the roles assigned to key players
- Providing operational guidelines for the implementation and its evaluation
- Organizing and monitoring the projects and implementation tasks
- Evaluating the outcomes of interventions and comparing the outcomes to those expected
- Adjusting the implementation procedures as needed
- Recommending continuation or discontinuation of the intervention to ensure the viability of the changes achieved
- Communicating the outcomes to clients so they can decide whether to continue the interventions.[32]

In contrast to the policy analysis stage, implementation planning is distinctly oriented toward organization, administration, and assessment of outcomes.

The Scope of the Social Policy Process

In practice, the two stages of the social policy process (Figure 2-5) can be either interrelated and sequential or relatively independent. For example, clients might request that policy planners focus either on one or on both of the stages. Each stage requires related but different skills and approaches. Policy analysis requires mainly cognitive skills, whereas implementation planning has mainly an organizational and planning orientation. Social policy planners may focus only on policy analysis and develop expertise in that area, or they may specialize in implementation planning.

In this book, the term *social policy planning* includes both social policy analysis and implementation planning theory, knowledge, skills, and tools. In practice, policy

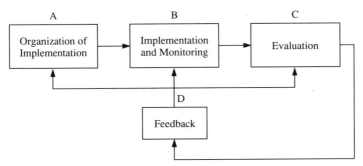

FIGURE 2-4   Phases of implementation planning

analysis and planning can converge to form a more comprehensive approach to problem solving.

Social work literature treats the similarities and differences of social policy analysis and social planning in varied ways. Kahn suggested that both social policy and social planning use rational, scientific concepts and techniques.[33] Mayer, focusing on social policy as a technical process, equated it with social planning for growth and development and with the rational decision-making process used by governmental bodies and large organizations that act in the public interest.[34] Patton and Sawicki, associating policy analysis with planning, focused on quick methods for resolving policy and planning problems.[35] Cox et al. emphasized strategic and tactical considerations in community policy making and planning.[36] Checkoway suggested that social planning and social policy practice activate people to plan for diverse domains and functional fields.[37]

Gilbert and Specht outlined the social planning process in social work as identification of a problem, selection of goals, program planning and development, and implementation of programs.[38] Austin uses the same phases to describe the social planning process in governmental activities for the "efficient, effective, and equitable use of resources in the implementation of social programs," including planning, programmatic skills, and strategic considerations.[39] Others describe the phases of social planning as problem analysis, needs assessment, decision making (program planning and budgeting, Delphi, and so on), and evaluation. However, some writers attribute these phases to the social policy process. Still others view the practice of social planning, social policy, and policy analysis as different technical processes in the context of values, social justice, and efficiency.

THE EVOLUTION
OF SOCIAL POLICY PRACTICE

Industrialization, Urbanization, and Modernization

Industrialization, urbanization, and modernization have spurred the emergence of social policy planning and practice as an important function of modern society. Modern governments spend billions of dollars to achieve many conflicting goals through

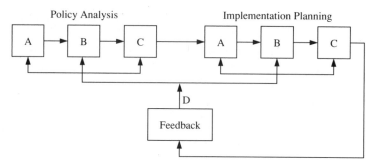

FIGURE 2-5 Stages of the social policy process

complex, competing public programs and projects. Legislators, administrators, government officials, and organizations in both the private and public sectors must plan their investments effectively, and before new appropriations are made, they must monitor and assess the outcomes of previous policies.

The roles of contemporary governments in protecting and improving the well-being of all citizens, and the competition in the economic market, require that strategies for growth and development be critically and systematically chosen. More important, governments and organizations are accountable to the taxpaying public. These factors necessitate continuous evaluations of the impact of social policy goals and programs on people and communities.

Spurred by increasingly complex social problems and by advances in technology, research, management, and decision making, social policy practice in social work has also emerged as an approach to analyze and alleviate social problems. Poverty, health care, homelessness, social welfare services, unemployment, crime, education, housing, the economic market, the environment, and hunger are examples of the social problems social policy planners address in practice. Social policy practice helps planners identify social goals and priorities that are in the public interest; analyze and resolve complex social problems to achieve societal goals; use scarce resources in the private or public sectors efficiently and equitably; and organize, manage, monitor, and evaluate interventions in large organizations or complex institutions.

Advances in Policy Analysis

Policy analysis has also emerged as a crucial component in public policy, governmental activities, management, and decision making. Placing little emphasis on content and conceptual issues, policy analysts typically synthesize technical and empirical data to formulate policies. Policy analysts come from several disciplines and backgrounds: management, administration, governmental policy and studies, urban planning, operations research, applied social sciences, and strategic organizational planning.

Policy analysts use one or more technical approaches, including operations research, systems analysis, cost-benefit analysis, cost-effectiveness analysis, and economic theory. Analytical tools can include linear programming, queueing theory, computer simulation, stochastic processes, and operational gaming. The emergence of policy analysis has promoted social policy planning in social work education and practice. Social policy planning in social work, however, has acquired social work characteristics.

Some professionals view policy analysis as an entity separate from other disciplines, including social work, sociology, economics, and political science. They consider analysis a separate, applied social science discipline that uses multiple technical methods of inquiry and rationale to produce and transform policy-relevant information to resolve policy problems.[40] From this perspective, policy analysis is a form of applied research carried out to acquire a technical, deeper, and more disciplined understanding of how to formulate policies and solve problems through their implementation.

Commentators supporting this view, including Dunn, focus on the development of technical and conceptual skills for analyzing policy problems.[41] Hogwood and Gunn, Stokey and Zeckhauser, Quade, and several others have presented repertoires of analytic techniques to assist policy makers at various stages of the policy process.[42] Transcending the boundaries of specific professions, these techniques and tools are frequently used in various fields, including social work. They are useful, effective technical tools because they provide a much-needed foundation for problem solving in modern society.

Some authors, including Dror, emphasize the inadequacy of contemporary, "normal" policy making and propose a supradiscipline that will encompass a different scientific approach. Carrying this movement and its labor market expansion to its highest level, these theorists have proposed using the term *policy analysis* to describe a new science and field of practice distinct from any other.[43]

In addition to the debate about a supradiscipline, crucial questions have been raised regarding the precise nature of policy analysis. Is policy analysis concerned only with the analysis of data to guide policy formulation, or does it include implementation of policy? Does policy analysis include normative concepts, or should it be considered a value-free, "scientific" process of technical approaches and tools? The debate on such questions is rather recent and, perhaps because of this, inconclusive.[44]

Critics of policy analysis point out that the technical approach has been tried but has not proven helpful enough to be worthwhile. Its emphasis on technique, and its exclusion of values, professional content, and commitments obscures unresolved basic policy issues, including the formulation of goals and which types of problems and analyses are appropriate.[45] As a scientific, technological, value-free process, critics point out, policy analysis is effective in determining the most appropriate means to achieve given goals, but it is not relevant in defining appropriate goals. Because goals are normative, their selection transcends the borders of "scientific" policy analysis.

Policy analysis tools are also used in other disciplines, including management, planning, organizational theory, decision making, and social policy. Thus, the use of certain tools does not readily distinguish policy analysis as a separate discipline.

Social Policy Practice and Social Work Methods

Social policy practice is central to social work. Social workers who focus on the interactions between people and their socioeconomic environment recognize that social policies influence clients' behavior.[46] Rather than operating in isolation, social workers analyze policies that influence the interactions both among people and among people and societal institutions. Social change and social action, central components in social work practice, can only be understood in the context of social policies.

Social work's historic commitment to distributive justice and to advocacy on behalf of the disadvantaged and powerless materialize in modern society through effective social policies. For example, social policy has provided social services and created appropriate human environments to meet the needs and interests of all citizens and to stimulate development.

In clinical social work practice, social workers must understand and analyze the macro forces of social policy for curative and preventive interventions with individuals and families. For example, freedom from powerlessness, alienation, and mental illness, sought through direct clinical service, is greatly strengthened when social workers do not focus solely on a client's freedom from his or her personal past. Rather, clinical outcomes can become more effective and lasting when clinical services are integrated with social policy reforms that are aimed at freeing clients from pressing wants created by dysfunctional environments.

In this context, social policy practice is central to social work services; it is a method of achieving social work goals and commitments. Social workers practice social policy when they try to improve social conditions for clients and achieve social work objectives, such as preventing societal ills and achieving well-being and social justice.

Social policy practice as a social work method is not as widely recognized as other, more traditional social work approaches. An increasing number of social work commentators, including Jansson, Pierce, and Tropman, have heralded the emergence of social policy practice. In their work, they refer to policy practice, the practice component of social welfare, and the practice of human services.[47] Emphasizing that social policy has always been a concern of the social work profession, they point out the inadequate integration of social policy content in social work curricula. These and other commentators argue for a broad recognition of social policy as a social work method, promoting social policy practice (or policy management) that is based on technical phases and steps, normative concepts, and social work commitments.[48]

Several commentators have suggested that the social policy method in social work practice includes problem definition, proposed decision, planning, and program evaluation—the steps to both policy formulation and implementation (policy analysis and implementation planning). Policy practice is perceived as a direct route to achieving social work's goals of institutional change, social reform, and provision of services to those in need.[49] As an integral part of social work practice, the social policy method is an intervention strategy to address clients' issues and institutional reform.

Approaches to social work practice vary with the problem being addressed; the client; the level of intervention required; the organizational setting; the social worker's style, creativity, training, and judgment; and the developmental stage of the intervention. In both clinical and macro social work practice, there are several modes of approaches. Macro social work methods include practice in social policy, social planning, social action, policy analysis, community organization, and administration. Each method has roots in different stages of evolution of social work practice, and each meets different client needs.

NOTES

1. U.S. Bureau of the Census, *Report for the House Select Committee on Children, Youth, and Families,* cited in *Educational Week,* March 28, 1990, 7. This report compared children in the United States with children in Australia, Canada, France, West Germany, Hungary, Italy, Japan, Norway, Sweden, the former Soviet Union, and the United Kingdom.

2. Statement by Senator Daniel Patrick Moynihan, cited in K. Phillips, *The Politics of Rich and Poor: Wealth and the American Electorate in the Reagan Aftermath* (New York: Random House, 1990); and in A. Hartman, "Children in a Careless Society," *Social Work* 35 (November 1990): 483.

3. U.S. Bureau of the Census.

4. U.S. Bureau of the Census.

5. C. Vitier, "Our America: An Indicator of Well-Being, 10.7: Cuba Reduces Its Infant Mortality Rate," *Granma,* (weekly English edition published by the Communist Party of Cuba), January 20, 1991, 4.

6. *S.O.S. America! A Children's Defense Budget* (Washington, DC: Children's Defend Fund, 1990), 3.

7. Ibid.

8. Ibid.

9. U.S. Bureau of the Census.

10. *The State of America's Children 1991* (Washington, DC: Children's Defense Fund, 1991), 56. And *A Vision for America's Children* (Washington, DC: Children's Defense Fund, 1989), 8.

11. J. Erickson and C. Wilhelm, eds., *Housing the Homeless* (Rutgers, NJ: Center for Urban Policy, Rutgers University, 1986), xxxi. Although estimates range from 300,000 to 3 million homeless in the United States, a 1984 Department of Housing and Urban Development report, cited by the editors, estimated the number at 3 million.

12. M. Cohen, "Social Work Practice with Homeless Mentally Ill People: Engaging the Client," *Social Work* 34 (November 1989): 505.

13. I. Klein, "Homeless," *NASW News* (October 1990), 4.

14. *The Hunger Project Newspaper* (San Francisco, February 1991), 13.

15. R. Pear, "Hungry Children Put at 5.5 Million," *New York Times,* March 26, 1991, A18.

16. Social workers can more effectively learn the specific techniques, procedures, and tools of social policy practice in special programs and through experience in practice.

17. For the identification of policy issues, see W. D. Coplin and M. K. O'Leary, *Public Policy Skills* (Croton-on-Hudson, NY: Policy Studies Associates, 1988).

18. W. Bower, "Our New Awareness of the Great Web," *Fortune* (February 1970).

19. S. Briar and H. Miller, *Problems and Issues in Social Casework* (New York: Columbia University Press, 1971).

20. M. Friedman, *Capitalism and Freedom* (Chicago: University of Chicago Press, 1982; and R. T. Selden, ed., *Capitalism and Freedom: Problems and Prospects; Proceedings of a Conference in Honor of Milton Friedman* (Charlottesville: University Press of Virginia, 1975); and G. F. Gilder, *Wealth and Poverty* (New York: Bantam Books, 1982).

21. D. Schon's highly regarded book, *The Reflective Practitioner: How Professionals Think in Action* (New York: Basic Books, 1983), has given these issues, particularly the dynamics of reflective practice, new form and legitimacy. See also D.A. Schon, *Educating the Reflective Practitioner* (San Francisco: Jossey-Bass, 1987). The book Schon edited in 1991, *The Reflective Turn* (New York: Teachers College Press, Columbia University), analyzes 14 case studies of reflective practice that illustrate a variety of theoretical frameworks and

methods and provide opportunities to explore several critical practice issues. In their 1974 publication, *Theory in Practice* (San Francisco: Jossey-Bass), C. Argyris and D. Schon analyzed the use of theory in practice situations. J. Forester, in "Anticipating Implementation: Reflective and Normative Practices in Policy Analysis and Planning" (in Schon, *The Reflective Turn*), examines what planners do and what kind of knowledge they call upon.

22. Parmenides of Elea (born 515 B.C.) changed the course of Greek cosmology, particularly metaphysics and epistemology, influencing Empedocles, Anaxagoras, the atomists, and Plato, who inherited from Parmenides the assumption that the object of knowledge must be found by the mind, not by the senses. Comments in this section are elaborated in G.E.L. Owen, "Eleatic Questions," in *Classical Quarterly*, n. s., vol. 10 (1960): 84–102; W. K. C. Gunthrie, *A History of Greek Philosophy*, vol. 2 (New York: Cambridge University Press, 1965); and P. Edwards, ed., *The Encyclopedia of Philosophy*, vol. 5 (New York: Collier Macmillan, 1972): 47–51.

23. Heraclitus of Ephesus, the first Greek speculative philosopher to raise the question of sensory perception ("I prefer things of which there is sight, hearing, learning"), believed the world was uncreated and that pairs of opposites exemplify the unity of all things. His theory of flux (comparing all things to a river) implied that all things change constantly, although total balance is always maintained. Life and death, as alternate states, are the same. Comments in this section are elaborated in G. Vlastos, "On Heraclitus," *American Journal of Philosophy* 76 (1955): 337–368; G. S. Kirk, *Heraclitus, the Cosmic Fragments* (New York: Cambridge University Press, 1954); and P. Edwards, ed., *The Encyclopedia of Philosophy*, vol. 3 (New York: Collier Macmillan, 1972): 477–481.

24. C. A. Lave and J. G. March, *An Introduction to Models in the Social Sciences* (New York: Harper & Row, 1975).

25. H. R. Hamilton, S. E. Goldstone, J. W. Millman, A. L. Pugh, E. B. Roberts, and A. Zellner, *Systems Simulation for Regional Analysis* (Cambridge, MA: MIT Press, 1969). Econometric models reflect a generation of models based on a causal structure. They are simulatable, and simulation analysis is used more and more extensively. See J. Dusenberry et al., *The Brookings Quarterly, Econometric Models of the U.S.* (Chicago: Rand McNally, 1965). See also L. R. Klein, ed., *Comparative Performance of U.S. Econometric Models* (New York: Oxford University Press, 1991); T. Baker and W. Peterson, eds., *The Cambridge Multisectoral Dynamic Model of the British Economy* (New York: Cambridge University Press, 1988); R. Heijmans and H. Neudecker, eds., *The Practice of Econometrics: Studies on Demand, Forecasting, Money, and Income* (Boston: Kluwer Academic, 1987); P. M. Robinson, "Best Nonlinear Three-Stage Least Squares Estimation of Certain Economic Models," *Econometrics* 59 (May 1991): 755–786; M. P. Clements and G. E. Mizon, "Empirical Analysis of Macroeconomic Time Series: VAR and Structural Models," *European Economic Review* 35 (May 1991): 887–917.

26. J. Forrester, "Counter-Intuitive Behavior of Social Systems," *Technology Review*, 73, no. 3 (January 1971): 52–68; J. Forrester, *Urban Dynamics* (Cambridge, MA: MIT Press, 1969); Hamilton et al., *Systems Simulation for Regional Analysis;* J. Forrester, "Systems Analysis as a Tool for Urban Planning," *IEEE Spectrum* 8, no. 1 (January, 1971): 48–54; G. Levin et al., "Narcotics and the Community: A System Simulation," *American Journal of Public Health* 62, no. 6 (June, 1972): 861–873; J. W. Forrester, "World Dynamics of Environmental Impact," *Proceedings of the 1972 Summer Computer Simulation Conference;* H. B. Weil et al., *Feedback Structures and Tenacity of Crime* (Cambridge, MA: Pugh-Roberts Associates, 1973); A. L. Pugh et al., "The Dynamics of Environmental Impact," *Proceedings of the 1972 Summer Computer Simulation Conference;* I. R. Hoos, *Systems Analysis in Public Policy* (Berkeley and Los Angeles: University of California

Press, 1972); and E. S. Quade and W. I. Boucher, *Systems Analysis and Policy Planning* (New York: American Elsevier, 1968).

27. D. Meadows et al., *The Limits of Growth* (New York: L. Potomac, 1972).

28. B. Commoner, *The Closing Circle* (New York: Knopf, 1971).

29. Ad Hoc Committee on Advocacy, "The Social Worker as Advocate: Champion of Social Victims," *Social Work* 14, no. 2 (1969): 16–22; and "NASW Code of Ethics," *Social Work* 25, no. 3 (1980): 184–188.

30. For types of planning, see G. T. Allison, "Conceptual Models and the Cuban Missile Crisis," *American Political Science Review* 63 (September, 1969): 689–717; T. R. Dye, *Understanding Public Policy* (Englewood Cliffs, NJ: Prentice-Hall, 1987); B. W. Hogwood and L. A. Gunn, *Policy Analysis for the Real World* (London: Oxford University Press, 1984); J. W. Kingdon, *Agendas, Alternatives, and Public Policies* (Boston: Little, Brown, 1984); R. M. Moroney, *Social Policy and Social Work* (New York: Aldine de Gruyter, 1991); R. B. Ripley, *Policy Analysis in Political Science* (Chicago: Nelson-Hall, 1985); and A. Wildarsky, *Speaking Truth to Power: The Art and Craft of Policy Analysis* (Boston: Little, Brown, 1979).

31. Planned Parenthood, *Planned Births, the Future of the Family, and the Quality of American Life* (New York: Alan Guttmacher Institute, 1977).

32. *Encyclopedia of Social Work,* 18th ed., vol. 2 (Silver Spring, MD: National Association of Social Workers, 1987) 593–631.

33. A. J. Kahn, *Theory and Practice of Social Planning* (New York: Russell Sage Foundation, 1969).

34. R. Mayer, *Policy and Program Planning* (Englewood Cliffs, NJ: Prentice-Hall, 1985).

35. C. V. Patton and D. S. Sawicki, *Basic Methods of Policy Analysis and Planning* (Englewood Cliffs, NJ: Prentice-Hall, 1986).

36. F. Cox et al., *Strategies of Community Organization,* 4th ed. (Itasca, IL: F.E. Peacock, 1987).

37. B. Checkoway, *Strategic Perspectives on Planning Practice* (Lexington, MA: Lexington Books, 1986), 1, 8.

38. N. Gilbert and H. Specht, "Social Planning and Community Organization," *Encyclopedia of Social Work,* 18th ed., vol. 2 (Silver Spring, MD: National Association of Social Workers, 1987), 602–619.

39. D. M. Austin, "Social Planning in the Public Sector," *Encyclopedia of Social Work,* 18th ed., vol. 2 (Silver Spring, MD: National Association of Social Workers, 1987), 620–625.

40. W. N. Dunn, *Public Policy Analysis* (Englewood Cliffs, NJ: Prentice-Hall, 1981), ix.

41. Ibid.

42. Hogwood and Gunn, *Policy Analysis;* E. Stokey and R. Zeckhauser, *A Primer for Policy Analysis* (New York: Norton, 1978); E. S. Quade, *Analysis for Public Decisions* (New York: North Holland, 1982).

43. Y. Dror, *Design for Policy Sciences* (New York: American Elsevier, 1971).

44. In a social work context, Tropman seems to equate policy analysis with social policy, referring to a general "policy" process that consists of several phases: problem, proposed decision, planning, and programming evaluation. In the social science literature, these phases are systematically identified as phases of policy analysis, social policy, and social planning. Tropman implies that the process is concerned with both the formulation and implementation of policy. Others maintain that it is sufficiently clear if and how the process of policy analysis differs from that of social policy, whether policy analysis includes both the formulation and implementation of policy, and whether policy analysis excludes normative notions.

45. Quade, *Analysis for Public Decisions,* chap. 2.
46. *Client system* (or *client group*) denotes that the client of a social worker may be an individual or a family, small group, committee, organization, neighborhood, community, or other social structure. See B.W. Sheator et al., *Techniques and Guidelines for Social Work Practice,* 2nd ed. (Boston: Allyn & Bacon, 1991), xv.
47. B. S. Jansson, *Social Welfare Policy: From Theory to Practice* (Belmont, CA: Wadsworth, 1990); and Jansson, *The Theory and Practice of Social Welfare Policy* (Belmont, CA: Wadsworth, 1984); D. Pierce, *Policy for the Social Work Practitioner* (New York: Longman, 1984); and J. Tropman, "Policy Analysis: Methods and Techniques," *Encyclopedia of Social Work,* 18th ed., vol. 2 (Silver Spring, MD: National Association of Social Workers, 1987) 268–281.
48. Tropman, "Policy Analysis."
49. N. L. Wyers, "Policy-Practice In Social Work," *Journal of Social Work Education,* 27, no. 3 (Fall 1991): 241–250; R. Dear, K. Briar, and A. V. Ry, "Policy Practice: A 'New' Method Coming of Age?" (Paper presented at the 32nd Annual Program Meeting of the Council on Social Work Education, Miami, Florida, March 1986); D. Pierce, *Policy for the Social Work Practitioner* (New York: Longman, 1984); A. Schorr, Professional Practice as Policy," *Social Service Review* 59 (1985): 178–196.

THE INSTITUTIONAL ENVIRONMENT

Part One's focus was the frameworks of social policy and its institutional environment. Part Two is an analysis of specific effects of key institutions on the practice of social policy. Part Two follows the theoretical model of the institutional environment of social policy presented in Chapter 1. As you will recall, this model highlights the interdependence of ideological, political, economic, and social institutions. In Part Two, the model is used to explore applied considerations of ideology and social justice (Chapter 3), distributions of political power associated with major models of political organization (Chapter 4), economic theories and rationales that influence approaches to social development (Chapter 5), major dilemmas of developing the welfare state (Chapter 6), and institutional effects on well-being and poverty (Chapter 7).

Ideology and
Social Justice

"China's rule has created a catastrophic situation for Tibetans, with discrimination and racism rampant. Today, Tibet is a human rights and cultural catastrophe."[1]

"At the U.N. Aristide stands up for Haiti, pledging creation of a just society. . . . We are on the way to democracy, struggling against injustice and exploitation. . . . We are proud to be Haitians, and . . . citizens of the world."[2]

"Governor Weld files abortion bills, draws blast by Cardinal Law. . . . The proposed liberalized abortion laws . . . drew biting criticism by Cardinal Bernard Law, including a pointed accusation that Weld 'seeks to make Massachusetts the Commonwealth of Death for the Innocent.' "[3]

"Judge Clarence Thomas . . . disavowed earlier controversial statements that a higher 'natural law' ought to be a guiding influence in interpreting the Constitution. . . . Natural law can be used to prevent government from regulating business and to restrict individual rights, including the right to privacy—and therefore abortion."[4]

"Thomas's railings against affirmative action and abortion were grounds enough for opposition to his nomination to the U.S. Supreme Court."[5]

"Americans bent on tax rebellion may wonder why Sweden, with the highest effective tax rate in the world, took so long to deprive the Social Democrats of power after they had governed for all but 6 of the past 60 years. The durability of the Social Democrats is, indeed, a tribute to the broad popularity of the wide-ranging social programs that a new government will dismantle at its political peril."[6]

"Greeks plan sale of some islands to help pay off the country's big budget deficits. . . . Opposition parties sharply criticized the government's plans."[7]

"President Bush urged the United Nations to repeal its 1975 resolution equating Zionism with racism. . . . The resolution has been a sore point between Israel and the Arab world."[8]

"Supporters argue that it is not affirmative action but centuries-old prejudice that stigmatizes blacks. . . . Beneficiaries find that access does not mean acceptance. . . .

Many chafe at the word *qualified,* which they say is used as a billy club by whites who question their credentials."[9]

"While the United States experienced more widespread, severe, and long-lasting poverty during the 1980s than did other Western democracies, she did the least to help her poor, so that the rich got richer and the poor poorer."[10]

THE SOCIETAL CONTEXT OF IDEOLOGY

Why do people and countries differ in their normative principles and attitudes about social justice, equality, patriotism, abortion, nationalism, and discrimination? What is the role of ideology in societal reform? Is it fair if the rich get richer and the poor poorer? How should social policy planners approach values and beliefs about the nature of human beings, society, and ethics? What social policy strategies are appropriate to achieve distributive justice and to eliminate discrimination?

Although answers to these questions vary widely, the theory of ideology and concepts of social justice are at the epicenter of these issues.

The Nature of Ideology

Few concepts have been so intensively discussed in the social sciences as ideology. Whether devalued as nonscientific and distorted or considered the necessary element of all social practice, ideology has become a necessary conceptual reference in social change and reform; class analysis and consciousness, and analysis of the power structure, political domination, social justice, scientific methodology, and the welfare state. Ideology is also a required reference in social policy practice: social workers in policy planning should promote social justice, eliminate discrimination, and strengthen the ideology that protects the rights of all people, particularly the poor and powerless.[11] Ideology consists of patterns of cognitive and moral beliefs about society, people, and the universe in the context of social relationships. Hence, ideology influences the role of the state, the institutional organization of society, the nature of governmental policy, and the climate for either societal reform or the maintenance of the status quo.

Supporters of social change in modern states use ideologies as tools to increase participation in collective efforts or to mobilize public opinion and resources. Positive action to improve human conditions is an indispensable requirement in the new frontiers of high technology and production. In both market and nonmarket countries, citizens are mobilized in mass efforts to accomplish the desired objectives of the state. In this sense, ideology defines situations in modern society and justifies people's actions. For example, attitudes about the welfare state, poverty, discrimination, equality, and social justice may well depend upon the prevailing ideology and values. Ideology can help people achieve desirable social changes (as in the civil rights movement) or undesirable social changes (such as social injustice and budgetary cuts for social programs), or it can promote desirable or undesirable resistance to social change.

The term *ideology*, however, has acquired several meanings and is one of the most debated concepts in the social sciences. In the late 18th century it was first used to mean the study of ideas in general, but it soon came to denote ideas about society and people. In contemporary societies, ideology generally means a comprehensive set of beliefs, attitudes, and opinions.[12] It includes true or false beliefs about everything from scientific knowledge to religion to everyday beliefs about proper conduct. All beliefs are socially determined in some way—by economics, the social structure, the interests of a particular social class, the power structure, or a political party.

Because social scientists do not agree on the exact definition of *ideology*, the term has been used in the social science literature in several ways, each of which has been challenged. Some commentators distinguish ideologies from outlooks, creeds, systems, and movements of thought. The latter, they suggest, are less systematized or integrated patterns of beliefs that surround an eminent value.[13] Other writers emphasize specific kinds of ideology; they perceive ideology to be a tightly knit body of beliefs organized around central values, including a political system (capitalism, communism, fascism, or nationalism) or a social transaction (racism, sexism, ageism, equality, laissez-faire economics, ethnic purity, or salvation). In the political realm, ideology denotes a specific theory, political orientation and beliefs, or party. Commentators from political science, such as Baradat, suggest that ideology is an action-oriented political theory (materialistic, popular, and simplistic) that originally, at least, was designed to accommodate the social and economic conditions created by the Industrial Revolution.[14] In the areas of social transaction or social value, racism[15] or sexism[16] are also regarded as ideologies. Although based on falsehoods and erroneous assumptions, these ideologies strengthen their advocates in resisting reforms for social justice and equality.

Some writers, including Therborn, suggest that ideologies are not just ideas, but social processes and practices on which people fail to reflect.[17] In this view, ideologies result in enduring, orderly, patterned relationships among institutional elements of a society; they are the medium through which people are socialized, individuals and groups acquire identity, and citizens become conscious social actors.

In brief, ideologies influence the behavior of individuals and institutions. Images and identities formed by ideologies tell us who we are and what kind of world we inhabit. Ideologies guide people, groups, and communities in selecting goals and choosing the means to achieve them. Not only do ideologies provide the basis for individual and institutional action, legitimacy, and status, but they also influence public commitment, priorities, and loyalties. Ideologies govern responses to such words as *poverty, equality, race, sex, abortion, welfare state, unions, democracy, freedom, and communism* by combining conceptions of existential reality, values, and memories and producing judgments and evaluations.

Ideology and Truth

Many people believe ideology masks interests or motives. For example, in the late 18th century, ideology acquired the connotation of ideas that were selective and distorted instead of factual, rational, or objective. In this view, ideology can either exaggerate or underrepresent the role a social value plays in the social system.

Ideology can also be perceived as unscientific. Those who equate science with objectivity or the absence of values exclude ideology and values from empirical inquiry because they are seen as subjective and irrelevant.[18] Some disciplines, including economics, exclude values from their scientific boundaries. They consider values exogenous to their scientific concerns, though appropriate to ethics and philosophy.[19]

Another school of thought opposes the exclusion of values and argues that nonideological or value-free social science inquiry is almost impossible. Any science describes the world through values.[20] Even though social scientists may claim to be scientific, they unwittingly allow values to intrude into their inquiries. As Weber suggested, even statistical data and empirical surveys that are essential to social science research have to be interpreted and evaluated.[21]

In brief, some authors narrowly define ideology as consisting only of distorted or unduly selective aspects of a system of social ideas. Others argue that ideology consists of selected or distorted ideas about a social system only when those ideas purport to be factual.[22]

Although false and true propositions can coexist in ideologies, some writers, including Marx and Engels, argue that ideologies are impelled by interest in defending the status quo of a social system.[23] Mannheim suggested that all ideas are determined by their holders' positions in the social system and are necessarily distorted; that the character of ideologies is largely determined by the economic arrangement of society; and that in class societies, ideologies are distorted by class interests and are imposed by the ruling classes.[24]

In this context, Althusser noted that although a general function of ideology (a theory of ideology in general) is to bring about cohesion in society, its specific function (a theory of a particular ideology) secures the domination of one social class.[25] He referred to an "ideological state apparatus"—consisting of communications media, educational and religious institutions, political parties, and trade unions—that incorporates all classes in societies within a dominant ideology.[26]

Weber and others have suggested that the same criteria of truth and validity apply regardless of the social origin of ideas.[27] Social workers who plan policy recognize the important role of ideology in influencing behavior. Both normative and scientific elements are used in social work practice, similar to the fusion of Parmenidean and Heraclitean views or the combination of order and conflict theories. In so doing, however, social workers must distinguish between personal value judgments (good and bad actions) and interpretations of values that establish goals to guide public policy.

Societal Change and Evolution

Reform and Institutional Structure

Major societal changes are associated with shifts in dominant ideologies. The societal structures of ancient Greece and Rome, early Christianity, feudalism, mercantilism, the transition from preindustrial to industrial society, the Industrial Revolution, capitalism, the domination of the United States in the 1980s by the neoconservative political right, and the rise and collapse of communism in Eastern European countries were all made possible by fundamental ideological changes in societal institutions, including the state, the family, the church, and the economy. These changes were also associated with beliefs about human nature, freedom, democracy, and social justice that differed from those of preceding eras. Several commentators, including Polanyi, Landes, Tawney, and more recently, Hunt, Heilbroner, and Samuelson, have illustrated the association between ideology and structural social change.[28] Analysts of the collapse of communism in Eastern Europe associate the rejection of old values or the acceptance of new beliefs with societal reform.[29]

Major social policy and institutional changes rarely occur without modifications in their ideological underpinnings. (see Figure 1-2 in Chapter 1). Social workers in policy planning understand societal reforms in the context of ideology. They also contrast social changes with the ideas of the previous era and their impact on societal organization.

For example, the destruction of feudalism and its ideology was necessary to pave the way for capitalist institutional arrangements. This included a repudiation of basic feudal values that condemned acquisitive, competitive behavior and individual greed and profit-seeking, as well as a shift away from the feudal emphasis on society as a collective, symbiotic whole. For early capitalism to emerge and dominate, a different ideology had to replace the feudal and mercantilist beliefs.

Precapitalist ideology prohibited the lending of money for interest, discouraged the accumulation of material goods, emphasized mutual-aid networks in the context of the medieval, paternalistic, Christian ethic, and was not conducive to the capitalist market-exchange system. By contrast, the new capitalist market ideology, which replaced eroding previous values, encouraged individualistic and competitive relations, the accumulation of wealth, usury, and governmental intervention. It was supported by a cumulative series of technological, social, and religious events that lasted several centuries.[30]

The emerging capitalist market structure was made possible by an ideological revolution that emphasized greater freedom to seek individual profits; an acceptance of "do acquire" Calvinistic beliefs (rather than the "do not acquire" orientation of the previous era); and a "work hard, be busy and thrifty, save, and thus prove that you are a godly person" philosophy. The new industrial ideology and industrialist class emphasized effective production and new "scientific" methodologies but deemphasized values incompatible with industrialization and capitalism. The transition in values fostered toleration of the human suffering and inhumane working conditions associated with the Industrial Revolution.

The Impact of Classical Liberalism

In brief, the introduction of a capitalist market economy and the resulting social conditions are associated with the ideology of classical liberalism from the 16th to the 18th centuries.[31] Classical liberalism (today's neoliberalism or neoconservatism) represented a new system of economic, political, social, and psychological thought that was intricately interwoven with laissez-faire capitalism. It introduced new beliefs about the nature of society, human behavior, economic relationships, and social justice that encouraged the emergence of a new merchant class.[32] Among other notions, four assumptions about human nature were postulated by advocates of classical liberalism: individuals are egoistic (motivated by self-interest), rationally calculating (they make choices that maximize pleasure and minimize pain), inert (lazy because they view work as painful), and atomistic (they value the individual as a more fundamental reality than society).

Classical liberalism, never totally triumphant in Western Europe, took root most deeply in the United States; hence, Europeans have been more amenable to public social welfare programs than have Americans.

Reaction to Classical Liberalism

Rather than accepting the beliefs of the economic market system, other theorists—including Robert Owen (1771–1858); pre-Marxist socialists Gracchus Babeuf (1760–1797), William Godwin (1756–1836), Claude Henri de Saint-Simon (1760–1825), Charles Fourier (1772–1837), and Pierre Proudhon (1809–1865); and Karl Marx (1818–1883)—provided a new ideology to replace capitalist notions. Proponents of the new ideology rejected the "inhumane" and "unjust" results of the free market; challenged the notion that the market is the best mechanism for determining societal production, distribution, and well-being; rejected capitalist property relations and capitalist productive forces; and refused to tolerate the high social costs and social ills of the market system (unemployment, inflation, deprivation among workers, poverty, and inequalities in income, wealth, and power).[33] Socialist theory paved the way for a shift to socialist governments in some Western European countries and to communism in the Soviet Union.

Societal Change in the East and West

Recent shifts in dominant ideologies are associated with major societal reforms in both market and nonmarket countries. For example, the swing to neoconservatism in the 1980s (the Reagan and Bush eras) from the liberalism of the 1960s (the Kennedy and Johnson eras) was also associated with an ideological shift to conservative beliefs about the state, the economy, the welfare state, and social justice.

The collapse of communism in Eastern Europe has also been associated with radical ideological shifts regarding individual freedom, human rights, the one-party system, dictatorship, social justice, the state, and the centralized planned economy. In both East and West, changes in economic, social, and political institutions have been mutually reinforcing. This supports the views of earlier commentators, including Weber, that change in one institution influences reforms in all others.[34] At the epicenter of these societal reforms were concepts of social justice, equality, and freedom.

To analyze America's social policies and their institutional context without knowledge of fundamental American ideology and intellectual thought is like trying to understand feudalism and the Reformation without knowledge of Christianity and industrialization. By the same token, institutions in modern society become fully comprehensible through exploration of their ideological context. For example, social workers planning policy analyze the ideological context of the role of the state and its commitments to the free market, private ownership, economic individualism, social justice, and limited welfare-state programs.

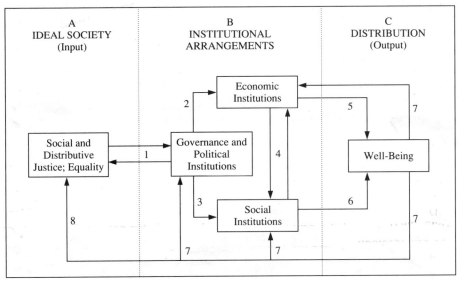

FIGURE 3-1   Justice in the context of social policy

SOCIAL AND DISTRIBUTIVE JUSTICE

The Central Role of Justice

Prevailing concepts of social justice and equality underlie and justify both social policy and ideologies. They also permeate societal structure, institutional functions, and human relationships. Society's distribution of resources, including wealth, power, knowledge, and human services, is associated with social justice and equality. Distributive justice demands that public policy allocate resources in a particular way (see Figure 3-1).

Fairness and equality demand that the distribution of goods and services not be left to random selection, to the needs of those in power, or to economic mechanisms that offend moral commitments. Political parties and subscribers to political ideologies tend to present their goals and programs in the context of social justice and equality. Capitalists, socialists, conservatives, liberals, and radicals all rationalize their policies in terms of social justice.

Underlying acceptance or rejection of capitalism and socialism are fundamental concepts of social justice. From its beginning, the capitalist market has been criticized as unfair in allocating resources and distributing goods and services. It tends to concentrate poverty and unemployment in lower classes and to distribute power unjustly. On the other hand, socialism has been criticized for its dictatorial concentration of power in the party elite, its democratic centralism in decision making, and its subordination of individual goals to collectivist ones. Differential concepts of justice are the main reason for acceptance or rejection of capitalism and socialism, societal reform, the status quo, and the welfare state.

Social work practice incorporates fundamental concepts of social justice. Clinical and policy interventions are justified or rejected by reference to specific ethics, moral commitments, and perceptions of social justice. Social action, social reform efforts, and clinical social work are perceived as just or unjust, and social workers recognize the critical impact of justice on identity, self-realization, actualization, and determination. Social work practitioners must have a clear, strong commitment to social justice as a dominant guiding value. Social work's code of ethics commits social workers to distributive justice, particularly for those who are most vulnerable in society.[35] Questions of what is just or unjust are basic in political and juridical thought. Does justice flow from religion, the nature of things, the human mind, the soul, the conscience, or human emotions and passions?[36]

The Nature of Social Justice

Right relationship

dis. justice

Although its precise meaning is controversial and defies consensus, *social justice* implies relationships among people (the organization of societal institutions) and the distribution of society's resources on the basis of valid claims (distributive justice). *Legal justice* (the practical side of justice) concerns the laws themselves and those who administer them.[37]

Central to the debate about social justice and equality is the distinction between "natural" and civil, social, or institutional sources of human differences. Natural or physical differences are established by nature—age, health, bodily strength, quality of mind and soul. Social and political differences, including wealth, power, status, discrimination, knowledge, and services of the welfare state, are authorized by the consent of people and thus are proper elements of social justice and equality.

Social policy planning is concerned with distributive justice, which concerns the justified distribution of benefits and burdens in society rather than the concepts of a just person or the laws and their application. The distribution of benefits and burdens is a cooperative societal project structured by various moral, legal, ideological, and cultural principles. These principles determine which individuals and institutions are obligated to cooperate, and social policy usually reflects these rules and their implications.

Models of Social Justice

The canons of distributive justice have roots in various philosophical sources and positions:

- *Divine law*: principles conceived in the mind of God[38]
- *Natural law*: the order of being that is inherent in the nature of things[39]
- *Reason*: rational, mathematical processes of the human brain[40]
- *Social contract*: principles centering on political authority and the contract between the citizenry and their sovereign: a king, parliament, or congress[41]

Principles of distributive justice include rights and freedoms guaranteed by civil institutions, such as the right to life, liberty, and private property; the inviolability of the person; the right to free expression and free association; the right to work; the right to health and to education; the right to participate in community decisions; the right to due process of law; freedom of religion and of conscience; the right to marry and to have children; and the right to develop one's personality.

In recent decades, four major models of justice have emerged in the literature. These include the *utilitarian model,* based on early classical liberalism; the *market model,* based on Adam Smith's variation of utilitarianism and on economic individualism incorporated into capitalism; the *fairness model,* based on social contract theory; and the *socialist-Marxist model,* based on Marxist theory.

The Utilitarian Model *Greatest happiness*

not = greatest common = good.

Early utilitarians, including Priestley, Beccaria, and Hume, emphasized the principle of "greatest happiness" or "utility" to defend the efficacy of the capitalist economic market.[42] In the generation that followed, Adam Smith, James Mill, Jeremy Bentham, and John Stuart Mill advanced the theory of utilitarianism to its current place in the discourse on capitalism and the free economic market. They placed the satisfaction of individual wants (utility) at the core of utilitarianism and capitalism.

As ordinarily understood, utilitarianism is an attempt to maximize the aggregate social utility by satisfying the wants of individuals. Institutions, laws, and actions are just not because of their intrinsic moral worth but because they promote happiness. Their value flows from the creation of surplus over pain, aggregated across all members of society.[43] Society, then, is just when its major institutions and distributions maximize both individual and aggregate utility. That is, the goal of utilitarian justice is to achieve the greatest net balance of satisfaction summed over all individuals in society. The greatest good is that which promotes the most happiness for the individuals within society as a whole.[44]

Utilitarianism implies that individual happiness is important insofar as it creates aggregate happiness, which is the ultimate goal in a utilitarian society. It also suggests that greater gains made by some should compensate for lesser losses of others. The violation of the liberty of a few should be made right by the greater good shared by many. By implication, institutions, laws, and actions have no intrinsic value. Rather, their value is determined by their utility—that is, by their consequences for aggregate well-being.

Critics of utilitarianism argue that the definitions of benefit, harm, and human wants are unclear. As values are rejected, their absence necessitates the use of cardinal scales that are difficult to construct. The emphasis on the greater good can result in inhumane, materialistic, and antidemocratic outcomes. For example, one portion of the population can be enslaved for the enjoyment and well-being of another. The concern with the total utility of production ignores distributive issues.[45] People will not necessarily act justly in enlightened self-interest or sacrifice their interest to that of others. In brief, the principle of total utility does not solve the problem of distributing aggregate satisfaction among individuals. The emphasis on aggregate utility (outcome) deemphasizes just procedures (due process).[46]

The Market Model

Adam Smith and other classical liberals, such as John Stuart Mill, provided variations of the earlier utilitarian school of thought. These models of distributive justice are the root of modern capitalism and the free economic market. Contemporary market theorists of justice, including economist Milton Friedman and philosopher Robert Nozick, have based their views of the economic market as a just distribution system for goods and services on the principles of Adam Smith and other classic liberals.

Adam Smith.   Although Adam Smith is often considered a defender of big business, he was opposed to the exploitation of the poor by the rising capitalist class. He sympathized strongly with the plight of the poor.[47]

Smith's view of social justice is reflected in his basic argument that the free economic market leads to greater individual liberty and greater prosperity for all members of society.[48] His crucial "invisible hand" theory is based on the concept of natural liberty prevalent in his time and on earlier utilitarian principles of justice. Smith argued that the free economic market functions through natural principles of liberty. The market is guided by an invisible hand that works through the instincts of the individual to create institutions that are necessary for the welfare of society.[49] While each individual is free and acts in individual liberty and self-interest, the aggregate of individual activity serves the best interests of society as a whole. This canon of individual liberty led Smith to a laissez-faire approach to the economic market in which governmental intervention was minimal. Smith's canon of justice is based on the rights to own property and work where one wants, bargaining for wages and profits in a freely competitive situation.[50]

Although Smith warned that in a free-market system inequality would normally favor the wealthy, his approach to justice was to improve the well-being of all by increasing the aggregate wealth of society. However, whether this would ensure that all classes of society would receive a larger and fairer distribution of goods and services was problematic even to Smith.[51]

John Locke.   Locke argued that a person justly owns what he or she has removed from the state of nature by labor. Along with Smith and David Ricardo, he formulated laissez-faire principles of justice based on the experience of early market societies. In an ideal, free, self-regulating economic market, Locke wrote, individuals are free to pursue competitively their self-interest (primarily pertaining to the right to acquire property).[52]

John Stuart Mill.   Mill also supported the utilitarian principle of greatest happiness and the free economic market as a canon by which to judge institutions and actions. However, he rejected the morality of utilitarianism and the economic market in the context of distributive justice. Deviating from the complete laissez-faire approach of classical liberals, he argued that society, not market forces alone, should determine how production should be distributed. Mill rejected the utilitarian hedonistic principle of maximizing materialism, asserting that it did not represent the social good. Instead, he called for maximum human development according to human capacities. He placed moral, intellectual, aesthetic, and productive capacities above the economic free market.[53] Mill argued that just distribution must be based on need, which ascribes to people a moral right to the material resources essential for subsistence. Distributions are also just, in his view, when they are based on desert, which rewards moral right in proportion to either productive contribution or effort.

Contemporary libertarians: Nozick and Friedman.   Current libertarian commentators advocate a minimal welfare state and oppose redistribution of goods and services among social classes.[54] For example, Friedman and Nozick argue that a just society is a capitalist economic market society[55] in which only a minimal state can be justified because more extensive involvement violates the people's rights.[56] In justifying the accumulation of wealth and society's skewed distributions of income and wealth, they argue that justice is a process whereby individuals receive what they are entitled to according to their efforts and skills.[57] To laissez-faire philosophers, including Locke, Nozick, Friedman, and neoconservative theorists, justice dictates that individuals receive what they earn by their efforts and skills in the economic market.[58]

This view of justice is based on the principle that different past circumstances and actions justify different entitlements.[59] The determination of entitlement is a normative decision best left to the economic market because it is impossible for unbiased decision makers to reach unanimity. One group's financial superiority should be accepted in society because its gain was not made at another group's expense. Libertarians also believe that the conditions of the poor should not be improved at the expense of those who are better off.

In his Principles of Entitlement, Nozick argues that if a person has come to own something within proper guidelines (such as through voluntary exchange and gifts rather than fraud or theft), then that ownership is just.[60] People who acquire holdings in accordance with just principles are entitled to their holdings; it is unjust for anyone to take them away. Thus, Nozick opposes redistribution that entails taking away one's legitimate holdings to increase equality of wealth or of other goods and services.

Critics of the market model of justice argue that only elitism, inequality, and injustice result from the market's historical entitlement principle. The market system can be fair to everyone only when it is in equilibrium, which is seldom the case. Buyers and sellers in the market profit by the errors, ignorance, or powerlessness of others. The "finders-keepers" ethic of Nozick's original entitlement position is a rejection of the very principles for which he recommended it; that is, original property was frequently acquired by exploitation (slavery, piracy, theft, or brutal power) rather than through justice.

Individual rights are not protected by the market as people are born into or otherwise enter society. Rather, only the first generation of society is protected. For example, only white male property owners were protected when American economic, social, and political patterns were established. Such groups as African Americans and women had neither rights nor equal opportunity.[61]

Modern American and European liberal critics believe in the marketplace as a just institution with just processes. But they also assert that governments must reduce sharp economic and social distributive inequalities that result from market functions. In their view, the value of a just action should also be determined by the social benefits and burdens for society's well-being. A strong commitment to property rights and to the free economic market can be an insurmountable obstacle to achieving collective societal goals. For example, in early America, John Adams, Alexander Hamilton, and John C. Calhoun voiced free economic market views that were applied in defense of slavery. Similarly, the market model of justice provides a "justification" for the accumulation of wealth by a small elite and for the tolerance of society's skewed distribution of goods and services.

distributive justice

The Marxist Model

The most radical and influential criticism of the free-market economy as a model of social justice is associated with the perspectives of Karl Marx. In the context of social justice, Marx's views on the relationship between economic life and other social institutions are particularly relevant.

Marx mounted his criticism of the free economic market amid the conditions of starvation and the popular revolts against several European governments in the mid-1800s. He rejected the free-market economy as a model of social justice because of the gross class inequalities and exploitation prevalent in market societies since the Industrial Revolution. In his view, since the Industrial Revolution, a dominant class of capital-owning bourgeoisie have exploited the labor of the dominated working class: the proletariat. This unequal social class relation has resulted unjustly in greater profit and accumulation of capital for the elite capitalist class through the fruits of the workers' labor.

Marx analyzed capitalism by its mode of economic production: The owners of the means of production, the bourgeoisie, oppose and exploit in the production process the proletariat, who own only their labor and sell it as a commodity. The main goal of the production process is the creation of surplus value—profit in the form of rents, interest, executive salaries, and fringe benefits. In this sense, all economic production is social and political.

Marx considered a person's relation to work a vital human experience. Conditions at work can make the working class dissatisfied and alienated. For example, alienation can result from negative conditions in the workplace, including unequal rewards, isolation of workers from the fruits of their own labor, and exploitation of workers in the production process. While alienation denotes the social estrangement of individuals, Marx transformed the concept into a sociological and economic idea. He rooted it in social structures and free economic markets that he believed denied people their essential human nature.

Alienation occurs when an individual no longer recognizes himself or herself in the product, which has become alien to the worker. Workers are then alienated from other people because, in Marx's view, the free economic market transforms human relations into market relations. People are judged by their position in the market and by their market acquisitions rather than by their human qualities. Marx asserted that capital accumulation generates its own needs, which reduce people to the level of commodities.

Marx believed that in a just workplace, workers would cooperate in creative and fulfilling activities, exercise their talents, accept responsibility, and produce socially useful products. Nonalienating labor is a fulfilling activity.[62] To accomplish distributive justice, Marx urged workers to eliminate the bourgeois class and form an egalitarian society based on principles of collectivism. Collective ownership would then replace private ownership. The resources in the new society would be distributed "from each according to his ability, to each according to his needs." Unequal distribution would be unacceptable. Private property would be collectivized under the joint ownership of the people and their government.

Critics of Marx's theory argue that his predictions based on class analysis did not materialize. His arguments that the state is the instrument of the ruling class are not supported by present theories that the state is relatively autonomous in responding to pressure from all groups. Most important, current socialist practice based on Marxism-Leninism has been criticized by those offended by the lack of individual liberties, the establishment of dictatorship and democratic centralism, the concentration of power in the party elite, and the subordination of labor unions to the Communist party.

The Fairness (Liberal) Model

This model is a version of the social contract theory as a basis of organizing society's institutions and distributive justice. Social contract theories are concerned with political obligation and government by consent. In the 17th and 18th centuries, social contract theories were used to justify political authority on grounds of individual rational consent and self interest: government is useful and ought, therefore, to be accepted by all reasonable people as a voluntary obligation.

Rousseau, one of the most notable supporters of this theory, along with Hobbes, Locke, and Kant, argued that laws resulted from people agreeing for mutual protection to surrender individual freedoms. For the first time in history a sense of moral and civic obligation was acknowledged. Government must rest on the consent of the governed.

The central idea of the social contract also concerns the intrinsic values of institutions, laws, and actions. Justice requires fair distribution of goods and services to preserve the humanness of each individual. Because they are human, all human beings must be treated the same way.

Rawls, the leading modern commentator on this view, deals with three major issues of justice: the definition of justice as principles of fairness, the organization of societal institutions to reflect justice as fairness, and the foundation of distributive justice on fairness principles. In so doing, he strongly opposes utilitarianism and challenges the free economic market's inequality.

Rawls charges that in seeking the greatest aggregate satisfaction, utilitarianism leads to gross and unacceptable inequalities in the distribution of liberties, resources, and opportunities. Such inequalities will be tolerated in a utilitarian society if they are perceived to lead to greater satisfaction for society as a whole.[63] He also disagrees that the loss of freedom for some is made right by greater satisfaction enjoyed by many.

For Rawls, the primary concern of justice is the basic structure of society—that is, the way social institutions distribute fundamental rights and duties and the manner in which the advantages arising from social cooperation are distributed.[64] Justice is the first virtue of all societal institutions. If any institution is unjust, it should be altered or abolished.

Solidarity

O for P

Replacing utilitarian principles with those of fairness, Rawls constructed a rational model of a social contract in which people agree to share one another's fate.[65] All people have equal rights to the basic liberties; rational beings can accept inequalities only if they work to the advantage of the least well-off.[66] Rawls's rational or fairness model of justice is based on two fundamental principles. The first concerns the equal right of all citizens to basic liberties that should be shared by all in a just society. Equal liberties include political liberties, such as the right to vote and to be eligible for public office; free thought, speech, and assembly; the right to have personal property; and freedom from arbitrary arrest and seizure.

The second principle, called the difference principle, stipulates that if social and economic inequalities are to exist, they must benefit the least advantaged. In other words, if inequalities of rank and fortune exist, they should be arranged so they will help the disadvantaged and powerless. The same principle must also apply to offices and positions to guarantee equality of opportunity.[67]

Rawls argues that natural distinctions are neither just nor unjust; what matters is how society's institutions deal with these differences. All social primary goods, including liberty, income, wealth, property, social services, education, power, self-respect, and self-determination, should be distributed equally unless their unequal distribution benefits the least favored.

Unlike advocates of utilitarianism, Rawls insists that in a just society both procedures and outcomes must be fair. For example, an examination or legal trial that is perfectly fair on procedural grounds (due process) must also have a fair outcome. In the fairness model of justice, procedure and outcome should always coincide.

For the implementation of this model, Rawls suggests that distributive justice, to be maintained by government and legal order, must be divided into four institutional branches. The allocation branch keeps the economy feasibly competitive to avoid unreasonable market power. The stabilization branch maintains reasonably full employment without wasting resources. The transfer branch determines the social minimum based on need. The distribution branch preserves and encourages a just distribution of income and wealth over time. (For example, it might intervene in the free economic market via taxes and proportional expenditures.)

For social workers committed to fairness and to the redistribution of goods and services to protect the least advantaged, Rawls's fairness model is extremely important. Rawls has also described self-respect as a primary social good. Rawls and social work commentators agree that when self-respect is undermined, so is the ability to be effective in life. According to Rawls, self-respect and self-esteem include a person's sense of his or her value and imply a confidence in one's ability to fulfill plans.[68]

Rawls's critics focus on five major points.[69] First, they challenge the original acquisition of holdings (the appropriation of unheld things), arguing that in the appropriation of resources, the model does not include past actions. They also claim past circumstances create different entitlements to resources.[70] These critics further challenge the assumption that original resource ownership may be unjust. They assert that a just distribution originates from another just distribution by legitimate means; individuals gain control over goods through a historical process. Finally, they challenge the rectification of injustice in holdings that Rawls suggested.[71] Injustice occurs, the critics claim, when governments or others transfer acquisitions from one person to another, thus distorting the historical distribution. The historical principle of acquisitions is the only valid criterion by which society can justly redistribute goods by taking them from one person and giving them to others. The accommodation of human needs or convention are arbitrary criteria for redistribution. If society does not protect ownership rights, chaos will result.

These arguments also reflect Nozick's theory of minimal governmental intervention and his rejection of redistribution of goods and services.[72] Nozick argues that Rawls's theory of social cooperation and redistribution would create more problems than it would solve. He calls it absurd that those with the least natural ability can insist that personal inequities entitle them to share in the holdings of others. A minimal state of noncooperation, he believes, will allow for the fairest distribution of resources if no external interference exists.

Models of Social Justice in Social Policy

Each model of social justice has competing implications for social policy practice, the distribution of goods and services, and the welfare state. For example, a government is faced with the problem of being able to help only one of two starving communities because of a food shortage. One community consists of terminally ill people for whom food will prolong life only briefly. The starvation of people in the other community is less advanced, but if not fed, they will be disabled for life. As a social policy planner, which community would you help? Why?

If utilitarian criteria are used in determining the distribution, the healthier community would be selected because a greater net societal benefit will result. If fairness (need) criteria are used, the terminally ill community would be selected because it is worse off and its right to survival is involved.

The fairness model supports the normative aspects of social policy practice and the ethical commitments of social work. It emphasizes humanness and the enhancement of being human. It also promotes welfare-state programs that redistribute goods and services in favor of the poor, the disadvantaged, and populations at risk. Demands on basic resources and entitlement programs are just when they strengthen humanness. Subsidies to business, banks, and military-industrial corporations are excluded unless evidence clearly shows that these entities enhance the satisfaction of basic human needs for all people or that allotting resources to these areas will not diminish the resources needed for satisfying basic human needs.

In contrast, the utilitarian-market model tolerates more inequality and poverty and accepts only limited welfare-state programs. It emphasizes individual contributions to production as a criterion of distributive justice. It also places priority on efficiency, increased production, and aggregate well-being, even at the expense of the disadvantaged. The idea that market forces—not society—should decide the distribution, accessibility, and affordability of basic resources (nourishment, health, clothing, shelter, education, services, and employment at a decent wage) is counterproductive and leads to gross inequality (see Table 3-1).

In the fairness model, it is government's responsibility to ensure that resource claims based on need have priority over claims of "merit" or "worth." Merit (or desert) needs are valid only if enough resources are available to satisfy claims of

TABLE 3-1 The utilitarian-market model versus the fairness model

	Utilitarian-market	Fairness
EPISTEMOLOGY (BASIS)	Teleology, pragmatism, materialism	Deontology, normative idealism, social contract
SOCIAL-CLASS BENEFITS	To powerful, rich property owners	To the worst off
DISTRIBUTIVE CANONS	Contribution to production; supply-and-demand	Need, collectivism
REDISTRIBUTION	Increases inequality	Increases equality
PRINCIPLES	Utility, maximization of the satisfaction of individual wants; intrinsic values are rejected; the market is just; embraces original acquisitions principle; minimal government is just	Fairness, humanness; liberty and equality for all; the market can be unjust; questions original acquisition; governmental intervention is just
FREEDOM	The loss for some is compensated by gains in aggregate utility	Slavery cannot be compensated by aggregate utility
EQUALITY	Impossible and undesirable	Possible and desirable
INEQUALITY	Unavoidable	Acceptable only if it protects the disadvantaged
STATE	Noninterventionist	Intervention is necessary
CRITERIA	Efficiency in production, growth in market output	Ethical commitment
SOCIAL POLICY FOCUS	Philanthropy, private-sector policy	Public-sector policy
WELFARE STATE	Discouraged	Encouraged

both need and desert. Although charity resides in the individual, distributive justice characterizes public policy, the relationships among people, and the allocation of resources. Charity is an arbitrary evaluation of worth made by a private individual or group.

While the market model operates mainly on the principle "to each according to his or her work," the welfare state operates on the principle "to each according to her or his needs." Bureaucracy operates on the principle "to each according to his or her rank." And political institutions operate on the principle "to each the same thing" (one vote).

EQUALITY

Equality in the Context of Justice

In social and political thought, justice has implied equality. Even when ideas about equality have shifted, equality itself has remained a central issue in concepts of justice.

But although equality and justice are related concepts, they are also distinct and separate. For example, a distribution of human services can be just but unequal, or unjust and equal. In a hierarchical society in which all people are not equal in all respects, only equal individuals receive equal rewards; unequal individuals do not. As early in history as Aristotle,[73] philosophers distinguished between justice and equality, suggesting that treating everyone equally might cause injustice to some members of society, particularly when the original distribution of resources is unequal.

It is not equality per se that constitutes the ideal of justice. Rather, equality is a logical implication of the necessity of applying one material rule to all members of some essential category. Equality means equal treatment before a common rule; formal justice rests on the idea of treating like cases alike. The challenge is to agree on some standard that specifies that certain cases are alike or to identify a rule that lays down the obligation to treat in a certain way all members of a given essential category. A substantive theory of equality declares which issues of justice can be properly adjudicated.

Concepts and Theories of Equality

As no consensus exists among reflective people about equality's central point of reference, concepts of equality vary significantly. So do the weights placed on the characteristics of equality. What do social workers demand when they want to promote equality? Equality in rights, in need, in merits, in social differences, in natural attributes, or in treatment? In the distribution of income, wealth, power, education, or services?

Even when commentators agree that moral equality among people exists, they may differ in their interpretations. Commentators agree, for example, all must be treated as moral people of equal worth; however, this does not mean that everyone must be treated identically. A child and an old, ill person should not be treated the same.

The complexity of equality as a concept becomes even more apparent when social workers consider its diverse aspects. Take, for example, the distinction or ambiguity between equality of opportunity and equality of results (or of condition). Equality of opportunity will inevitably result in inequality of condition because some people are more able, healthy, fortunate, or energetic than others. Some commentators believe, however, that equality of opportunity ought to lead to equality of condition. They argue that failure to achieve this goal is irrelevant or immaterial or reflects "externalities" (that is, other socioeconomic arrangements).

The polarity between these conceptions of equality also appears in other aspects. Examples include equality of treatment versus equal satisfaction of basic needs; equality of rights only, versus equality of natural characteristics; ex-ante (before the fact) equality versus ex-post (after the fact) equality;[74] individual versus group equality; and equity (fair shares) versus equality (equal shares).[75]

Central to the debate about the characteristics of equality is the distinction between so-called natural sources of human differences and civil or social (institutional) sources. Differences in the first category (natural or physical) are established by nature: age, health, bodily strength, and quality of mind and soul, as suggested by Rousseau. By contrast, the second category (moral or political characteristics or privileges), which includes wealth or power, is authorized by people's consent.

The term *equality* can also refer to certain kinds of treatment. For example, all people are entitled to be treated equally and have the same moral and legal rights to freedom. Moral rights imply freedom to exercise them, whereas legal rights flow from law. Equal treatment implies that benefits and burdens allotted to people must be equal, including voting, legal duties, liabilities (such as taxes), and opportunities to hold certain positions or offices.

Some conservative commentators have recently argued that inequality is a necessary and desirable condition of modern social organization. They argue that social differentiation and social stratification are indispensable to the very existence of social structures that prescribe the nature and degrees of inequality to be tolerated.[76] Critics of this position argue that this represents a covert return to the classical and medieval antiegalitarian or despotic principle of hierarchy as the basis of social order. The antiegalitarian mode of thought is closely associated with discrimination, racism, sexism, Nazism, and Fascism.

Inequality in the United States

For social workers, inequality means broadly that people in some communities live well, enjoying many material benefits, personal freedoms, and opportunities for development; those living elsewhere have fewer or none of these advantages. In this sense, inequality is one of the most serious social policy problems. Compared with other advanced industrial countries, the United States is a remarkably unequal democratic society.

Social workers recognize that inequality and distributive justice affect certain populations disproportionately and more frequently. For example, the most unequal, vulnerable, and oppressed Americans are the lowest socioeconomic classes, children, women, single-parent families headed by women, and minorities.

Socioeconomic Class

Historically, the lowest socioeconomic class of Americans is one of the most powerless and oppressed groups. Although large, this group receives greatly uneven and much smaller shares of the Gross National Product (GNP) than do the upper socioeconomic classes. For example:

• The rich got richer and the poor got poorer in the 1980s. Those in the richest fifth of families gained an average income of $7,200 per family over the decade; the middle fifth of families gained an average of just $140 in income, and the poorest lost an average of $350.[77]

• In 1989, the poorest fifth of families received 4.6% of total national family income; the richest fifth received 44.6%[78]

• Between 1979 and 1989, the poorest fifth of families lost $559 (or 5.6%) in average before-tax family income; the richest fifth gained $13,238 (or 16.7%).[79]

• Although the per capita GNP in constant 1987 dollars expanded from $10,740 in 1980 to $12,287 in 1987, the weekly per-worker income was reduced from $318 in 1980 to $312 in 1987.

• While the poorest fifth of American households lost $2,834 in real income from 1972 to 1987, the income of the richest fifth increased by more than

$10,000. The gap between the two groups is now wider than at any time in the last 50 years.

- Half the benefits from mortgage interest deductions go to the wealthiest 10% of the population, and three-quarters of all itemized deductions are taken by individuals earning $50,000 or more per year.[80]
- Only four in ten American workers have retirement plans.[81]

Wealth is even more unequally distributed:

- Eleven percent of households have zero or negative wealth, and 26.2% have wealth of less than $5,000. At the high end of the spectrum, 26.3% have a net worth of over $100,000; the "super-rich" (about one-fifth of 1%) own almost 60% of the corporate wealth.[82]
- The top 1% of families own nearly one-fourth of all the net wealth, although they receive only 11% of all money income. The top 10% of families hold 70% of all net wealth.[83]

Education, a major pillar of societal infrastructure, is a crucial source of inequality. Schools in the United States remain separate and unequal.[106] Commentators argue that schools frequently exist in a state of "educational apartheid," where minority and needy children are doomed to failure and reform movements meet institutional gridlock.[107]

- Affluent communities spend more money on education, and suburban students enjoy far better facilities and higher-quality education than their urban and rural counterparts.[108]
- The major source of funding for education in this country is the local property tax. The gulf between the wealthiest and poorest school districts, based on per-pupil expenditures, varies greatly from Delaware, where the wealthiest district spends 1.43 times as much as the poorest, to Texas, where the difference is more than 6.7 times.[109]

In spite of *Brown* v. *Board of Education,* the pivotal U.S. Supreme Court ruling that struck down the principle of "separate but equal" education in 1954, school segregation remains firmly entrenched across the nation. It has been reproduced by economic inequalities that are, in turn, reproduced by unequal access to education. Several recent state rulings, including rulings in Texas, California, and Arkansas, have sought to establish a legal foundation for an equitable public school system. However, equalization efforts are often met with great resistance.

Children

Since the mid-1970s, children have become the poorest Americans. The big economic losers of the last two decades, they are frequently oppressed, neglected, and abused.

- In 1974, children displaced the elderly as the poorest group in America. In 1991, children represented 26% of the population, but they constituted 40% of the poor. By contrast, the elderly comprised 12% of the population and only 11% of the poor.[84] Young children are most likely to be poor.[85]
- The 1991 child poverty rate of 21.8% was the highest recorded since 1983.[86]
- The United States has more children in poverty than other industrial countries. In this country, 17.1% of children live below the poverty line, compared with

5.1% in Switzerland, 5.2% in Sweden, 7.6% in Norway, 8.2% in the former West Germany, 9.6% in Canada, 10.7% in the United Kingdom, and 16.9% in Australia. Since 1979, child poverty in this country climbed to nearly 21% in 1987.[87]

• About one-third of the annual $4 billion in child-care tax credits allowed by the federal government benefits families with yearly incomes of more than $50,000. On average, these households pay just 6% of their income for child care, compared with 23% for families earning under $15,000.[88]

Women

Historically, women are one of the most unequal, powerless, and abused groups. Violence against women is becoming more visible in this country.

• Women are paid less than men with the same qualifications for the same job. The average weekly earnings of women are 52 to 82% of men's earnings.[89]

• Two of three adults whose incomes fall below the official poverty line are women.[90]

• Far fewer elderly men than women are poor, and elderly women are especially vulnerable to a retirement in poverty. Although more than 90% of the elderly receive some Social Security benefits, only 27% of women over 65 received employer-provided pensions in 1990, with average benefits of $5,478 a year. In contrast, 49% of older men received employer pensions averaging $9,756.[91]

• Families headed by women are five times as likely to be poor as are all other families. Although members of this group constitute one-fifth of the U.S. population, they account for over half of the population in poverty.[92]

• In 1988, the median household income for families headed by women was only $16,051; the median household income for all families was $32,491; for married couples, $36,436; and for single-parent families headed by men, $28,642.[93]

• Children living with only one parent are almost five times as likely to be poor as children living with both parents.[94]

• Between 1979 and 1987, the average annual rate of violent crimes against women by current or former spouses, boyfriends, and other family members was 6.1 per 1,000 females age 12 or older.[95]

• In 1992, President Bush vetoed a bill that would have allowed many new mothers (and fathers) to take 12 weeks of unpaid leave from their jobs.[96]

African Americans and Other Minorities

Minority families, children, and women suffer even greater inequality and oppression than do whites.

• The average African American family's income is only 61.5% of the income of the average white family; African American females head 56.2% of the families headed by women, while white females head 17.3%.[97]

• In 1988, the median income of males 15 years of age and over was $18,909. White males received $19,959; African Americans, $12,044; and Hispanics, $13,030. By contrast, the median income of females was $8,884. White females received $9,103; African Americans, $7,349; and Hispanics, $6,990.[98]

• African American children fare the worst among racial and ethnic groups, with 39.8% living in poverty. By contrast, the poverty rate is 38.8% for Native

Americans, 32.2% for Hispanics, 17.1% for Asian Americans, and 12.5% for whites.[99] Minority children are more likely than white children to be poor—46% of African Americans and 40% of Hispanics are poor, compared with 17% of whites.[100]

- Almost half of all African American children are poor. One in two grows up without a father, more than 50% of African American families are headed by single women, and over 50% of these children live in poverty.[101]
- Of the 10.3% of all families living below the poverty line, 7.8% are white, 27.8% are African American, and 23.4% are Hispanic. Of the 19% of all children living below the poverty line, 14.1% are white, 43.2% are African American, and 35.5% are Hispanic.
- Members of minority groups are roughly 60% more likely to be denied a mortgage than whites even when they are equally creditworthy.[102]
- Americans aged 18 to 24 are more likely than older ones, and African American and Hispanic workers are more likely than white workers, to work in low-wage jobs.[103]
- In the distribution of occupations, whites are almost twice as likely as African Americans (1.7 times) and Hispanics (1.9 times) to hold professional and managerial jobs.[104]
- As children move from the 6-8-year-old group to the 9-11-year-old group, their rate of enrollment below grade level increases by 5% for whites, 11% for African Americans, and 14% for Hispanics.[105]

Distributive Criteria

Social workers in policy planning recognize several frequently antithetical criteria for the distribution of goods and services. Extensive literature refers to nine major canons of distributive justice: equality, need, ability (or desert), effort, productivity, public utility, supply and demand, rank, and legal entitlement.[110]

Equality as a distributive criterion refers to the treatment of all people as equal. Everyone is treated exactly the same, even though differences exist between individuals or groups. In practice, it is crucial to agree about how equality is to be perceived. In spite of varied interpretations of equality, the dominant societal values usually provide guidelines for the precise meaning of equality.[111] Otherwise, users of this criterion can be oblivious to the reality of differential claims.

If based on varied criteria and points of reference, equality and egalitarianism can remain operationally unclear notions. For example, in the previous section on concepts of equality, we discussed different types of equality encountered in practice: equality of sacrifice, equality of results, equality of opportunity and risk, equality of rights, equality of considerations, and ex-ante and ex-post equality. Social workers recognize that in practice equality can be fixed and constant or varying and proportionate. The regressive sales tax represents a fixed-equality perspective, and the progressive income tax represents a varying or proportionate tax.

Similar issues arise in the case of affirmative action and reverse discrimination. Justice requires not only the equal treatment of equals, but under varied circumstances, it requires the reverse: the unequal treatment (appropriately measured) of unequals. The treatment of people as equals without reference to their differential claims may violate rather than strengthen social justice, as in the case of distributions among social classes and individuals whose legitimate claims to this distribution are diverse.

Need, a distributive criterion with a socialist bent (to each according to individual needs), recognizes that individuals enter this world with different possessions, opportunities, and natural endowments. People should be treated in a way that will make them as equal as possible in those respects in which they are equal, namely, in human dignity and personality strengths. Because no widely accepted definition of need exists, the value system of society must define and prioritize the needs to be included: real needs, felt needs, materialistic needs, or social and emotional needs.

Ability, or *desert,* refers to treatment according to merit, achievement, or some equivalent. As a distributive criterion, its focus is the qualities of people or groups.

Social policy planners attempt to distinguish in practice the meritorious components of this criterion from its natural-endowment aspects. Some may allocate rewards solely according to innate ability without regard to how the abilities in question are used or abused. Others keep in mind that natural ability is not a matter of desert (merit).

Effort refers to treatment according to effort and sacrifice. This criterion relates to the Puritan ethic: God helps those who help themselves. It also relates to the assertion that in a natural society acquisitions are proportional to individual labor. In practice, this criterion tends to discount achievement and ability; it may weaken incentive or encourage the inefficient and incompetent. Effort in and of itself can be fruitful or vain, well-directed or misguided.

Productivity as a distributive criterion refers to treatment according to actual productive contribution. It links personal characteristics to work or production. This essentially economic principle excludes need, effort, and merit if used as a single-factor criterion. In explaining and measuring collective efforts, productivity cannot be operationally associated with intelligence, education, or ability—the forces that contribute to it.

Public utility refers to the treatment of all people according to the requirements of the common good, the public interest, or the good of a greater number. This partly utilitarian principle guarantees in practice that all individual claims can or will be recognized and acceded to. This can be problematic, however, particularly when rejection of such claims (however socially advantageous) might constitute an unjust action.

Supply and demand refers to treatment according to the scarcity of socially useful resources or services in the context of the economic market and its forces of supply and demand.[112] Unlike productivity, which is based on contributions to the value of products, this laissez-faire criterion is based on relative economic scarcity.

Rank refers to treatment according to status. In a hierarchical society, masters are treated differently from slaves, managers differently from rank-and-file workers, and the wealthy differently from the poor.

Legal entitlement refers to treatment according to what the law allows: *cuique suum.* Justice follows the "rules." A challenge arises, however, when the rules are unjust or biased in favor of the status quo.

In social policy practice, each criterion is homogeneous (not pluralistic) and usually excludes the others. Social policy planners who use one of these distributive criteria may achieve different results than those who use other criteria. As a rule, policy planners consider various canons of distributive justice and use those most appropriate in a given situation. Need, for example, is considered mainly in programs for the poor; contribution is used in social insurance schemes. The concept of supply and demand prevails in the distribution of goods and services by the economic market; equality is basic to law and legal processes. In selecting distributive criteria for equality, policy planners are also influenced by the model of social justice supported by social work. For example, social workers opting for fairness are more likely to use the equality criterion and the rational model of justice. On the other hand, business managers using the market model are more likely to use the criterion of supply and demand.

Strategies to Reduce Inequality

Social policy planners use various strategies to reduce inequality and distribute or redistribute goods and services. Some social workers seek to improve the position of those with the fewest advantages by increasing their minimum share. Planners using other strategies try to decrease either the ratio or the absolute difference between those with greater and lesser entitlements in society. Still other approaches are attempts to reduce the advantages of those who have more. Although the aim of all strategies is to reduce overall inequality, each emphasizes a different approach.[113]

MAXIMIN. Shorthand for "maximizing the minimum share," the aim of this strategy is to improve the position of the least advantaged. By maximizing the minimum, social workers can increase the rights and income of the least advantaged in society. Welfare-state programs reflect this strategy and the fairness model. MAXIMIN allocations give more to those with less and therefore are thought to be more equal. This is the notion of egalitarian redistribution, which tends to change the status quo. Other factors being equal, Rawls's model is a MAXIMIN principle. Pareto's principle also reflects this strategy: any increased utility of at least one person increases the aggregate welfare as long as it decreases the utility of no one.[114]

Ratio. This strategy is based on distributions that increase the ratio between the lesser entitlement and the greater. That is, it increases the ratio of the amount of rights and wealth held by the least advantaged to the amount held by the most advantaged. Such allocations emphasize the importance of relative differences and are considered more equal. Relative (rather than absolute) definitions of the official poverty line are based on this strategy. A crucial policy issue concerns how much to take from the advantaged and give to the disadvantaged.

Least Difference. Strategies of this type decrease the absolute difference between greater and lesser entitlements. In other words, they narrow the arithmetical difference between the absolute amount of rights and wealth held by the most and least advantaged. The emphasis is on absolute differences, not on ratios. Absolute definitions of the poverty line reflect this strategy.

In absolute equality, the ratio and least-difference strategies converge precisely: any 1:1 ratio will also have a difference of zero. In inequality, however, the two strategies are clearly distinct: poverty-line strategies can increase the ratio while decreasing the difference or can decrease the ratio while increasing the difference.

MINIMAX.   Shorthand for "minimizing the maximum share," this strategy is an attempt to diminish the entitlement of the more advantaged. It is based on distributions that reduce the rights and wealth held by the most advantaged in society. Progressive income taxes reflect this strategy.

There seems to be no single strategy that policy planners use in all cases because each strategy produces different results under varied circumstances.[115] Thus, eliminating poverty may require different strategies in different situations. For example, during economic growth, the most effective strategy to benefit the least advantaged is usually MINIMAX. Limiting the absolute amount for the most advantaged results in a top-down redistribution of growth from the most to the least advantaged. MAXIMIN is less effective here because it sets an absolute social minimum that does not necessarily rise during economic growth.

By the same token, during economic recession, MAXIMIN tends to be most effective in giving benefits to the least advantaged.

Arguments against Redistribution

Social workers are committed to social change and redistribution of goods and services to improve social justice and equality for all people, particularly the powerless and disadvantaged. The distinct inequalities in the United States not only undermine the collective interest of society and violate basic human rights, but also condemn the powerless and the oppressed to continuous socioeconomic underdevelopment. Commentators who support the market model of justice, however, argue that the redistribution of goods and services to improve equality can undermine the economic market. In their view, inequality is unavoidable and desirable in the structure of modern hierarchical society and its market economy. They say the economic market distributes goods and services justly and fairly, so redistribution is unnecessary and undesirable. These arguments frequently take the form of economic efficiency (the market model) versus social justice and equality (the fairness model).[116]

In opposing the redistributive programs of the welfare state, these commentators (usually neoconservative) argue as follows. First, most economic inequalities are "earned" through one's capabilities and motivations and therefore are "deserved." It is only fair that those who produce more should enjoy a higher income. Hence, inequality is both desirable and unavoidable, and redistribution conflicts with the individual right to property in a free market.

Second, no matter how unequal the distribution, it is just if it is based on a just process, such as the marketplace. Market arrangements are free, voluntary, and based on free competition and equality of rights and opportunity. Income derived from market processes is produced by the recipients and the resources they own.

Third, redistribution is more likely to depress than to raise living standards for the poor. Redistribution transfers resources from people who are productive in the market to others who are less so. Hence, ambition and energy are diverted from productive economic activity.

Fourth, equality and egalitarianism undermine economic freedom in an open society. Political decisions to remove economic differences entail extensive coercion, which increases the actual inequality of power between rulers and subjects in exchange for reducing economic inequality.[117]

Proponents of fairness and the welfare state challenge the fundamental assumption that marketplace outcomes are "just" simply because they emerge from "right" procedures in the marketplace. These theorists point out that determining who is deserving or whether the market process is just depends on normative perceptions of the production process in the marketplace. They also challenge the assumption that the rich produce correspondingly more than the poor. They disagree that property owners normally produce their income and the resources they own; production based on the joint use of different resources by different people makes it impossible to separate which people or which resources produced how much of the total output. Also, in the past, wealth could be accumulated through unfair and illegal ways (such as slavery, piracy, coercion, power, or theft).[118]

If the economic market were not seriously flawed, producing unemployment and inflation, redistribution and the welfare state would be almost unnecessary. Rather than accept and tolerate inequality, proponents of fairness call for the reform of the economic market and the introduction of principles of justice into the marketplace to prevent gross inequalities.

NOTES

1. Report by the International Campaign for Tibet, a U.S. rights group, "Report Assails China Over Tibet," *Boston Globe,* September 23, 1991, 12.
2. P. Constable, "At U.N. Aristide Stands Up for Haiti," *Boston Globe,* September 26, 1991, 28.
3. F. Phillips and B. McGrory, "Weld Files Abortion Bills, Draws Blast by Law," *Boston Globe,* September 20, 1991, 1.
4. W. V. Robinson, "Thomas Disavows Old Stance and Statements on Natural Law," *Boston Globe,* September 11, 1991, 1, 14.
5. "Judiciary Should Say No to Thomas," editorial, *Boston Globe,* September 10, 1991, 12.
6. "The Restless Swedes," editorial, *Boston Globe,* September 23, 1991, 10.
7. "Greeks Plan Sale of Some Islands," *Boston Globe,* September 24, 1991, 2.
8. "Jewish Leaders Hail U.S. Appeal on Zionism," *Boston Globe,* September 24, 1991, 27.
9. I. Wilkerson, "A Remedy for Old Racism Has New Kind of Shackles," *New York Times,* September 15, 1991, 1, 28.
10. DeFao, "Worst of West's Poverty Was in U.S., Study Finds," *Boston Globe,* September 19, 1991, 3, and M. K. Frisby, "Rich Got Richer, Poor Poorer, Another Study on Taxes Finds," *Boston Globe,* September 13, 1991, 79.
11. Code of Ethics, National Association of Social Workers; and B. W. Sheafer et al., *Techniques and Guidelines for Social Work Practice* (Boston: Allyn & Bacon, 1991).
12. N. Abercrombie, S. Hill, and B. S. Turner, *Dictionary of Sociology* (New York: Penguin, 1984), 104.
13. E. Shil, "Ideology: The Concept and Functions of Ideology," in D. L. Sills, ed., *The Encyclopedia of Social Sciences,* vol. 7 (New York: Free Press, 1968), 66.
14. L. P. Baradat, *Political Ideologies: Their Origins and Impact* (Englewood Cliffs, NJ: Prentice-Hall, 1991), 264.
15. *Racism* refers to attitudes, and policies (either overt and individual or covert and institutional) that oppress individuals or subordinate social groups. Central to this doctrine in the United States are discrimination against African Americans and ethnic minorities as biologically inferior to whites and the assumption that any attempt to extend all human

rights to minorities debases the biological conditions of civilization and destroys the American way of life.

16. *Sexism* refers to doctrines, attitudes, and actions that result in discrimination against women purely on grounds of their sex.

17. G. Therborn, *The Ideology of Power and the Power of Ideology* (London: Verso Editions, 1980), 2–11.

18. The most widely abused meaning of *ideology* sets it in opposition to science, in which ideas are tested against empirical evidence. It suggests that ideology convinces one of the truth without proving it. However, this is not the meaning applied here. Moreover, the alleged antagonism between ideology and science is artificial, dating back to developments that resulted in the introduction of capitalism between the 16th and 18th centuries.

19. This view rejects the teleological context of social science inquiry (explanations of social processes that refer to an end state they allegedly serve).

20. *Science,* is not immune to the subjectivity of its predictions; it can even function as ideology. The works of Adam Smith, Karl Marx, and Charles Darwin, for example, are works of science, but they have also operated as ideologies ("economic liberalism," "scientific socialism," and "social Darwinism").

21. Abercrombie, Hill, and Turner, *Dictionary of Sociology,* 231.

22. H. M. Johnson, "Ideology and the Social System," in D. L. Sills, ed., *The Encyclopedia of Social Sciences* (New York: Free Press, 1969), 77.

23. For some Marxists, the economic base determines the superstructure of beliefs. They stress the causal importance of the superstructure and the causal role of objective economic conditions.

24. K. Mannheim, *Ideology and Utopia: An Introduction to the Sociology of Knowledge* (New York: Harcourt, Brace, & World, 1954).

25. L. Althusser, *For Marx* (London: Penguin, 1969); L. Althusser and E. Balibar, *Reading Capital* (London: New Left Books, 1970); and T. Bottomore et al., eds., *A Dictionary of Marxist Thought* (Cambridge, MA: Harvard University Press, 1983), 223.

26. In this context, A. Gramsci argued that the domination of the capitalist class could not be secured by economic factors alone but required political force and, more important, an ideological apparatus that secured the consent of the dominant classes. See Abercrombie, Hill, and Turner, *Dictionary of Sociology,* 97.

27. For a discussion of the works of Marx, Mannheim, and Weber in this context, see R. K. Merton, *Social Theory and Social Structure* (Glencoe, IL: Free Press, 1957).

28. For more information about the ideological evolution of concepts in this section and highlights of the evolution from tradition to command and to the market, see K. Polanyi, *The Great Transformation* (New York: Farrar, Rinehart, 1944); D. Landes, *The Unbound Prometheus* (Cambridge, England: Cambridge University Press, 1969); P. Mantoux, *The Industrial Revolution in the Eighteenth Century* (New York: Harcourt-Brace, 1928); R. H. Tawney, *Religion and the Rise of Capitalism* (New York: Harcourt-Brace, 1937); R. L. Heilbroner, *The Economic Problem,* 9th ed. (Englewood Cliffs, NJ: Prentice-Hall, 1990); J. F. Bell, *Economic Evolution* (New York: Roland Press, 1967); E. K. Hunt and H. J. Sherman, *Economics: An Introduction to Traditional and Radical Views* (New York: Harper & Row, 1981); and P. Samuelson and W. Nordhouse, *Economics,* 13th ed. (New York: McGraw-Hill, 1989).

    For more information about American ideology and treatment of minorities, see S. Carmichael and C. V. Hamilton, *Black Power: The Politics of Liberation in America* (New York: Random House, 1967); R. Huber, *The American Idea of Success* (New York: McGraw-Hill, 1971); "If the Indian Tribes Win Legal War to Regain Half of Maine," *U.S. News and World Report,* April 4, 1977, 53–54; R. L. Means, *The Ethical Imperative:*

The Crisis in American Values (Garden City, NY: Doubleday, 1970); and "Should We Give the U.S. Back to the Indians?" *Time,* April 1, 1977, 51.

29. T. G. Ash, "Poland after Solidarity," *New York Review,* June 13, 1991, 46–47; F. Feher and A. Arato, eds., *Crisis and Reform in Eastern Europe* (New York: New School for Social Research, 1991); A. Brumberg, "The Turning Point?" *New York Review,* June 28, 1990, 52–59; M. Meurs and R. Schauffler, "Not According to Plan: The Collapse of the Soviet Planned Economy," *Dollars and Sense* (July/August, 1990), 6–9; T. G. Ash, "Eastern Europe: Après Le Déluge, Nous," *New York Review,* August 16, 1990, 51–57; R. Heilbroner, "Reflections: After Communism," *New Yorker,* September 10, 1990, 91–100; O. Friedrich, "Headed For the Dustheap," *Time,* February 19, 1990, 36–38; and A. G. Papandreou, "What Does Socialism Mean Today?" (Lecture given at the University de la Complutense, on October 7, 1991, Madrid.)

30. The chain reaction of forces included developments in the agricultural economy between the 11th and 13th centuries, the rapid growth of population and the increase in urban concentration, the increase in long-distance trade, the enclosure movement, the creation of new nation-states, the emergence of Protestantism, and the Industrial Revolution.

31. Several eminent liberal philosophers and political economists have contributed to classical liberalism and its interpretation of nature, human and economic behavior, social relations, government, democracy, social justice, and public social welfare, including Thomas Hobbes (1588–1679), John Locke (1632–1704), Adam Smith (1723–1790), Jeremy Bentham (1748–1832), Thomas Malthus (1766–1834), David Ricardo (1772–1823), and John Stuart Mill (1806–1873).

32. Classical liberalism is the belief that the free market should be self-regulated by the naturally acquisitive, competitive character of human beings; people should have equal opportunity to practice civil and political freedoms in pursuing their self-interest. For notions of classical liberalism in this section, see H. K. Girvetz, *The Evolution of Liberalism* (New York: Collier, 1963), 1–49; W. D. Grampp, *Economic Liberalism* (New York: Random House, 1965); and E. K. Hunt and H. J. Sherman, *Economics* (New York: Harper & Row, 1981).

33. Critics of modern capitalism include R. C. Edwards et al., *The Capitalist System* (Englewood Cliffs, NJ: Prentice-Hall, 1972); E. Fromm, *The Sane Society* (New York: Rinehart, 1955); E. Greenberg, *The American Political System* (Cambridge, MA: Winthrop, 1980); M. Zeitlin, ed., *American Society, Inc.* (Chicago: Markham, 1970); *Catalyst, A Socialist Journal of the Social Services;* and the Union for Radical Political Economics, *U.S. Capitalism in Crisis* (New York: URPE, 1978).

34. M. Weber, *The Protestant Ethic and the Spirit of Capitalism* (New York: Scribner's, 1958).

35. A. Morales and B. Sheafor, *Social Work: A Profession of Many Faces* (Needham Heights: Allyn & Bacon, 1992), 225.

36. A. Brecht, *Political Theory* (Princeton, NJ: Princeton University Press, 1959), 136.

37. See R. Dworking, *Taking Rights Seriously* (Cambridge, MA: Harvard University Press, 1978); J. Rawls, *A Theory of Justice* (Cambridge, MA: Harvard University Press, 1971); D. T. Meyers, *Inalienable Rights: A Defense* (New York: Columbia University Press, 1985); and G. Sher, *Moral Philosophy* (Orlando, FL: Harcourt Brace Jovanovich, 1987).

38. The U.S. Catholic bishops claim that the right to human dignity comes from God. National Conference of Catholic Bishops, *Economic Justice for All: Pastoral Letters of the Catholic Social Teaching and the U.S. Economy* (Washington, DC: U.S. Catholic Conference, 1986).

39. For natural rights, see H. C. Black, *Black's Law Dictionary,* 5th ed. (St. Paul, MN: West, 1979); and H. Sidewick, *Outlines of the History of Ethics* (Indianapolis, IN: Hackett, 1988).

40. Brecht, *Political Theory,* 55, 136.
41. Social-contract theories postulate a "state of nature" and political authority. Hobbes thought that humankind overcomes its natural state of being antisocial by placing political authority in a government (through a social contract) that guarantees human relations. Rousseau believed that people overcome their natural state by becoming social beings. He and Locke placed authority in a political community. Hobbes attributed absolute sovereignty to government; Rousseau, to people; Locke asserted the right of individuals to transfer to government or community a public right, including political authority.
42. R. Posner, *The Economics of Justice* (Cambridge, MA: Harvard University Press, 1981) 33.
43. In contrast to Locke, who suggested that within natural law there are certain rules of nature governing human conduct, Bentham suggested that the utility of anything can be measured by the amount of pleasure or pain it brings to society as a whole. He proposed that general happiness is *summum bonum:* the greatest happiness to the greatest number. In conflicts, he believed that the greater number of people will judge by reason.
44. J. Rawls, *A Theory of Justice* (Cambridge, MA: Harvard University Press, 1971), 6, 19, 21, 24–25; and W. A. Galston, *Justice and the Human Good* (Chicago: Chicago University Press, 1980), 108.
45. Aggregate utility favors productivity (members A, B, and C receive two units each, for a total of six) at the expense of distribution or average utility (members A, B, and C receive one unit each, for a total of three).
46. A problem arises when just procedures and just outcomes do not coincide. A perfectly just outcome may be unjust on procedural grounds.
47. T. Sowell, "Adam Smith in Theory and Practice," in G. O'Driscoll, Jr., ed., *Adam Smith and Modern Political Economy: Bicentennial Essays on the Wealth of Nations* (Ames: Iowa State University Press, 1979), 4.
48. R. Solomon and M. Murphy, eds., *What is Justice? Classic and Contemporary Readings* (New York, Oxford: Oxford University Press, 1990), 164.
49. L. Schneider, "Adam Smith on Human Nature and Social Circumstances," in O'Driscoll, *Adam Smith and Modern Political Economy,* 53.
50. Sowell, "Adam Smith," 5; and R. Heilbroner and L. Thurow, *Economics Explained* (Englewood Cliffs, NJ: Prentice-Hall, 1982), 4.
51. D. Reisman, *Adam Smith's Sociological Economics* (New York: Barnes and Noble, 1976), 153.
52. J. Locke, *Two Treaties of Government* (New York: Mentor, 1965); and D. C. McPherson, *The Political Theory of Possessive Individualism* (New York: Oxford University Press, 1962).
53. J. S. Mill, *Principles of Political Economy* (Clinton, NJ: Kelley, 1965); and R. Krouse and M. McPherson, "The Logic of Liberal Equality," in J. D. Moon, ed., *Responsibility, Rights, and Welfare: The Theory of the Welfare State* (Boulder, CO: Westview Press, 1988), 134–135.
54. Solomon and Murphy, *What is Justice?* 130.
55. M. Friedman and R. Friedman, *Free to Choose* (New York: Harcourt Brace Jovanovich, 1979), 135.
56. R. Nozick, *Anarchy, State, and Utopia* (New York: Basic Books, 1974), 149.
57. Ibid.
58. Nozick, *Anarchy, State, and Utopia;* Friedman and Friedman, *Free to Choose.*
59. K. Arrow, *Social Choice and Individual Values* (New York: Wiley, 1963), 18.
60. Nozick, *Anarchy, State, and Utopia;* R. Nozick, "Distributive Justice," in J. Sterba, ed., *Justice: Alternative Political Perspectives* (Belmont, CA: Wadsworth, 1980), 148–149.

61. J. Paul, *Reading Nozick* (Totowa, NJ: Rowman & Littlefield, 1981).
62. E. Nell and D. O'Neill, "Justice Under Socialism," in *Justice: Alternative Political Perspectives,* 200, 205, 207; and R. Heilbroner, *Marx For and Against* (New York: Norton, 1980), Chapters 4 and 5.
63. Rawls, *A Theory of Justice,* 26.
64. Ibid., 440.
65. Ibid., 82.
66. Ibid., 303.
67. Ibid., 302–303.
68. Ibid., 440.
69. For critiques of Rawls's theory, see N. Daniels, ed., *Reading Rawls* (New York: Basic Books, 1974); and R. M. Hare, "Rawls' Theory of Justice," *Philosophical Quarterly* 23, 1973.
70. Nozick, *Anarchy, State, and Utopia,* 155.
71. Ibid., 150–161.
72. Ibid.
73. The principle of proportional equality, based on the classical and medieval assumption that society and the cosmos are necessarily hierarchical, was elaborated by Aristotle in Book V of the *Ethica Nicomachea* and Book III of the *Politics,* Aristotle, *Ethica Nicomachea,* translated by W. D. Ross (Oxford: Clarendon Press, 1925); and Aristotle, *Politics* (London: Heinemann; Cambridge, MA: Harvard University Press, 1959).
74. Ex-ante equality is concerned with a standard before the fact; ex-post equality is concerned with after-the-fact considerations. For example, a group of six people having the same wealth would make a payment of $60. Ex-ante approaches would allocate the burden of payment by assigning numbers from one to six to each person and then rolling a die to determine which individual should pay the entire $60. Thus, each individual has before-the-fact equal chance of incurring the obligation of payment. Risks or opportunities are equalized. The ex-post approach would require each person to make a payment of $10. Other factors being equal, if individuals dislike risk, they might opt for an ex-post approach.

    A random system to select individuals for military service is equitable only in an ex-ante sense: it equalizes the risk of being drafted. This is not true in an ex-post sense because not all young people would bear equal shares of the burden of national defense.
75. Equality gives each person one-third of a pie, but equity gives a hungry person a larger slice.
76. T. Parsons, K. Davis, and W. E. Moore, among others, have argued that social stratification is indispensable in modern society.
77. *Boston Globe,* August 28, 1992, 15.
78. Center on Budget and Policy Priorities; U.S. Census Bureau; and *The World Almanac and Book of Facts 1992,* 135.
79. Center on Budget and Policy Priorities; and U.S. Census Bureau.
80. J. Birnbaum and D. Wessel, "Tax Breaks: Who Gets What," *Wall Street Journal,* July 20, 1990, section A, p. 3; and R. Reischauer, "The Federal Budget: Economics and Subsidies for the Rich," in A. Woldauski and M. Baskin, eds., *The Federal Budget* (San Francisco: Institute for Contemporary Studies, 1989), 247.
81. Phillips, *Politics of Rich and Poor.*
82. *Statistical Abstract of the United States 1991* (Washington, DC: U.S. Government Printing Office), section 14, p. 469.
83. A Levinson, "Racism Cost U.S. Millions of Dollars," *Springfield Sunday Republican* (MA), August 1992, B-1.
84. Ibid., 2.

85. D. L. Cohen, "Despite Widespread Income Growth, Study Finds Increase in Child Poverty," *Education Week,* August 5, 1992, 24.

86. National Commission on Children, *Poverty, Welfare, and American Families: A Hard Look* (Washington, DC: Author, 1992), 1, 2.

87. T. Smeeding, B. Boyle Torrey, and M. Rein, *Patterns of Income and Poverty: The Economic Status of Children and the Elderly in Eight Countries* (Washington, DC: Urban Institute, 1991).

88. D. Ribadeneira, "Day Care Credits Said to Favor Well-Off," *Boston Globe,* September 18, 1992, 3 (from a national study released by Harvard University).

89. M. F. Fox and C. H. Biber, *Women at Work* (Palo Alto, CA: Mayfield, 1981), 34.

90. B. Ehrenreich and F. Piven, "The Feminization of Poverty," *Dissent,* (Spring 1984), 162–170.

91. S. Rich, "A Spending Limit at 65," *Boston Globe,* September 22, 1992, 3.

92. S.A. Levitan, *Programs in Aid of the Poor.* (Baltimore, MD: Johns Hopkins University Press, 1990), 7.

93. U.S. Bureau of the Census, *Statistical Abstract of the United States 1991,* 11th ed. (Washington DC: U.S. Government Printing Office, 1991).

94. U.S. Department of Commerce, Bureau of the Census, Current Population Reports, ser. P-60, no. 181, *Marital Status and Living Arrangements: March 1991* (Washington DC: U.S. Government Printing Office, 1992), 43, table 6.

95. L. Ginsberg, *Social Work Almanac* (Washington, DC: National Association of Social Workers, 1992), 58.

96. F. Barringer, "In Family-Leave Debate, a Profound Ambivalence," *The New York Times,* October 2, 1992, 1, A22.

97. S. A. Levitan, *Programs in Aid of the Poor* (Baltimore, MD: Johns Hopkins University Press, 1990), B-1.

98. U.S. Bureau of the Census, *Statistical Abstract of the United States 1991,* 11th ed. (Washington, DC: U.S. Government Printing Office, 1991).

99. D. L. Cohen, "Despite Widespread Income Growth, Study Finds Increase in Child Poverty," *Education Week,* August 5, 1992, 24.

100. U.S. Department of Commerce, Bureau of the Census, Current Population Reports, ser. P-60, no. 181, *Poverty in the United States, 1991* (Washington, DC: Government Printing Office, 1992), 10, table 5.

101. M. W. Macht and J. B. Ashford, *Introduction to Social Work and Social Welfare* (New York: Macmillan, 1990), 295; and S. A. Levitan, *Programs in Aid of the Poor* (Baltimore, MD: Johns Hopkins University Press, 1990), 3, 7.

102. M. Zuckoff, "Study Shows Racial Bias in Lending," *Boston Globe,* October 9, 1992, 1.

103. *Education Week,* May 27, 1992, 3.

104. E. Bonacich, *Capitalism and Racism, Race, Class, and Gender* (Belmont, CA: Wadsworth, 1987), 101.

105. Gutterman, 1992, 13.

106. J. Kozol, "Whitle and the Privateers," *The Nation,* 1992, 255, 272–278.

107. L. Robinson, "Boston Schools Short of Books Despite Vows," *Boston Globe,* October 20, 1992, 1, 19.

108. *Boston Globe,* October 12, 1992, 14.

109. *Education Week,* 1992.

110. Sophists in ancient Greece, denouncing morality as an invention of the weak to neutralize the strength of the strong, declared that "might is right"; justice is the interest of the strongest and represents a compromise between persons of roughly equal power. According to Plato, justice is relations among individuals depending on a just social organization.

It is harmony and order; each shall receive the equivalent of what he or she produces and shall perform the function for which he or she is best fit (innate ability). For Aristotle, a just and legitimate society was one in which inequities of property, status, or power are necessary for the common good.

111. Until 300 to 400 years ago, inequality was assumed to be inevitable and desirable. The counterassertion that equality is both desirable and attainable is associated with the French and American Revolutions, as well as with socialist goals. Contemporary neoconservatives assert that equality would lead to intolerable degrees of uniformity and to new forms of inequality and that it would undermine the capitalist economic market. In this view, redistribution to achieve equality offends those who justly earned resources in the marketplace.

112. These and other principles of distributive justice are discussed in J. A. Ryan, *Distributive Justice,* 3rd ed. (New York: Macmillan, 1942); J. P. Sterba, *Justice: Alternative Political Perspectives* (Belmont, CA: Wadsworth, 1980); J. A. Buss, "A Comparison of Distributive Justice in OECD Countries," *Review of Social Economy* 47 (Spring 1989), 1–14; R. C. Solomon and M. C. Murphy, eds., *What Is Justice?* (New York: Oxford University Press, 1990).

113. D. Rae et al., *Equalities* (Cambridge, MA: Harvard University Press, 1981), 114–118, 117–122.

114. V. Pareto, *Manual of Political Economy,* A. S. Shwier, trans., A. S. Shwier and A. M. Page, eds. (New York: Augustus Kelly, 1970).

115. Rae, *Equalities,* 112–121.

116. Among three class societies, A produces the lowest gross national product (GNP) but has a perfectly equal distribution. B is second in production and distribution. C produces the highest GNP but has the most unequal distribution. As a policy consultant, which society would you recommend?

117. P. I. Baver, *Just Deserts* (Cambridge, MA: Harvard University Press, 1981).

118. If person A has produced some food unaided and persons A and B need that food equally, then the case for A rather than B having the food may be strong. However, what if person A has produced the food but has little need for it, while B, who is hungry, or C, who is sick, needs it desperately? Furthermore, the conservative view is based on the assumption that production is personal—a difficult notion to sustain in the case of modern interdependent production.

CHAPTER 4

Political Power
and Social Policy

"Greece celebrates the 2,500th anniversary of the world's first recognizable democracy."[1]

"Europeans OK political union treaty."[2]

"Center-right Social Democrats won in Portugal vote."[3]

"Despite a threatened European trade embargo, Yugoslavia's warfare intensified."[4]

"After the recent upheavals in the Soviet Union, a common market among politically independent republics is now evolving."[5]

"The Food and Drug Administration (FDA) felt the impact of the Reagan administration's pledge in the 1980s to deregulate American business. A protracted period of indecisiveness ensued at the FDA, which had rarely before had its hands tied in carrying out its responsibilities."[6]

"Reagan aide admits guilt in cover-up. Former Assistant Secretary of State, Elliot Abrams . . . pleaded guilty to charges that he misled Congress as part of the cover-up of U.S. aid to the Nicaraguan rebels."[7]

"At gunpoint, Haitians pick new leader."[8]

"European Community finance ministers back $2.4 billion aid to USSR."[9]

"U.N. chief weighing panel on Iran-Iraq war."[10]

"Mobutu hints at sacking new premier of Zaire."[11]

"Senate approves natural gas regulation."[12]

"Spanish king bids U.N. to intervene in Gibraltar."[13]

"Women still hold few leadership positions in unions."[14]

"The Senate postponed a vote on Judge Clarence Thomas's nomination to the Supreme Court, so it can investigate sexual harassment charges against him."[15]

"Taboo issues of sex and race exploded in glare of Senate hearing."[16]

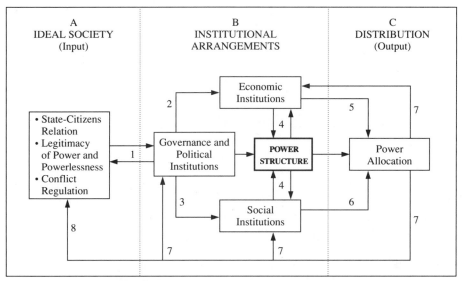

FIGURE 4-1   Power structure in social economy

THE SOCIETAL CONTEXT OF POLITICS

Why did a new Western Europe without borders replace the old nationalistic Western European nation-states? Why did the United Nations begin to play a new role in world politics? Why do countries have different political systems, institutions, and mechanisms for electing their governments and for achieving political change?[17] What role does government play in society? Which groups have the greatest influence in determining governmental policies? What power should the government have to protect consumers and achieve more equality of opportunity among groups, including women and minorities? How can holders of political power be made more accountable to those who are affected by the exercise of political power and to the people in a democratic context?

Answers to these and similar questions are complex and vary among the contending theoretical approaches. However, all the approaches include major beliefs regarding social justice, political power and legitimacy, the distribution of power, and the nature of the relationship between the state and its citizens in allocating burdens and benefits in society. The sources of power in the political system, the legitimation of the state, nationalism, the ideology of specific social orders, the rules of the political process, and cultural and political movements influence the character of social policy and the welfare state (see Figure 4-1).

Politics is concerned with who gets what, when, and how; therefore, a country's political institutions are one of the foundations of public policy and the welfare state.[18] Since World War II, popular political movements have moved beyond who gets what to identify social needs, such as sexual and racial equality, environmental protection, nuclear disarmament, and world peace. The contemporary political scene and democratic theory increasingly include not only the state but also form_ of oppression in the economy and the family as arenas of domination and political contest in which solidarity, collective identity, and interests are a part of political activity. Rather than reject the importance of control over resources, these new cultural and political movements have expanded the politics of "getting" to the politics of human development.[19]

THE STATE IN SOCIETY

Two major issues link the nation-state—the most powerful political idea of the past several hundred years—to social policy and the welfare state: the role of the state in society and the forces that control the state and state policy. The first issue concerns the degree of responsibility the state assumes for socioeconomic policy, the welfare state, and human development, including guidance of the economic market. Should the state intervene to increase social justice and equality, provide welfare-state services for human development, and distribute benefits and burdens among citizens and social classes? Should the state guide the economic market and the distribution of its products? The second issue concerns the state's bias or neutrality as a regulating institution in the context of the conflicting interests and needs of individuals and groups in society. Should the state represent the power class and the elite, the poor and the disadvantaged, or everyone (that is, the whole society) equally, without bias?

The modern state is usually identified with specific spatial boundaries and is perceived as a set of institutions (the legislature, the executive branch, central and local administrations, the judiciary, the police, and the armed forces) acting as the system of political domination and having a monopoly over the legitimate use of violence.[20] The legitimate use of power is a crucial component of the concept because it justifies the existence of the state and its specific hierarchical social orders and forms the basis of a population's acceptance of a specific polity and system of rule. The idea that all political systems ultimately rest upon the consent of the governed is directly associated with legitimacy.

Legitimacy and Justification of the State

Historically, the justification and evolution of the state were based on varied assumptions and theories. Supporters of *natural theory,* including Plato, Aristotle, and Saint Thomas Aquinas, assumed that the state is a natural phenomenon—the result of people's natural inclinations to interact and the ultimate expression of people's intrinsic capacity for social action and society's natural environment. Early supporters of the *divine theory,* including Jews, Christians, and Islamic fundamentalists, assumed that some people are chosen by God, implying that God is the only true source of political authority. Supporters of *force theory,* including Hegel and Nietzsche, viewed the state as the most powerful and total form of human organization, distinctly above the people. Supporters of *contract theory,* including Hobbes, Locke, and Rousseau, focused on the assumptions that the ruler governs by the consent of the governed, that the state is created by all the individuals within it, and that the state is of the people, who are also a part of it.[21]

Supporters of *nationalism* (the ideology of the nation-state) assume that the interest of the nation is the supreme interest; that its power is ultimate; and that its rules, exercised through the state, are final.[22] The concepts of nation and state are not the same. *Nation* is mainly a sociological term denoting a unit of society with common language, tradition, and culture that may or may not coincide with state boundaries. The concept of *state,* as the instrumentality of sovereign power and as a political term, includes the following essential properties: population, territory, diplomatic recognition, and a government with the monopoly of force to preserve peace and order and to promote the common good of its citizens. The virtues proper to the purely nationalist state are the soldierly ones of obedience, duty, and courage. In an unstable world of nation-states, supporters of nationalism assume that the people must be continuously available and controllable to be mobilized for the national purpose, including that of waging war against other nations. State membership is defined in terms of the bonds of common characteristics, including language, religion, or ethnicity: one people, one land, one law, one currency, one sovereign.

Although nationalism was not known in this form before the 18th century, it spread quickly from Western Europe and North America to the Third World. By the middle of the 19th century, it had become (and still is) a universal political force that centers the supreme loyalty of most people upon the nation-state.[23] By the end of the 19th century, it was assumed that nationalism would decline and be replaced by internationalism and global sociopolitical structures.[24]

With its several faces and applications, nationalism is reflected in the most varied and diametrically opposed ideologies—capitalism, fascism, and communism—as well as in industrialized countries and the Third World.[25] Nationalism is associated with Abraham Lincoln's deep and abiding patriotism, Adolf Hitler's national socialism (racial purification and the deified affinities of the German nation as "blood and soil"), European colonialism, war, political extremism, and xenophobia.[26] Trying to cope with poverty and neocolonialism, Third World states developed strong nationalist movements and turned to economic nationalism and versions of socialism to eradicate colonialism, achieve self-government, and promote social development.[27]

In the Soviet model of communism, nationalism took several forms: instructing the Communist parties of other countries to follow policies favoring the national interests of the former Soviet Union, suppressing the independence of the Soviet republics, and occupying Eastern European countries. But nationalism also made it difficult for the former Soviet Union to establish a new federation (or commonwealth) of the various republics. Nationalism in the republics was reflected in their hostility toward the Soviet plan and their push for independence, as well as in the division of Czechoslovakia and Yugoslavia. From its beginning, nationalism has been a politically revolutionary movement characterized by attempts to overthrow or transform the "legitimate" governments of the past whose claim to authority was based upon divine ordination or hereditary rights.

The emergence of more democratic, intercultural, and international views accelerated the shift from the maximal nationalist state, which is command based and in which the individual must be subordinate to the national interest, to the minimal democratic state, in which supreme social value is accorded to the liberty, satisfaction, and fulfillment of the individual. In the minimal democratic state, social well-being is simply the sum of individual satisfactions, and the social purpose is the aggregation of individual purposes. The state is subordinated to the individual, protecting the security of the individual and to facilitating the individual pursuit of personal values and private ends. "Rugged individualism" is aggressively promoted without significant concern for collective and common interests. The role of the state regarding the economic market and other societal functions is usually nominal and supports individual goals.

To what extent should the state intervene in societal functions, and on whose behalf? For the supremacy of the individual or of collective and common interests? Modern states attempt to establish policies that balance individual and common interest, viewing them as complementary rather than antithetical.

Control of State Policy in Democratic Societies

The basic theoretical models of the state and democracy have emerged from debates on who should control state policy and how burdens and benefits are distributed in society. Some contemporary political theorists, including pluralists, view the state as a partly independent force that can be influenced democratically by different, politically represented interests. Other theorists, including Weber, see the state in capitalist and socialist societies as an independent force that has its own rules of action and dominates all social groups. Still others, including Marxists, regard the state in capitalist countries as tied to the interests of the capitalist class.[28] The debate about who controls state policy, about direct and indirect democracy, and about pluralism and elitism is crucial to understanding the direct influence of the state and its political institutions on the welfare state and on policies for human development. Because the democratic process is equated with the state's policy-making process, the relationship between the people and policy making is an important criterion in distinguishing among the various democratic systems.

Direct Democracy

In pure, participatory democracy and self-government, the people act as their own state decisionmakers. Governing without representatives, the people eliminate the division between ruler and ruled. Ancient Athens, the Paris Commune of 1871, some cantons in Switzerland, Israeli kibbutzim, and some New England town meetings practiced direct democracy in which all individuals in society represented themselves. Some states in the United States allow their citizens to pass or repeal laws themselves in statewide referenda, as, for example, Massachusetts statewide 1988 referendum to approve or disapprove a salary increase for the members of the legislature.[29]

The concepts of classic participatory democracy in the 17th and 18th centuries stressed that democracy is a holistic ideal in which the participation of all in decision making is essential to protect the individual's private interests.[30] Smith's idea that the individual's pursuit of economic interests automatically promotes the society's interest also applies to participatory democracy, in which rational, active, informed people, furthering their private individual interests, ensure good government and promote universal interests. Because participation is central to establishing and maintaining democracy, a participatory society must educate its people to the point where their intellectual, emotional, and moral capacities have reached their full potential and the people join freely and actively in a genuine community. Rousseau maintained that democracy hinges on the participation of each citizen in political decision making and that sufficient economic equality and independence are required to prevent political inequality. Mill saw government and political institutions as primarily educative but rejected Rousseau's argument that political equality is necessary for effective participation. He believed, however, that cooperative, participatory democratic patterns in industrial organization lead to increased productivity and a "moral transformation" of the participants.[31]

The faith in the capacity of ordinary human beings to govern themselves wisely was later reaffirmed during the American Revolution. Thomas Jefferson, Thomas Paine, Samuel Adams, and other leaders of the American Revolution believed in the ability of people to rule themselves and by so doing to become better people. Dewey later maintained that the foundation of democracy is faith in the capacities of human nature, in human intelligence, and in the power of pooled, cooperative experience.[32] Cole, a 20th-century political theorist who provided a framework of participatory democracy in the context of a modern, large-scale industrialized society, wrote that democratic governments should have more than the passive or implied consent of the governed.[33] A truly democratic society is self-governing; the object of social organization in this view is not only material efficiency but also the fullest self-expression of all the society's members. Self-expression involves self-government, which means the people must fully participate as equals in society's development and law-making. Not only should individuals participate in decision making to regulate the associations of which they are members, but all associations must be free and roughly equal in power. In Cole's theory, associations hold society together.

Critics of direct democracy assert that the size and complexity of modern societies prohibit significant participation by citizens in state policy.[34] These critics argue that the ideal of direct democracy is unattractive and unrealistic given modern political realities, such as the lack of political interest and activity by the majority and the fragility of democratic political systems. They further contend that for democracy to work, individuals must know what they want, and ordinary people have inadequate levels of rationality;[35] that classic participatory theory ignores modern leadership requirements; and that mass participation in decision making is inefficient and undermines modern bureaucratic, hierarchical, and industrial social organization.

Indirect, Representative Democracy

Indirect democracy refers to a system of elected representatives who determine state policy. The people do not make public policy themselves; elected representatives do it for them.

Theorists of indirect democracy, including Berelson, Dahl, Sartori, and Eckstein, emphasize that the stability of the state is enhanced by the representative, elite system.[36] Criticizing the direct-democracy model as unrealistic in the context of modern societies, Berelson suggested that contemporary states must limit the intensity of conflict, restrict the role of change, maintain economic stability, and secure a pluralist social organization and basic consensus. Limited participation in state policy and citizens' apathy have a positive function for the modern political system because they cushion conflict, adjustment, and change.[37]

Dahl, who defined a political system as any persistent pattern of human rela-tionships that involves a significant amount of power, rule, and authority, regarded contemporary democracy as polyarchy: the rule of multiple minorities.[38] Dahl claimed that modern democratic theory is concerned with processes by which ordinary people exert a relatively high degree of control over leaders rather than participate directly to control the state. He contended that citizens' increased participation in decision making can endanger the stability of a democratic system because lower socioeconomic groups include more authoritarian personalities and greater political activity; therefore, bringing the masses into the political arena will cause polyarchy to decline. Sartori extended Dahl's model by stressing that democracy is rule not just by minorities but also by competing elites, and active participation of the people in the political process leads directly to totalitarianism.[39] The people must not be proactive, Sartori stated; instead, they must react to the policies and initiatives of the competing elites. Eckstein argued that democratic stability can be attained and strain avoided only if congruency is achieved through public education and if political democracy is adapted to the economic organization.[40]

In brief, supporters of representative democracy introduced the model as a value-free, empirical, and descriptive modification of classical participatory democracy. The model includes competition among leaders (the elite) for people's votes, ensures limited or no participation by the masses, and provides for the masses' restricted control over their leaders so that the masses will not undermine leadership and material efficiency. In the model, universal suffrage—one vote per citizen—ensures political equality and equal influence over leaders.

Representatives or delegates.   A debate about the nature of representatives and their freedom to vote as they wish also focuses on the people's role in representative political systems. Locke thought popularly elected representatives should be delegates, who are obliged to vote as their constituents wish. Burke and Madison believed that elected representatives should be true representatives, not delegates, and should vote as they wish on any issue; the people could defeat them in the next election if they disagreed. The more freedom representatives are given to make state policy based on their own judgments, the less control people have over policy making.[41]

Critics of representative democracy assert that citizens have little formal control over state policy, that the people are not sovereign and do not control the laws of society. In the United States, for example, the representatives, not the people, directly control who will serve as president or as a member of the Supreme Court, whether war will be declared, what amendments to the Constitution will be proposed and ratified, what the fiscal and monetary policies of the state will be, and what welfare-state services will be curtailed or added. Representative democracy is unsatisfactory because it restricts the freedom of the minority.[42]

There are several versions of representative democracy. The most typical are pluralism and elitism.[43]

Pluralism

Modern pluralists have branded direct democracy a romantic notion that is impossi-ble to attain.[44] Hence, pluralists, advocating representative democracy, created a new democratic model: pluralist democracy or, simply, pluralism.[45] This model accounts for current political behavior, preserves democratic values in the modern world, and supports the market system; it does not endanger existing democratic systems by giving rise to unrealistic, potentially disruptive expectations of direct control by the people. In brief, the pluralist model adjusts traditional participatory democracy to contemporary life in the United States. It assumes that the prerequisites for participatory democracy have not materialized in the United States; that citizens are not sufficiently rational, informed, or interested in political life; that the capacity of ordinary people for knowing what should be done is restricted; and that few Americans have an adequate framework and world view for modern governing. Advocates of pluralism further assume that democracy works even though the masses are apathetic and uninvolved in public life; that in the absence of mass participation, democracy depends on representatives to defend the democratic system; and that too-active involvement by the masses leads to mediocrity, which should be feared more than should elitism and aristocracy. According to this model, the American system works as it is, and people are basically satisfied with pluralism.

The theory of balance, equilibrium, or pluralism dominated the past few decades in the United States. It defines society as an aggregate of dissimilar, equally influential special-interest groups and associations (including labor unions; corporations; religious, economic, professional, educational, and cultural groups; political parties; and business associations) with diverse and conflicting interests. Developed by English liberals and socialists in the early 20th century, pluralism reflects a political adaptation to the transformation of the social and economic structures associated with the Industrial Revolution, the organizational revolution, and urbanization. The individual who enjoys an approximate autonomy and self-sufficiency, expressing his or her individual will through personal choice, is no longer at the center of things. In practice, the once-private being is now encompassed by the group, and personal volition is subsumed in complex organizational systems that are beyond the individual's comprehension or control. Pluralism represents a political adaptation to the shift of the individual from a central to a relatively marginal role in society and to the emergence of organizational structures as the mediating, dominant forces in determining state policy.

Under pluralism, power should be diffused widely among a variety of associations, and the government should be fragmented into decentralized units so that society is dominated neither by the state nor by a single class. The state thus has a reduced scope and acts as a neutral mediator between the conflicting interests of groups.

In modern societies, pluralists perceive state policy as the balanced product and representation of these conflicting group pressures. The political process tends to maximize the interests and concerns of all participants.[46] As in laissez-faire capitalism (in which power is distributed among labor, management, and capital), governmental policy under pluralism is the equilibrium determined by the relative influence of interest groups.

Pluralists, including Bentley, Truman, Latham, de Tocqueville, Dahl, Polsby, Rose, Easton, and Key, assume that interacting social groups rather than individuals are the units of political behavior that influence state policy.[47] State policy is the product of conflicting pressures from society's dissimilar and equally influential special-interest groups and associations. Corporations, labor unions, religious groups, and professional associations have highly diverse and often competing interests. No one group can be dominant. Instead, the various groups must negotiate with one another to reach a mutually agreeable outcome for each contested issue. That politics is a group struggle to influence public policy implies that individuals are important only when they act as part of or on behalf of group interests. Thus, the group links individuals and governments. The task of political systems, then, is to manage group conflict by establishing the rules of the game, by enacting and enforcing compromises, and by balancing group interests. Changes in policies result from changes in the relative influence of interest groups. Public policy shifts toward the interests of groups that are gaining influence and away from those of groups that are losing influence.

Group influence results from wealth, organizational strength, size of the membership, leadership, access to decision makers, and internal cohesion, with wealth being decisive in wielding power and shaping policy. The complex web of cross-pressures in society prevents the dominance of any one group, avoids systematic conflict, and guarantees the political system's stability. According to pluralist theorists, it does so because contestants for state policy are ambivalent about victory, consider other groups' viewpoints, avoid totally destroying the opposition, have overlapping membership in several groups, and develop mutually advantageous compromises to minimize harm to contending groups. Pluralism is an adaptation of political thinking to accommodate the group's emergence as a mediator between the individual and the elected representatives of the people.

Critics of pluralism, including Domhoff, Mills, Bachrach, and Kariel, challenge this political philosophy.[48] They claim that pluralism is less democratic, allows only certain groups to dominate, and constitutes a political adaptation to today's oligarchic, corporate, economic market system. Furthermore, these critics argue that a contradiction exists between democratic theory and pluralistic practice: pluralism removes the individual a step further from state policy and has changed the nature of direct democracy to bring it into line with the capitalist market.

The critics contend that pluralism is not an accurate description of the political system because the visible and apparently pluralistic exercise of power in democracies can conceal the fact that some interest groups actually dominate state policy. Under the pluralistic appearance of capitalist society is an elitist core structural arrangement in which the ruling class dominates, so pluralism is limited to only marginal domains. Historically, small groups have ruled large societies by controlling the normative institutional apparatus, making power self-perpetuating, and favoring the status quo rather than a pluralistic consensus on values.[49]

Opponents of pluralism argue that the state is not essentially a political marketplace in which different groups and social classes compete and alternate in determining state policies. Even if the state is structurally within the influence of all classes, it is systematically biased toward the development of the economic market, maintaining the interests of the capitalist class. The state and its policies are dominated by the wealthy, who hold the most powerful positions in socioeconomic institutions and protect their own interests. The poor and disadvantaged do not have an equal opportunity to contest public policies.[50] Thus, rather than being a broker, the state becomes an instrument of the ruling class, rendering pluralism impossible. Government-appointed directors of regulatory agencies are frequently members of the military-industrial complex (retired high-ranking officers of the armed forces and business executives) who vote against consumers when regulatory interventions threaten the formation of capital and retard the accumulation and expansion of capital throughout the economy. The government's responsibility to promote and defend market functions (capital formation, property relations, and the reproduction of capitalist-class structures under continual changing socioeconomic circumstances) contradicts democratic prerequisites that the government should be responsive to all groups.[51] The capitalist economic market, rather than the balance of interest groups or their relative strengths, determines public policy. Distributive justice, equality, the eradication of poverty and unemployment, or significant reforms of the welfare state are problematic when public policy is committed to capital formation.[52]

Opponents of pluralism also claim that society is not composed of equally powerful groups, that groups do not reflect the interests of most people,[53] and that groups are asymmetrical in power per member.[54] Lobbying, though legally open to all interest groups, is the province of only the affluent groups. Congress itself frequently represents the interests of upper-class males and has severely curtailed funds to regulatory agencies that threaten the interests of giant corporations or that serve or empower women.

The existence of pluralism does not necessarily legitimate it. Far from being value-free or empirical, the pluralist model is normative. It prescribes the kind of democracy that ought to be by selecting criteria that are inherent in the organizational structure of today's market society. What ought to be—the economic market system—is what is.

Elitism

This perspective, which some commentators consider a variation of pluralism, takes several forms. It suggests mainly that Western representative political systems, including the United States, are oligarchies (governments ruled by a few people) rather than democracies. A small number of people, called the elite (who have an innate drive for power), control the economy, interest or pressure groups, and state policies.[55] Atypical of the governed masses and drawn disproportionately from society's upper classes, the elite shape society's basic values to preserve the system. Even revolutions that overthrow the elite are led by other elite, who later become equally powerful and privileged.[56] The elite might focus on different aspects of public policies and compete with one another, but they all seem to operate under a common frame of reference that promotes the stability of the system. In the United States, the bases of elite consensus are the sanctity of private property, limited government, limited mass participation of citizens in decision making, an emphasis on individual economic liberty, and the legitimacy of laissez-faire capitalism.

Aristocratic versions of elitism emphasize that all large societies have elite leaders who rule the vast majority, shape mass opinion on policy questions, and promote their own interests.[57] Because public officials and administrators merely carry out policies decided upon by the elite, policies flow downward from the elite to the masses rather than arising from the demands of the masses. According to this view, the state and its policies are organs of a minority because the majority is incapable of or indifferent to government. Without an elite to provide the will, ability, and interest to make policies and to inspire the masses, there can be no effective societal organization. The masses engage in irrational behavior, including revolutions, demonstrations, and rioting for food, unconstrained by traditional law-and-order institutions.

Radical elitists, such as Mills and Domhoff, also see the political system as divided between the elite and the passive masses who are manipulated by them.[58] But elitists disagree that the masses are incapable of governing themselves. Rather, they attribute the passivity of the masses to the manipulative influence of the mass media. Both pluralists and elitists believe that the political system responds to group pressures. Pluralists, however, say that the members of interest groups have enough power to control their leaders democratically. Elitists believe the system is undemocratic because the members of interest groups do not control their leaders. Elitists do not suggest that all decisions are made by the same group of leaders. Rather, as Mills suggested, each policy issue is associated with its own elitist group. Elitist commentators suggest that thousands of the elite form ad hoc or more permanent alliances as needs and issues arise.

Elitist theorists, such as Schumpeter and Lipset, have provided a basis for a modern interpretation of democracy that defends the parliamentary form of the modern state.[59] These critics of direct democracy claim that their interpretation reflects modern political practices in market countries and is based on the empirical behavior of modern political institutions in the market economy.[60] The vital feature of this version of democracy is the competition among potential decision makers (leaders) for the people's vote. The citizen's role is to select representative leaders and then to withdraw from participation. Schumpeter wrote that modern representative democracy is a due process in which people have the right to elect their representatives.[61] It is an institutional method for arriving at political decisions in which leaders acquire the power to decide by competing for the people's vote.[62]

Applying Adam Smith's economic market principles to the political market, Schumpeter explained that voters, like consumers, choose among political products offered by competing political entrepreneurs. The political parties regulate the competition, just as trade associations regulate the economic market. The participation of citizens in decision making has no central role in this version of democracy, which assumes that the electoral mass is incapable of any action other than a stampede.[63] Lipset, following Schumpeter, interpreted modern democracy as a political system that provides systematic, regular opportunities for electing governing officials. But unlike Schumpeter, Lipset proposed that the system must allow for the largest possible participation of the population to influence major decisions among contenders for political office. In this version of democracy, government by the people becomes government approved by the people: the participation of citizens is achieved through representation.

Critics of elitism argue that elitist notions are undemocratic and erroneous.[64] People resist domination, control, and manipulation by the elite and occasionally force social revolutions. In exaggerating their power, elitists fail to explain social change and class struggle over public policies; they say social change can only be incremental and slow, favoring the status quo. Accepting that the elite disagree and compete among one another, these critics contend that elitism implies that competition centers on a narrow range of issues on which the elite agree more than they disagree. Elitist policy is exclusionary because the only policy alternatives considered fall within the shared elitist consensus. The system's survival and stability are not necessarily enhanced, even though they depend upon the elitist consensus about fundamental societal values. Contrary to what elitists believe, the masses are consistent and reliable.

Control of State Policy in Socialist, Nonmarket Countries

To understand the vague and controversial socialist concept (including the nature of the state and its policy) one must realize that there are several competing approaches to state socialism with major differences among their theoretical foundations (including egalitarian communalism, utopian socialism, and scientific socialism with its diverse movements—orthodox, revisionist, and Fabian socialism)[65] and their applied forms (including the Marxist-Leninist-Stalinist model, the Yugoslav associative socialist model, the Marxist-Maoist model, and Fidel Castro's variation).[66] Although one cannot properly speak of some essential core that any of the various definitions of socialism must include, most classical definitions of socialism have involved collective or social control of economic decision-making.

In theory, socialist democracy has three main features, all of which are characteristics of socialist justice designed to achieve a new social order in which human cooperation is the basis of all social institutions, social relations, and economic productivity:

1. The achievement of freedom and egalitarianism, including self-government and mass participation of citizens in the control of state policy. Socialist justice and egalitarianism necessitate self-government and a long process of societal transformation to achieve direct democracy (decentralism). Socialism rejects the concept of a state erected above society as a constraining power (centralism).

2. The exercise of a collective or state concern and responsibility for the well-being of all citizens, including a comprehensive welfare state that provides universal programs as a right to all citizens. The comprehensive welfare state (in which social policy planning coordinates all societal institutions) reflects the socialist, collective concern with not only production but also the fair distribution of the goods and services produced in the society. (Fair distribution is achieved by eliminating major differences in material status and by narrowing the gap between higher- and lower-income groups.) The establishment of an extended welfare state as a human right for all people reflects the socialist thinking that all people must be allowed to refine their own humanity and to reach their highest potential.

3. The control or elimination of the free market through the establishment of centralized social and economic planning and nationalized or cooperative ownership of the major means of production.[67] National or cooperative ownership of the major means of production and centralized planning are central to socialist efforts to distribute goods fairly (by eliminating profit and private property that, according to Karl Marx, create unfair distributions of capitalist production) and to eliminate the economic and social waste that result from the unavoidable ups and downs of the capitalist free market.

Applied socialism, however, is different. The major tenets of theoretical socialism either failed to materialize or were achieved at great social costs, including brutal coercion by the state and the elimination of political freedom and individual human rights. In the decades before 1990, great economic inefficiency and lack of productivity in the Soviet Union and Eastern Europe were associated with the formidably complex tasks of central command planning and the lack of effective work incentives. The trial-and-error efforts to implement socialism through the Leninist-Stalinist model took forms that deviated from and in some respects contradicted the tenets of theoretical socialism. This model imposed a totalitarian, statist political system; the dictatorship of the Communist party; an elitist social class; an extended bureaucracy; an inflexible central-command planning system that undermined direct participation of the people in economic decision-making and alienated the working class; and democratic centralism. Above all, it suppressed individual freedom and human rights. Far from withering away, the state in this model increased in dominance and was transformed into a massive bureaucratic entity. During the early 1990s, these socialist practices brought about the collapse of applied socialism in Eastern Europe and the Soviet Union.[68]

Self-government is incompatible with the existence of a strong statist political and economic system and the establishment of an inflexible bureaucracy. Certain applied socialist models, therefore, including the Yugoslav model of associative socialism,[69] decentralized and significantly reduced the power of the state, delegating policy-making to production enterprises at the local and regional levels in efforts to establish decentralized self-government.

The trial-and-error effort for self-government in applied socialism was stimulated by the two extremes of centralization state power (statism) and decentralization (supreme individualism or anarchy). Appearing first as a utopian idea of individual visionaries, including Thomas More (1478–1535), Tommaso Campanella (1568–1639), Comte de Saint-Simon (1760–1825), and Etienne Cabet (1788–1856), self-governance originally had a distinctly centralist orientation. In the late 18th and early 19th centuries, social reformers and anarchists, including William Godwin (1756–1816), Pierre Joseph Proudhon (1809–1865), Mikhail Bakunin (1814–1876), and Prince Kropotkin (1842–1921), questioned the advisability of the centralist order in socialist self-government. Instead, they advocated the elimination of the state (individualistic anarchy) and the decentralization of state policy. Marxists who favor centralization as a means to transform society and Marxist anarchists who oppose centralization because it generates elitism and statism have struggled continuously.

Earlier philosophies of self-government emphasized cooperative work communities and collectivized, federated forms of production and exchange. Federations of cooperative communities governed by producers (Robert Owen, 1772–1858) and self-governing and collectivized groups (phalansteries) cultivating equally sized agricultural areas (Charles Fourier, 1772–1837) are typical earlier models which were put in practice but failed because of inexperience, limited scale, improper financing, or the broader antagonistic environment. Early models abolished hard labor, guaranteed the right to work, provided material security for members, distributed income in equal shares, and encouraged the state's eventual abolition. The same principles, but with a distinct state orientation through nationalization, provided models in in which egalitarian society and personal interests merge in the common good. Louis Blanc (1811–1882) visualized nationalized key industries, banks, insurance companies, and railways so that the state would regulate national production and establish "national workshops" for industrial workers. The commitment was, "To each according to his needs, from each according to his abilities." This thinking later became famous through Marx's model.

More holistic models of new economic and sociopolitical orders include that of Proudhon, who first used the word *anarchist*.[70] Proudhon's scheme of communes (established through a contract among heads of families) federated into provinces and states stipulated that decisions of the central organs would become obligatory only when they were accepted by the communes. Believing that representative democracy is unsatisfactory because it restricts the freedom of the minority, Proudhon wanted all individuals to participate in political decision-making without a hierarchical political organization. Full participation in economic organization would dissolve the state's economic infrastructure by transferring all power to communes. The principal instrument would again be the contract as a basis of reciprocal justice that would prelude the violation of individual freedom while leading to equitable exchange, equalization of business conditions, and equitable cooperation among individuals. Non-earned incomes and exploitation would be eliminated, and no coercion would be necessary for the maintenance of the new social order. According to Proudhon, if wealth is equally distributed, people can cooperate without the intervention of an authoritarian state. The Paris Commune of April 1871, with its cooperative workers' societies that took control of abandoned, closed factories, is an example of this scheme.

Supporters of self-government assume that a model of society based on self-determination applied to all aspects of the creative praxis is superior to any authoritarian, statist model and to liberal capitalism, which reduces human emancipation only to political liberation.

Another debate in applied socialism concerns the issue of revolution versus reform. When 19th-century Europe experienced revolutions by the ruled classes and trade unions were legalized in the second half of that century, activists, including Louis Blanc and Ferdinand LaSalle (1825–1864), claimed that it is possible to reform society nonviolently without revolution. Supporters of this approach include leaders of Eurocommunism, who believe that national communist parties should be independent of the former Soviet Union's Communist party guidelines and that communist parties in various countries should participate in the regular political processes as legal entities.

IMPLICATIONS FOR SOCIAL WORK AND THE WELFARE STATE

Social work practitioners, who help people and society change by solving problems and enhancing social functioning, have a major stake in the role of the state in society, its political organization, and its policy orientations. As the state intervenes or does not intervene to regulate the distribution of resources, benefits, and burdens among citizens and population groups, it sets the parameters of distributive justice and equality, social development programs, and the empowerment of the powerless.

Social workers must understand the function and influence of state policy, the different types of political organization of the state, and relationships between the state and its citizens. In implementing the profession's Code of Ethics, social workers support social policies ensuring that all people have access to the resources, services, and opportunities they require. Social workers have a commitment to expand choice and opportunities for all, especially the disadvantaged or oppressed. In so doing, they advocate changes in policies and legislation to improve social conditions and to promote social justice. They also inform the public and encourage citizens to participate in changing social policies and institutions.[71] Social workers engaging in social action must understand the sociopolitical and economic organization of the society in which they work and the beliefs that generate its functioning. They also recognize that political arrangements and state orientations influence the lives of their clients. In the political arena social workers identify interventions to prevent or resolve social problems or to improve social functioning.

Because the state is a central regulative instrument for change and development in modern society, a biased or neutral state or a participatory, elitist, socialist, or fascist state can significantly affect social work practice and the achievement of professional objectives. A state that represents the power class and the elite is more likely to establish social policies that favor the interests and needs of these groups. In contrast, authentically representative states can encourage the participation of citizens in public decision-making and can empower the disadvantaged, the poor, the powerless, women, children, and racial and ethnic minorities: the main concern of social work.

If state policy is controlled by an elite that favors the ruling class, social action cannot improve the status quo, achieve full citizenship rights, eliminate poverty, or empower the disadvantaged. Thus, social work's efforts to enhance self-determination, self-actualization, self-government, and the meaningful participation of citizens in decisions that affect their lives are more difficult in the context of elitism. The new interpretation of democracy as merely a due process of competing elites also discourages citizen participation in decision-making. Representative and elitist political systems are hostile toward direct democracy and its full, effective participation of citizens.

Social work's efforts are more likely to be enhanced by classic, direct political democracy, which promotes self-governing, self-determination, and full participation in decision-making. The growth of the welfare state can be stifled by the erosion of the alliance between the middle and working classes. This class struggle is due to demographic changes or regressive tax policies.

Neoconservatism justifies power differences in society and accepts inequitable treatment of individuals and classes as inevitable and palatable. It also rewards those in important positions who wield power and wealth and discourages public welfare transfers to those who are least productive or to the working poor. Neoconservatives argue that the welfare state provides work disincentives and disinvestments in the formation of capital. They also attribute the existence of unequal power, status, and development of individuals, communities, and geographic regions to differential needs or individual performance rather than to societal or economic market dysfunctions.

In contrast, liberal states recognize the need for collectivist, humanitarian societies because they accept that unequal power is internalized in key social institutions, particularly the economic market. In their view, inequalities are created by excessively unequal material rewards. Liberal states promote policies that favor the welfare state and the redistribution of income, wealth, and services.

Laissez-faire, noninterventionist states focus on promoting a healthy economic market as the ultimate goal of government. They neglect social policy and the welfare state, which then can operate only within the constraints of market operations and interests. Laissez-faire states promote incomplete employment and allow wages to provide full-time income that is less than the official poverty line. In contrast, interventionist states with policy based on Keynesian economics (or macroeconomics, introduced by J. M. Keynes during the depression of the 1930s) can promote the Keynesian welfare state and social services, as was the case in the 1960s and 1970s.[72]

The participation of workers in workplace decisions is also crucial in industrial welfare and self-management. Elitist, hierarchical management and Weberian state policy oppose management by workers. Elitists argue that participation undermines efficiency and organizational obedience. In contrast, liberal states believe that management by workers improves discipline, increases production, and decreases absenteeism and waste. Trade unions focus on wages and on the control of working conditions; but workers also want to participate in consultation, codetermination (sharing power), and self-management.

Noninterventionist states assume that the best government governs least. The free economic market, rather than the state, should make decisions about production, distribution, and social well-being. Modern state interventions in the market and the welfare state obstruct economic growth, undermine the capitalist economic market, cause declining investment and productivity, and raise taxes and inflation. Passive states do not establish effective state controls but try instead to enhance the economic market, efficiency, and entrepreneurship. Since passive states reinforce the powerful in the market, neoconservatives see egalitarian reformers as adversaries and enemies of the market. Neoconservatives fear that activists will transform the government into a vast, counterproductive system of overprotection against the unavoidable social risks inherent in a modern industrial society.

In contrast, interventionist states can guide the economic market toward social justice, citizenship, and welfare-state objectives. They can oppose systemic oligarchy and monopolistic trends that defy competition and efficiency in the market. They constrain the excessive powers of giant corporations and the military-industrial complex. Interventionist states can guarantee the social development of all people and can protect the physical environment, consumers, the powerless, the alienated, and the disadvantaged.

A crucial component of social work practice is social action for legislation and social policies that promote the development of all individuals and communities.

NOTES

1. K. E. Meyer, "Demes, Demos, Democracy," *New York Times*, September 29, 1991, 16E.
2. C.A. Radin, "Europeans OK Political Union Treaty," *Boston Globe*, December 11, 1991, 1.

3. "Center-Right Party Wins in Portugal Vote," *Boston Globe,* October 7, 1991, 4.

4. C. J. Williams, "Fighting Rages in Yugoslavia," *Boston Globe,* October 7, 1991, 2.

5. M. Feldstein and K. Feldstein, "A Single Soviet Currency?" *Boston Globe,* October 8, 1991, 38.

6. C. J. Raubicheck, "It's Time to Set the FDA Free," *Boston Globe,* October 8, 1991, 38.

7. J. A. Farrell, "Reagan Aide Admits Guilt in Cover-Up," *Boston Globe,* October 8, 1991, 1.

8. P. Constable, "At Gunpoint, Haitians Pick New Leader," *Boston Globe,* October 8, 1991, 1.

9. J. Haverman, "EC Finance Ministers Back \$2.4b to Aid USSR," *Boston Globe,* October 8, 1991, 2.

10. "To Get Help on Hostages, U.N. Chief Weighing Panel on Iran-Iraq War," *Boston Globe,* October 8, 1991, 6.

11. "Mobutu Hints at Sacking New Premier of Zaire," *Boston Globe,* October 8, 1991, 11.

12. "Senate Approves Natural Gas Rules," *Boston Globe,* October 8, 1991, 18.

13. "Spanish King Bids U.N. to Intervene," *Boston Globe,* October 8, 1991, 18.

14. D. E. Lewis, "Women Fail to Land Top Union Posts, New Study Claims," *Boston Globe,* September 30, 1991, 10.

15. W. V. Robinson, "Hearings Set to Air Charge of Harassment," *Boston Globe,* October 9, 1991, 1.

16. M. Dowd, "Taboo Issues of Sex and Race Explode in Glare of Hearing," *New York Times,* October 13, 1991, 1. Judge Thomas has since been appointed to the U.S. Supreme Court.

17. Because politics extends beyond the actions of the state, the political system includes various branches of governmental and extragovernmental institutions, along with the political parties, laws, lobbyists, and private interest groups that affect public policy.

18. H. Lasswell, *The Political Writings of Harold D. Lasswell* (Glencoe, IL: Free Press, 1951). See also M. H. Fried, "The State," in D. L. Sills, ed., *International Encyclopedia of Social Sciences,* vol. 15 (New York: Free Press, 1968), 143–150.

19. Movements of the right, including the political turn to religious fundamentalism, nationalism, and the right-to-life movement, also reflect a focus on the cultural aspects of politics. See S. Bowles and H. Gintis, *Democracy and Capitalism* (New York: Basic Books, 1986), 8–11.

20. The modern state is the product of earlier struggles to overcome the difficulties associated with the outgrowth of the Middle Ages. By the 16th century, Niccolo Machiavelli had introduced the word *state* in its modern sense. He suggested that politics is a struggle for power and that the proper objective of political action is to maximize the power of the state. To him, the state was a work of art created by the skill of statesmen. See F. M. Watkins, "State: The Concept," in D. L. Sills, ed., *International Encyclopedia of Social Sciences,* vol. 15 (New York: Free Press, 1968), 150–152.

21. J. Bennett, *Unthinking Faith and Enlightenment: Nature and the State in a Post-Hegelian Era* (New York: New York University Press, 1987); M. Lessnott, *Social Contract Theory* (New York: New York University Press, 1990); P. Riley, *Will and Political Legitimacy: A Critical Exposition of Social Contract Theory in Hobbes, Locke, Rousseau, Kant, and Hegel* (Cambridge, MA: Harvard University Press, 1982).

22. For nationalism, see G. Pockock, "Nation, Community, Devolution, and Sovereignty," *Political Quarterly* 61 (1990): 318–27; A. D. Smith, "The Supersession of Nationalism?" *International Journal of Comparative Sociology* (Leiden, Netherlands) 31 (1990): 1–31; E. B. Haas, "What Is Nationalism and Why Should We Study It?" *International Organization* 40 (1986): 707–744; A. D. Smith, "Nationalism and Classical Social Theory," *The British Journal of Sociology* 34 (1983): 19–38; H. Meadwell, "Ethnic Nationalism and Collective Choice Theory," *Comparative Political Studies* 22 (1989): 139–54; H. Patterson, "Neo-Nationalism and Class," *Social History* 13 (1988): 343–349; Ma Shu Yun,

"Ethnonationalism, Ethnic Nationalism, and Mini-nationalism: A Comparison of Connor, Smith, and Snyder," *Ethnic and Racial Studies* 13 (1990): 527–541.

For Marxist views, see E. Nimni, "Marx, Engles, and the National Question," *Science and Society* 53 (1989): 297–326; P. G. Mitchinson, "The 'Pigheaded' Nation: Marxism Grapples with the National Question," *East European Quarterly* 25 (1991): 223–235; S. Avineri, "Toward a Socialist Theory of Nationalism," *Dissent* 37 (1990): 447–457.

For a critique of nationalism, see W. A. Douglas, "A Critique of Recent Trends in the Analysis of Ethnonationalism," *Ethnic and Racial Studies* 11 (1988): 192–206.

23. G. Stokes, "How is Nationalism Related to Capitalism?" *Comparative Studies in Society and History* 28 (1986): 591–598.

24. J. Mayall, *Nationalism and International Society* (New York: Cambridge University Press, 1990).

25. W. Bloom, *Personal Identity, National Identity, and International Relations* (New York: Cambridge University Press, 1990).

26. V. Reynolds, V. Falger, and I. Vine, eds., *The Sociology of Ethnocentrism: Evolutionary Dimensions of Xenophobia, Discrimination, Racism, and Nationalism* (Athens: University of Georgia Press, 1987).

27. R. V. Salisbury, *Anti-Imperialism and International Competition in Central America, 1920–1929* (Wilmington, DE: S. R. Books, 1989).

28. Pluralists include B. Beselson, P. Lazarsfeld, R. Dahl, C. Lindbloom, V. O. Key, S. M. Lipset, G. Sartori, and J. Shumpeter. See also M. Weber, *The Protestant Ethic and the Spirit of Capitalism* (London: Allen & Unwin, 1930); M. Weber, *Selections in Translation,* ed. W. G. Runcimay (Cambridge, England: Cambridge University Press, 1978); M. Weber, *From Max Weber: Essays in Sociology,* (London: Routledge & Kegan Paul, 1946). For Marxist views, see R. Miliband, "The Capitalist State: Reply to Nicos Poulantzas," *New Left Review* 59 (1970): 53–60; N. Poulantzas, "The Problems of the Capitalist State," *New Left Review* 58 (1969): 67–78.

29. Formulated first by the Greek historian Herodotus, the word *democracy* means rule by the masses in their own interest. Etymologically, *democracy* comes from two Greek words, *demos* ("the populace") and *kratia* ("rule"). Hence, direct democracy means direct government by the masses, as distinguished from indirect, representative democracy, which means government through representatives. Pericles suggested that the Athenian state was called a democracy because it was in the hands not of the few, but of the many, the masses, the common people. See D. Easton, *The Political System* (New York: Knopf, 1957).

30. J. Bentham, *Works,* ed., J. Bowring, (Edinburgh: Tait, 1843); J. Mill, *An Essay on Government* (Cambridge, England: Cambridge University Press, 1937); J. J. Rousseau, *Emile* (New York: Everyman, 1911); J. J. Rousseau, *The Social Contract* (New York: Penguin, 1968); J. S. Mill, *Representative Government* (Everyman, 1910).

31. A. Smith, *The Wealth of Nations* (New York: Modern Library, 1937); Rousseau, *The Social Contract;* J. J. Rousseau, *Political Writings* (London: Nelsa, 1952); Mill, *Representative Government;* J. S. Mill, *Collected Works,* ed. J. M. Robion (Toronto: University of Toronto Press, 1961).

32. J. Dewey, *The Public and Its Problems* (New York: Holt, 1927), 311.

33. For Cole, it is industry that must lead to a truly democratic policy. In his theory of guild socialism, he outlined a scheme of how a participatory society might be organized. Cole has applied Rousseau's insights to a modern setting. G. D. H. Cole, *Self-Government in Industry* (London: Methuen, 1920); G. D. H. Cole, *Guild Socialism Re-Stated* (London: Parsons, 1920). For the development of guild socialism, see S. T. Glass, *Repressive Society* (London: Longmans, 1966).

34. For criticism of contemporary theories of democracy, see L. Davis, "The Cost of Realism: Contemporary Restatements of Democracy," *Western Political Science Quarterly* 17, no. 1 (1964): 37–46; G. Duncan and S. Lukes, "The New Democracy," *Political Studies* 11, no. 2 (1963): 156–177; P. Bachrach, *The Theory of Democratic Elitism: A Critique* (Boston: Little, Brown, 1967).

35. J. A. Schumpeter, *Capitalism, Socialism, and Democracy* (London: Allen & Unwin, 1943), 253–254.

36. B. R. Berelson, "Democratic Theory and Public Opinion," *Public Opinion Quarterly* 16 (1952): 313–330; B.R. Berelson, P. F. Lazarfield, and W. N. McPhee, *Voting* (Chicago: University of Chicago Press, 1954); R. A. Dahl, *Preface to Democratic Theory* (Chicago: University of Chicago Press, 1956); R. A. Dahl, "Further Reflections on the Elitist Theory of Democracy," *American Political Science Review* 60 (1966): 296–306; R. A. Dahl, *Modern Political Analysis* (Englewood Cliffs, NJ: Prentice-Hall, 1963); G. Sartori, *Democratic Theory* (Detroit: Wayne State University Press, 1962); H. Eckstein, "A Theory of Stable Democracy," Appendix B of *Division and Cohesion in Democracy* (Princeton, NJ: Princeton University Press, 1966).

37. Berelson, "Democratic Theory and Public Opinion," 313–330.

38. Dahl, *Modern Political Analysis*, 6.

39. Sartori, *Democratic Theory*, 77.

40. Eckstein, "A Theory of Stable Democracy," 234.

41. J. Locke, *The Second Treatise of Government and a Letter Concerning Toleration*, ed. J. W. Gough (New York: Macmillan, 1956); E. Burke, *Reflections on the Revolution in France* (Chicago: Reguery, 1955); R. P. Fairfield, ed., *The Federalist Papers: Essays by Alexander Hamilton, James Madison, and John Jay* (New York: Anchor Books, 1961).

42. Critics of representative democracy include G. W. Domhoff, *The Higher Circles* (New York: Vintage Books, 1970); C. W. Mills, *The Power Elite* (New York: Oxford University Press, 1957); P. Bachrach, *The Theory of Democratic Elitism* (Boston: Little, Brown, 1967); and H. Kariel, *The Decline of American Pluralism* (Stanford, CA: Stanford University Press, 1961).

43. Functionalism is also a variation of pluralism but is rapidly declining in importance. It refers to the basic needs of a society that have to be met for the society to survive as a functioning system. Functionalism suggests that a societal activity can help maintain the stability of a social system by satisfying basic social needs or functional prerequisites. Proponents of this controversial perspective accept power inequality as a functional, unavoidable, and desirable necessity to achieve collective goals that reflect the groups' ability to mobilize and follow a given course. Elections are deposits of power (like fund deposits in laissez-faire capitalism) that express people's confidence in government, increase political power, and mobilize for the attainment of collective goals. See T. Parsons, *The Social System* (New York: Free Press, 1964); T. Parsons, *The Systems of Modern Societies* (Englewood Cliffs, NJ: Prentice-Hall, 1971); T. Parsons, "The Distribution of Power in American Society," in *Structure and Process in Modern Societies* (New York: Free Press, 1960); and T. Parsons, *Politics and Social Structure* (New York: Free Press, 1969). Other functionalists include K. Davis, *Human Society* (New York: Macmillan, 1949); K. Davis and W. Moore, "Some Principles of Stratification," in *American Sociological Review* 10, no. 2 (1945): 242–249; and R. Williams, *American Society* (New York: Knopf, 1970). For criticism of functionalism, see C. W. Mills, *The Sociological Imagination* (New York: Oxford University Press, 1959); A. Szymanski, "The Value of Sociology: An Answer to Lidz," *Sociological Inquiry* 40, no. 1 (1970): 21–25; and A. Szymanski, "Dialectical Functionalism," *Sociological Inquiry* 42, no. 2 (Spring 1972): 145–153.

44. Pluralism is actually the kind of system foreseen by Madison. It denotes a decision-making process in which the people's interests are represented by various pressure groups; governmental policy is a compromise between their competing interests. For further discussion of pluralism, see W. E. Lambert, *Coping with Cultural and Racial Diversity in Urban America* (New York: Praeger, 1990); R. Panikkar et al., *Pluralism and Oppression: Theology in World Perspective* ed. P. F. Knitter (Lanham, MD: University Press of America, 1990); D. Mattei, ed., *Comparing Pluralist Democracies: Strains on Legitimacy* (Boulder, CO: Westview Press, 1988); R. A. Dahl, *Dilemmas of Pluralist Democracy: Autonomy vs. Control* (New Haven, CT: Yale University Press, 1980); S. Ehrlich, *Pluralism On and Off Course* (New York: Pergamon Press, 1982); M. Walzer, *Spheres of Justice: A Defense of Pluralism and Equality* (New York: Basic Books, 1983); R. E. Flathman, *Toward a Liberalism* (Ithaca, NY: Cornell University Press, 1989); R. E. Goodin and A. Reeve eds., *Liberal Neutrality* (New York: Routledge & Kegan Paul, 1989); T. R. Dye and L. H. Ziegler, *The Irony of Democracy: An Uncommon Introduction to American Politics* (Pacific Grove, CA: Brooks/Cole, 1981); I. M. Young, *Justice and the Politics of Difference* (Princeton, NJ: Princeton University Press, 1990).

45. The discussion in this section is based on seminal works of pluralism, including those by B. Berelson, Paul Lazarsfeld, Robert Dahl, Charles Lindbloom, V. O. Key, Seymour Martin Lipset, Giovanni Sartori, and Joseph A. Schumpeter.

46. The father of American pluralism, Arthur Bentley, suggested that the balance of group pressures is the existing state of society. Pressure is always a group phenomenon (push and resistance among groups). See A. Bentley, *The Process of Government* (Cambridge, MA: Belknap Press, 1908), 258–259.

47. Following Bentley, D. Truman, in *The Government Process* (New York: Knopf, 1951), suggested that interest groups make claims upon other groups and become political when they make a claim upon governmental institutions. E. Latham, in "The Group Basis of Politics," in Eulaw et al., eds., *Political Behavior: A Reader in Theory and Research* (Glencoe, IL: Free Press, 1956), suggested that public policy is actually the equilibrium reached in group struggles and represents the balance that the contending factions constantly strive to tip in their favor. See also A. de Tocqueville, *Democracy in America* (New York: Knopf, 1945); R. Dahl, *Who Governs* (New Haven, CT: Yale University Press, 1963); N. W. Polsby, *Community Power and Political Theory* (New Haven, CT: Yale University Press, 1965); A. Rose, *The Power Structure* (New York: Oxford University Press, 1967); D. Easton, *The Political System* (New York: Knopf, 1971); and V. Key, *Parties, Politics, and Pressure Groups* (New York: Crowell, 1954).

48. G. W. Domhoff, *The Higher Circles: The Governing Class in America* (New York: Random House, 1970); C. W. Mills, *The Power Elite;* (New York: Oxford University Press, 1957); P. Bachrach, *The Theory of Democratic Elitism* (Boston: Little, Brown, 1967); and H. Kariel, *The Decline of American Pluralism* (Stanford, CA: Stanford University Press, 1961).

49. Capital and management have far more power than does labor and thus compel the workers' cooperation.

50. Domhoff, *The Higher Circles;* Mills, *The Power Elite;* Bachrach, *The Theory of Democratic Elitism;* R. Hamilton, *Class and Politics in the U.S.* (New York: Wiley, 1972): H. Kariel, *The Decline of American Pluralism;* and G. McConnell, *Private Power in American Democracy* (New York: Knopf, 1966). For criticism of contemporary theories of democracy, see L. Davis, "The Cost of Realism: Contemporary Restatements of Democracy," *Western Political Quarterly* 17 (1964): 37–46; G. Duncan and S. Lukes, "The New Democracy," *Political Studies* 11 (1963): 156–177; P. Bachrach, *The Theory of Democratic Elitism.*

51. R. C. Edwards et al., *The Capitalist System*, 3rd ed. (Englewood Cliffs, NJ: Prentice-Hall, 1986).

52. Basic economic conditions and their imperatives of anti-inflationary and production-increasing policies provide a limited number of effective options that states can follow in any area without causing general disruption. Investors have central power and veto over the public sector and its managers. The corporate class as a whole is intricately linked to protection and promotion of its goals. Of the more than 200,000 industrial corporations in the United States, the top 100 controlled 54.9% ($495 billion) of all industrial assets, while the 5 largest industrial corporations, Exxon, General Motors, Mobil, Texaco, and IBM, controlled 13% of all industrial assets, according to R. Dye, *Who Is Running America?* (Englewood Cliffs, NJ: Prentice-Hall, 1979), 21–22. Interlocking directorships, mergers, and governmental regulatory agencies of business form a powerful network that pressures the state for policies favoring profit objectives.

53. Only about half the people in the United States belong to even one voluntary association, and most groups, at best only peripherally interested in politics, make their decisions without consulting most of their members. See A. Szymanski, *The Capitalist State and the Politics of Class* (Cambridge, MA: Winthrop, 1978), 1–6.

54. The AFL-CIO, with membership in the millions, has less clout than does the Council on Foreign Relations—the business group on foreign affairs—with only about 1,000 members.

55. For discussions of elitism, see J. W. Riddlesperger, Jr., and J. D. King, "Elitism and Presidential Appointments," *Social Science Quarterly* 70 (1989): 902–910; and V. Rich, "Democratic Elitism," *Nature* 311 (October 13, 1984): 598.

56. G. Mosca, *The Ruling Class* (New York: McGraw-Hill, 1939), 50.

57. Aristocratic elitists include V. Pareto, *The Mind and Society* (New York: Dover, 1935, 1963); R. Michels, *Political Parties* (New York: Collier, 1915, 1962); and Mosca, *The Ruling Class*. See also E. A. Albertoni, *Mosca and the Theory of Elitism* (New York: Blackwell, 1987); and E. D. Baltzell, *Philadelphia Gentlemen* (New York: Free Press, 1958).

58. Radical elitists include Mills, *The Power Elite*; G. W. Domhoff, *Who Rules America?* (Englewood Cliffs, NJ: Prentice-Hall, 1967); and Domhoff, *The Higher Circles*.

59. J. S. Schumpeter, *Capitalism, Socialism, and Democracy* (New York: Harper & Row, 1950); and S. M. Lipset, *Political Man* (Garden City, NY: Doubleday, 1960).

60. Opponents of classical theory of democracy, including Schumpeter, claim that in today's context, the traditional concepts of democracy are erroneous because individuals do not have a political will, cannot observe and interpret facts, and cannot make a reliable choice on the basis of their will and knowledge of the representatives who will implement their will.

61. Schumpeter, *Capitalism, Socialism, and Democracy.*

62. Ibid., 269.

63. Ibid., 283.

64. For criticism of elitism, see P. H. Sniderman, J. F. Fletcher, and P. H. Russell, "The Fallacy of Democratic Elitism: Elite Competition and Commitment to Civil Liberties," *British Journal of Political Science* 21 (1991): 349–378; R. M. Herman, "Danger: Expediency and Elitism," *Trial* 25 (1990): 7; H. Aptheker, *The World of C. Wright Mills* (New York: Marzani & Munsel, 1960); G. W. Domhoff and H. Ballard, *C. Wright Mills and the Power Elite* (Boston: Beacon Press, 1968); N. Poulanzas, *Political Power and Social Class* (London: New Left Books and Sheed & Ward, 1963); and J. Mollenkopf, "Theories of the State and Power Structure Research," *The Insurgent Sociologist* 5 (1975): 245–264.

65. For the theoretical frameworks of socialism, see L. P. Baradat, *Political Ideologies: Their Origins and Impact,* 4th ed. (Englewood Cliffs, NJ: Prentice-Hall, 1991); G. McLennan, *Marxism, Pluralism, and Beyond: Classic Debates and New Departures* (Cambridge, MA:

Blackwell, 1989); P. O. Hirst, ed., *The Pluralist Theory of the State: Selected Writings of G. D. Cole, J. N. Figgis, and H. J. Laski* (New York: Routledge & Kegan Paul, 1989); L. Johnston, *Marxism, Class Analysis, and Socialist Pluralism* (Boston, MA: Allen & Unwin, 1986); K. Marx, *Critique of Hegel's Philosophy of Right* (1844) *Critique of the Gotha Program* (1866), and *The Civil War in France* (1871), in E. Kamenka, ed., *The Portable Karl Marx* (New York: Penguin, 1983), and in K. Marx, *Economic and Philosophic Manuscripts of 1844,* 5th ed. (Moscow: Progress Publishers, 1977). See also C. W. Mills, *The Marxists* (New York: Penguin, 1982); R. L. Heilbroner, *Marxism: For and Against* (New York: Norton, 1980); M. Albert and R. Hahnel, *Marxism and Socialist Theory* (Boston: South End Press, 1981); H. Selsam and H. Martel, eds., *Reader in Marxist Philosophy: From the Writings of Marx, Engels, and Lenin,* 5th ed. (New York: International Publishers Press, 1981); G. Novack, *An Introduction to the Logic of Marxism,* 5th ed. (New York: Pathfinder Press, 1986); M. Salvadori, *Modern Socialism* (New York: Walker, 1968); E. Fromm, *Marx's Concept of Man* (New York: Unger, 1961); and N. Poulantzas, *State, Power, and Socialism* (London: New Left Books, 1978).

66. For the Marxist-Leninist-Stalinist model, see M. Albert and R. Hahnel, *Socialism Today and Tomorrow,* and L. P. Baradat, *Political Ideologies: Their Origins and Impact,* chap. 9; Mao Tse-tung, *Selected Reading from the Works of Mao Tse-Tung* (Beijing: 1971); and Che Guevara, *Man and Socialism in Cuba* (New York: Pathfinder, 1968).

67. See B. Horvat, *The Political Economy of Socialism* (New York: Sharp, 1982); B. Horvat, M. Markovic, and R. Supek, eds., *Self-Governing Socialism,* vols. 1 & 2 (White Plains, NY: International Arts and Science Press, 1975); G. D. H. Cole, *A Short History of the British Working Class Movement* (London: Allen & Unwin, 1938), and *Socialist Thought,* Vols. 1–3 (London: Macmillan, 1967); R. Garaudy, *Crisis of Communism* (New York: Collins, 1972); M. J. Brockmeyer, ed., *Yugoslavian Workers' Self-Management* (Dordrecht, Holland: Reidel, 1970); J. Y. Tabb and A. Goldfard, *Workers' Participation in Management* (New York: Pergamon Press, 1970).

68. For the transition to capitalism, see *Transition to Freedom: The New Soviet Challenge, Cato Policy Report* 13 (1991):1; International Monetary Fund, *The Economy of the USSR: Summary and Recommendations* (Washington, DC: International Monetary Fund, 1990).

69. See D. Milenkovitch, *Plan and Market in Yugoslav Economic Thought* (New Haven, CT: Yale University Press, 1971); B. Horvat, *Towards a Theory of Planned Economy* (Belgrade: Yugoslav Institute for Economic Research, 1964); and B. Horvat, "An Institutional Model of Self-managed Socialist Economy," reprinted in *Eastern European Economics* 10 (1972): 369–392.

70. S. Edwards, *Selected Writings of Pierre Joseph Proudhon* (London: Macmillan, 1970).

71. National Association of Social Workers, *Code of Ethics, Policy Statement No. 1* (Silver Spring, MD: National Association of Social Workers, 1980), 2–3, 6–7.

72. G. H. Vatter and J. F. Walkere, *The Inevitability of Government Growths* (New York: Columbia University Press, 1990).

CHAPTER 5

Economics: The Epicenter of Social Policy

"Recession forces states to turn budget ax on programs to support children, families."[1]

"Lots of pressure to fix the economy, but few options. . . . Who should try to make the economy grow again: the President, Congress, the Federal Reserve Board, or you, the consumer?"[2]

"Dollar is down across the board. As economy lags, both parties split on solutions."[3]

"Lithuania . . . would have a full-fledged market economy by the end of the year."[4]

"Finland suddenly let its currency float . . . costing high-yield investors millions of dollars."[5]

"Japan lowered its discount rate to 5 percent from 5.5 percent. The economy is a little out of breath."[6]

"A single currency for the European Community seems pretty likely now."[7]

"The President of Argentina . . . arrived in the United States for a whirlwind tour to drum up much-needed investment and loan funds."[8]

"Median household income in 1990, adjusted for inflation, was $29,943, or $1,000 less than it was in 1973. For all but the 20% of the American population with incomes above $80,000 annually, income has stagnated."[9]

"Total government revenue is at a postwar peak. . . . Despite all the talk of tax cuts, people can expect to pay more."[10]

"Many voters are telling pollsters they are extremely worried about the state of the economy."[11]

"Managers have rewarded themselves at the expense of workers. Members of Congress have doubled salaries from $60,000 to $120,000 in a decade of proven failure."[12]

"A provision of the Senate banking reform bill . . . would relieve banks of virtually all liability for contaminated sites for which they grant loans or hold title."[13]

"Domestic violence is on the rise in Massachusetts in part because of the state's dismal economy. . . . The number of women killed in domestic violence is also rising."[14]

THE SOCIETAL CONTEXT OF ECONOMICS

What links these social conditions together is the economic system: the production and distribution mechanism of modern society. Hardly anything has figured more prominently in the struggles for freedom, justice, and social development than the issue of how the economy can increase the efficiency of production and distribution of goods and services, promoting at the same time the rights and responsibilities of the individual, family, community, and state.

The Centrality of Economics in Modern Society

Everyone is interested in the health and future of the economy. Unemployment, depression, recession, fiscal and monetary policy, inflation, national deficit, borrowing money, saving, investing, and basic economic indexes (including the Gross National Product and per capita income), have now become as much political and social as economic terms.

People tend to accept that the economic markets establish the boundaries of what is possible and even desirable in most domains of organized life, including social policy. For example, capitalist economic policy in modern society frequently precedes, sets the parameters for, or becomes a synonym of social policy. Some hope that this will result in more efficient ways of organizing production, distribution, and economic exchanges in the marketplace. But it also creates disinvestments in human capital and causes social underdevelopment. Economic planners in capitalist countries tend to cut back social programs to balance their budgets. This includes appropriations for health, housing, education, public welfare, food projects, and social services to children, pregnant women, the mentally ill, and older people. Alternatively, why not raise taxes or reorganize the economic market?

What are the implications for social work clients? What is the social work view of society and the economy? Inflation, rather than unemployment and poverty, is the main enemy when market economies prosper. What is the impact of this approach on the disadvantaged and powerless? In the most advanced capitalist countries a large part of the population lives in poverty. Is this unavoidable in the context of the economic market system?

Answers to these and similar questions vary among contending theoretical approaches. However, at the center of these approaches are fundamental views regarding the nature of the economic system in modern society and crucial assumptions regarding the economic market, production, distribution, and economic exchanges.

Social philosophies regard the state as either providing sufficient freedom to the market to be efficient or granting too much liberty and undermining the societal context. Social policy is frequently a function of these competing views.

Economics as a Subsystem of Social Organization

Capitalist economists tend to view economics as independent of and overarching other societal policies, including social policy. More importantly, they also view society mainly as a marketplace in which self-serving individuals compete with one another, enhancing the general welfare in the process.

The economic view of production, distribution, and economic exchanges in the marketplace as an independent system reflects a utilitarian orientation and is based on the philosophy of radical individualism. It sees individuals as seeking to maximize their utility (pleasure, happiness, consumption, or profit), rationally choosing the best means to serve their goals. Individuals are the decision-making units of the economic system. The coming together of these individuals in the competitive marketplace is said to generate maximum economic efficiency and well-being. The notion of community, if it enters at all, is often seen as the mere result of the aggregation of individual rational decisions.

Thus, classical and neoclassical economists have argued that the market economy can be treated as a separate system that is basically self-containing, whose distinct attributes can be studied by the use of a perfect competition model.

Social Economics

Other social commentators, including social workers, tend to view the economic market in a broader context that perceives economics as a subsystem of societal organization. Social economics places production, distribution, economic exchanges, and the economic market within the context of society, culture, polity, and social organization. It is this societal context that determines the liberty, morality, and efficiency of the economic market.

In this view, the dynamics of the economy cannot be studied without integrating social, political, and cultural factors. Production, distribution, economic exchanges in the marketplace, and the extent to which the market is competitive are functions of societal organization. Moreover, social collectivities, far from being mere aggregates of individuals, have structures and influence of their own. The individual cannot be viewed as detached from the community and from shared values. Economic production, distribution, and exchanges are intricately related to all societal domains. The economic market is an integral part of society's structure and function, including public policy.

Human and material resources are interdependent in modern society. As citizens, producers, and consumers, people and their collectivities are a basic part of economic activities. With ever-growing urgency, the modern age has tied the fate of societal development to the design of social economics. Even conventional wisdom says that economics is essential to individual, family, community, and institutional development. The integrated use of human and material resources is a prerequisite for socioeconomics. Society's development and well-being, even its survival, freedom,

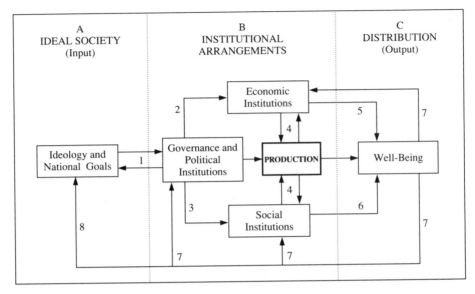

FIGURE 5-1 Production in the social policy context

distributive justice, and human rights, depend on the successful fusion of human and material resources.[15]

Economics is thus a human institution in which both material and human resources are integrated in social governance (the way people manage their own affairs) and in social development (the way people cultivate human resources). The economic and social orders are linked. In turn, they join with the state to manage growth and development, democratic well-being, and social justice.[16] Even if efficiency is the highest goal of the economy, it should lead to the attainment of people's needs. Economic success, on the other hand, can only be assessed in reference to the needs of human beings who constitute the economy.

Economic Production Depends on Social Organization

Economic production is not solely or even primarily a physical and technical economic issue but is also a social organization concern. Production depends on social organization and social institutions, which are necessary to mobilize human energy for productive purposes. (See Figure 5-1.) Mobilizing the productive effort is a challenge to social organization; success or failure determines the volume of human effort that can be directed to economic activity.

Society also determines the proper allocation of the social effort of production among people. Whether children or parents of young children should become members of the labor force, whether prisoners or slaves should work, and so forth is a function of the social system and the way it allocates the productive effort. Society's existence, survival, and development depend directly on the production of goods and services, including food.

Economic production hinges on the tacit precondition that social organization will function effectively. Rich nations survive because an army of people produces what we need and cannot produce ourselves. This enormous division of labor in social organization supports the economic functions of the market. Failure of any social institution and the division of labor would cripple production, the economy, and society itself. For example, when we face a large strike, our entire economic machine may falter because a strategic population group ceases to perform its social tasks.

Material abundance through economic production is assured only by organized social cooperation, division of labor, and specialization. Social organization and the relations of people provide the bonds that forge us into a collective, social whole.

THE CAPITALIST ECONOMIC SYSTEM

Two things stand out in the history of capitalism. First, it can create and at the same time destroy. It has produced goods and services unprecedented in history. Capitalism has surpassed all prior economic systems because of its special virtues: unprecedented high production, rapid increase in the abundance of goods produced (social surplus), and productive reinvestment of the social surplus in capital to form wealth.

Historically, capitalism was able to use and benefit from several societal developments, such as the religious promotion of hard work and frugality that was established in the postmercantilist era. The discovery of precious metals in the New World had a profound impact on economic classes and on the distribution of income in Europe. The emergence of nation-states fostered and directly provided for the formation of capital in the form of capital goods. In this environment of unprecedented material abundance engineered by the capitalist system, people could for the first time in history develop their own humanity, freedom, leisure, creativity, and culture.

This creativity, however, has been coupled with the destruction of existing technologies, forms of business organization, and jobs. In the long run there are more jobs, greater productivity, and higher levels of output. In the short run industries are closed down, workers left without jobs, and whole communities devastated. The arms buildup, especially in the 1980s, while promoting prosperity in regions where weapons were built, left huge sections of the economy vulnerable to foreign competition and many communities in steep decline.

Second, capitalist development has proceeded very unevenly between countries and among regions and social classes within countries. This tends to increase the inequality of income, wealth, and power and the distance between social and ethnic classes. For example, some regions and social classes became dynamic centers of development. While others stagnated on the periphery or became powerless under capitalist development the rich become richer and the poor poorer, raising crucial questions as to whether the marketplace is just and moral. Economic growth has also proceeded cyclically through economic booms and busts in each country and region, raising central questions of undue destruction, poverty, and unemployment.

The Economic System:
The Roots and Essence of Microeconomics

The behavior of individuals and businesses is the concern of *microeconomics*. The economic system as a social organization explains how a society is knit together by the market. Businesses and individual consumers interact in the marketplace to determine what, how, and for whom goods and services are produced. Buyers and sellers of a commodity determine its price and quantity, rejecting tradition or command.

The central concepts of microeconomics include the division of labor and specialization, competition and pricing, self-regulation of the market, private property, profit, voluntary labor, and a distribution of goods and services according to contributions in the marketplace.

Adam Smith, the architect of capitalism's order and of the classical school of economic analysis, saw in society's division of labor and specialization the key to the wealth of nations.[17] The key to economic growth, he contended, is to improve productivity through the division of labor and specialization.[18] This increases the demand for labor and, in turn, wages. As wages rise and workers are able to buy better food for their families, infant and child mortality decline, leading to a larger labor force. In turn, this prevents wages from rising excessively.

While Smith saw in the division of labor the key to productivity and economic growth, Marx thought increased productivity could be realized only in a higher stage of communist society. So far, Marx's view has proved to be an illusion. Rather, the giant corporation has proved to be the most effective instrument for promoting science and technology and for harnessing them to produce goods and services. In the United States today the means already exist for overcoming poverty, for supplying everyone with the necessities and conveniences of life, and for giving to all a genuinely rounded education and the free time to develop faculties to the fullest. However, nothing of the sort has happened. Specialization has led to increasing economic insecurity.

Social Class Division

Fundamental to any version of capitalism are the relations between the owners and nonowners of the means of production. Private owners of nonpersonal means of production such as land, mines, and industrial plants are collectively known as capital. They make production decisions for profit. On the other hand, voluntary workers do not own capital and make no production decisions. Instead, they sell their labor to employers for wages and salaries. Highly productive people get high incomes, while those who produce nothing get no income. Class division leads to income inequality.

Those who own, use, and need resources and those who work are usually of different social classes. Among major industrialized countries the United States has the highest income inequality after Australia for 1980–1988 (See Table 5-1).

The relations between capitalists and laborers are crucial in organizing efficient ways to allocate scarce resources, create a surplus, and raise general living standards. Social class relations based on slavery used a master-slave social class distinction. Those based on feudalism were characterized by a lord-serf arrangement. Those of socialism are based on a state-workers relationship.

Evolving through John Stuart Mill in the mid-19th century, the core of classical economic analysis is the model of competitive market capitalism and pricing. The best way to confront economic problems is to rely on the individual's pursuit of self-interest in a private property system, regulated by the forces of market competition. Mainstream economists believed that an uncoerced person would act rationally to maximize individual self-interest.

TABLE 5-1   Rankings of income inequality for industrialized nations 1980–1988 (for varying years)

	Ratio of highest 20% to lowest 20%	*Income share of lowest 40%*
Hungary	3.0	26.2
Poland	3.6	23.9
Japan	4.3	21.9
Sweden	4.6	21.2
Belgium	4.6	21.6
Netherlands	5.6	20.1
Germany (West)	5.7	19.5
Spain	5.8	19.4
Norway	5.9	19.0
Finland	6.0	18.4
Italy	6.0	18.8
France	6.5	18.4
Israel	6.6	18.1
United Kingdom	6.8	17.3
Yugoslavia	7.0	17.1
Canada	7.1	17.5
Denmark	7.1	17.4
Switzerland	8.6	16.9
New Zealand	8.8	15.9
United States	8.9	15.7
Australia	9.6	15.2

SOURCE: United Nations Development Programme, *Human Development Report, 1992;* and *Dollars and Sense,* July/August 1992, p. 23.

Smith asserted that a society of competitive, profit-seeking individuals can assure orderly material provisioning through the self-regulating, competitive market and price mechanism, resulting in capital accumulation, productivity, and wealth. In the market process and the price mechanism people produce things for sale that other people demand most and are willing to pay the highest prices for. When people demand more of something, shortages develop in that market, and the price is forced up. When people demand less of something, surpluses develop, and the price is forced down. The lower price discourages the production of that item, and producers shift to the production of something else. Businesses and households respond to the price mechanism by selecting cheaper goods—a powerful force that works automatically in a free market. Households and businesses interact to determine prices as well as what, how, and for whom goods and services are produced.

The interaction of households and businesses is crucial. Households decide how to spend their income, while businesses produce the highest-profit commodities by the lowest-cost techniques. Whenever the price of something goes up much, more of it will be produced and less consumed. Whenever the price of an item goes down much, more will be consumed and less produced. The price mechanism directs the economic choices that individuals and businesses make and influences the market process itself (rational choice theory). This mechanism automatically solves the basic output question: What should society produce? It also answers the input question: How will the products be produced? Producers will use the most plentiful, cheapest materials and the lowest-cost production techniques.

Distribution is also automatically handled by the market. The people who produce the most valuable, most popular things and do it most efficiently will earn the most income. This is the productivity principle of distribution. The more valuable the productive contribution, the greater the income and the distributive share of the output received.

Self-Regulation

The market acts as its own guardian through the price mechanism, which automatically responds to changes in demand and supply. The price mechanism encourages production and discourages consumption of higher-priced goods. It also discourages production and encourages consumption of lower-priced goods. If prices, wages, or profits stray from competitive levels, they will be driven back. Smith thought that an automatic, self-regulating mechanism to manage the economy was possible if built on basic human nature.

Although Smith recognized the mean ways of the business class (the manufacturing class in his time) and the suffering of workers, he also believed that laissez-faire and the complete liberty of the economic market would ultimately benefit the general public. Smith asserted that the system of perfect liberty (the market left to its own devices) would grow due to the drive for self-betterment and the thirst for profits. Free individual choices were expected to overcome scarcity and result in the common good through the automatic adjustments of free exchange in markets. Competition would ensure that the economy most efficiently produced the goods people desired. The government should simply act as the referee of the economic game.

The Utilitarian Invisible Hand

Smith wrote of an "invisible hand" that would lead the selfish activities of individuals to the best outcome for all and to the production of goods and services that society needs.[19] Therefore, any governmental interference with free competition and pricing, according to Smith, is almost certain to be injurious.

In Smith's view, market actors are driven to gain profits and better their condition, but competition and pricing prevent them from exploiting fellow citizens. This generates a socially workable arrangement from the unsocial motivation of capitalist self-interest. Each person, wanting only self-betterment, confronts similarly motivated people in the market. In buying or selling, each market actor is forced to meet the prices offered by competitors.[20]

The market mechanism produces the goods that the society wants in the desired quantities without anyone issuing an order. Businesses expand in response to increasing demand for their products: they hire more workers, add more space, and buy more capital equipment. Businesses contract in response to reduced demand for their products: they fire workers, give up leases on space, and cut down on their capital investment. The output of items that people want will rise, and that of items that people don't want will fall.

Classic, theoretical capitalism (no governmental interference and no restrictions from tradition) is also characterized by the institution of private property: the right of all people to private ownership and control of the means of production. Capitalism is further characterized by a market framework that regulates economic activity for profit. This contrasts to the precapitalist dictates of tradition or personal authority.

The capitalist system provides a regular flow of profits, which are appropriated by the owners for capital (subject to taxes). It also provides voluntary labor by people who freely respond to the opportunities and discouragements of the market, as opposed to involuntary laborers such as slaves, serfs, or tradition-bound artisans.[21]

This economic system of competition and laissez-faire prevails when people and markets are free to follow the influences of the price mechanism to produce whatever is profitable in the most efficient ways and to earn as much income or profit as possible.

The Behavior of the Economic System as a Whole: Macroeconomics

Macroeconomics, or Keynesian economics, was introduced during the 1930s depression by John Maynard Keynes (1883–1946). It is concerned with totals: the total levels of production, output, employment, spending (by consumers, investors, and the government), and national income.

Keynes is known as the savior of capitalism in the 1930s and the father of macroeconomics—the behavior of the economy as a whole. His macroeconomic insights provided an additional rationale for the expansion of the welfare state and social services; he argued that governments must provide macroeconomic stabilization of the economy. Thus, he rejected the notion of a self-correcting economy that tends toward a balance of full employment automatically. Without governmental economic intervention, full employment is problematic, the market remains prone to recession, and economic stabilization is unattainable.

Most importantly, Keynes argued that social welfare payments, public jobs, social security, unemployment compensation, and similar governmental subsidies increase consumption and in turn production. Thus, governmental expenditures for the welfare state, far from undermining the economic market as some classic economists suggest, stimulate production, augment the national income, and increase human capital.

Keynes asserted that government must use its ability to spend. In a recession the government must spend money on public transfers, including social welfare benefits to the poor, even if this creates a budget deficit. This spending permits the economy to recover and creates budget surpluses that can pay off prior deficits. This is why some commentators refer to the welfare state as the Keynesian welfare state. Its expansion was made possible by the macroeconomics of Keynes, particularly the concept of budget deficits to fund and expand the welfare state even when the economy is in decline.

Microeconomics is concerned with individual and business choices about what to do with available resources. The Great Depression of the 1930s, however, made it crucial to study the economy as a whole. Keynes focused on what causes the economy to speed up and slow down and on what causes recessions, depressions, unemployment, and inflation. He tried to explain aggregate poverty, perennial unemployment, and affluence. Macroeconomics helps policymakers understand how to devise more effective policies to stabilize the economy. Most importantly, it helps

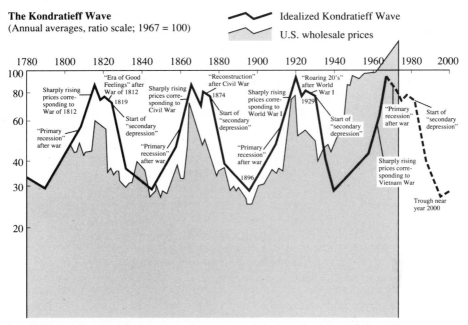

The Kondratieff Wave
(Annual averages, ratio scale; 1967 = 100)

Idealized Kondratieff Wave

U.S. wholesale prices

FIGURE 5-2   Economic booms and busts, 1780–2000. From "Boom and Bust Theory Shines New Lite," by P. Lewis. In *The New York Times,* Oct. 12, 1982, p. E2. Copyright © 1982 by The New York Times.

them appreciate what role, if any, the government should take in this effort. For example, why does the economic system speed up and slow down at regular and perhaps predictable intervals? What can the government do about it?

Nicolai D. Kondratieff, a Russian statistician, fell out of favor with the former Soviet authorities because his theories suggested that capitalism recovers from its periodic crises and is not doomed to collapse, as Marx believed. In 1925 he drew the Kondratieff Long Economic Wave based on prices, interest rates, and production (see Figure 5-2).

The Kondratieff Wave showed four major 50-year boom-to-bust cycles since the 1790s and a gloomy outlook for the world economy. The first cycle began in the late 18th century. It reached its peak about 1815 at the end of the Napoleonic wars, reflecting the spread of steam power and the beginning of the Industrial Revolution. Then it dropped to a trough around 1848. A second upswing lasted into the 1870s, coinciding with the expansion of railroads, steamboats, and trade. After that, a decline set in again. The world economy turned around for the third time at the start of this century, fueled by the harnessing of electric power and the invention of the internal combustion engine and receiving further impetus from World War I. It reached a third peak about 1920, Kondratieff thought, with another downswing lying ahead—the Great Depression of the 1930s.

Kondratieff's followers traced the fourth upswing from World War II to the 1970s. It was helped along by the new plastics and durable-goods industries and by the postwar expansion in air and road transportation. Then in 1973 the world economy turned down again with the first rise in oil prices.

According to this theory, the global recession of the 1980s and 1990s may last until the end of this century. While there is a tendency for wars to occur as the upswing nears its peak (the Napoleonic Wars at the top of the first cycle, the American Civil War and the Franco-Prussian War at the top of the second cycle, World War I in the third cycle, and World War II and the Vietnam War near the top of the fourth upturn), the explanation for this is unclear and remains controversial.[22]

Economists try to explain the erratic yet regular behavior of the market to assist continuous governmental efforts to stabilize the economy through monetary and fiscal policies. The objectives of macroeconomic policy are to avoid the sharp boom and bust business cycles and to achieve high levels of output and employment, low involuntary unemployment, stable prices and exchange rates. Macroeconomic policy also strives for equilibrium between exports and imports through fiscal policy (governmental expenditures and taxation) and monetary policy (control of the money supply affecting interest rates).

Ever-Changing Forms of Capitalism

Since its inception capitalism has evolved, acquiring different forms in the same and different countries. Early classical forms of 19th-century capitalism in Great Britain and the United States were characterized by a large number of small capitalist firms. They were owned by individuals or families who directly managed them. The economy was regulated by competition between the suppliers of goods and services and demand from consumers. The labor market determined wages and allocated workers among employers according to the same forces of supply and demand. The state allowed the market to determine economic activity.

In contrast, other countries, including Japan, Germany, and Italy, have opted for detailed public control of economic life to enhance national power, maintain healthy state revenues, and preserve social order or social justice. Hence, the state in these countries directly subsidized private entrepreneurs, guided credit and investment capital, and established state-owned firms. It also regulated labor and product markets by political means, established governmental contracts and protective tariffs, and granted firms monopoly rights to produce certain goods or to sell in certain markets.

In the 20th century, capitalism evolved into a powerful promoter of technological change and moved away from the early classical model because of internal and external forces, including the shift from commercial to industrial capital and changes in technology and organization. At the same time, an increasing range of economic decisions shifted from the private (capitalist) to the public (governmental) sector.

The new capitalist form ("oligarchy," "financial," or "corporate" capitalism) is marked by economic concentration, joint-stock ownership, the decline of family-owned firms, and market domination by a small number of large firms rather than competition among numerous small ones. Businesses try to enter agreements to limit competition, manipulate markets, and increase profitability and stability. Ownership and the managerial function have become disconnected with the rise of institutional ownership by banks, holding companies, insurance companies, and pension funds.

Most importantly, laissez-faire policies have become less prominent. The state seeks to create economic stability and protect the interests of indigenous capital and

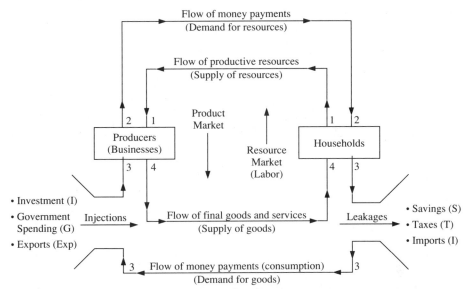

FIGURE 5-3 Circulatory flows of market activities. Modification and combination of two diagrams from R. H. Leftwich and A. M. Sharp, *Economics of Social Issues* (4th edition, Dallas, TX: Business Publications, 1980), pp. 279 and 284.

labor with state investments, subsidies, and public ownership of parts of industry. The state also intervenes to guide private investments and regulate the formation of companies, including the control of mergers and takeovers. At times the state also tries to control wages, salaries, and prices.

The resulting and still-evolving "mixed economy" capitalist system contains elements of market, command, and tradition. In this context, it is quite different from the earlier classical, theoretical form of capitalism.

THE FREE MARKET MODEL

The Classic View

The most direct way to understand the basic causes of economic behavior is the basic model of circulatory flows of market activities that illustrates the theoretical foundation of the capitalist system (see Figure 5-3). This model represents the view of classical mechanics: the economy runs like a clockwork machine in perpetual synchrony.

Players with Equal Power: Households and Businesses

The model describes households as both consumers and owners (and hence suppliers) of production resources. Businesses are both producers of final goods and users that demand productive resources. Both interact, are interdependent, and are equal. When households that own the factors of production sell them to firms (see Figure 5-3, line 1), income flows to households (line 2). When households spend money (line 3) to buy products from firms (line 4), households get the goods and the firms get back the money. Thus income flows from firms to households in the form of wages, salaries, rents, interests, and profits (line 2). This money then flows back to firms as consumer spending when the households buy goods and services (line 3). As long as firms sell all they have produced and make satisfactory profits, the circulatory flows of income and spending continue.[23]

These circular flows of income and spending serve as a fundamental economic tool that describes the relationship between resources and final goods and services and also that between the national income—the total income earned in the nation or gross national product (GNP)—and the national product (the GNP minus depreciation). The national income and product accounts (the GNP accounts) show the income and product flows of the nation and indicate the rate at which the economy is running.

The model reflects several assumptions regarding the interdependence, equivalence, and equal power of its components: (1) Income depends on production, production depends on spending, spending depends on income, and the demand for resources depends on the demand for products; (2) the flows of money and goods arise jointly and are quantitatively equal; and (3) the national product value is equal to the sum of wages, interests, rents, and profits (the total price that products must fetch when marketed).

Hence, the national income and national expenditures are constantly transformed into one another. If households continuously spend the income they receive, entrepreneurs have no sales difficulties. Increases in production create income to buy extra production; this is known as *equivalence assumption.*

In justifying the egalitarianism of capitalism, the model suggests that households and firms have equal power in production and consumption decisions. Households control resources by deciding how, when, and whether their resources will be used. They also control consumption by determining what, when, and how much they will spend. Households therefore influence firms and final social output in the labor, capital, and consumer-goods markets. In labor markets, for example, the household rejection of physical jobs reduces the number of such jobs, and products that require physical labor are produced only in small amounts. Locational preferences and working conditions are similarly affected.

Households also influence capital markets. By providing their financial capital to or withholding it from firms according to the degree of risk and return households influence production decisions. When households save more and spend less, they buy fewer goods and services, so firms produce fewer products. By saving or spending, consumers make their wishes known to entrepreneurs, who adjust their prices and production accordingly.

In consumer goods markets, consumers influence the commodity composition of the GNP through purchase decisions. To profit, firms in this area must produce goods that households want, are willing to buy, and prefer to similar alternatives. The better a firm is at complying with consumer wishes, the more profitable it will be.

Each firm, too, has equal powers. Firms decide the kind and quantity of resources they purchase, which products and how much output they produce, which technical processes they use, and where operations will be located. In so doing, they maximize their profits (the difference between revenues and the cost per dollar of ownership capital in the firm). Firms also influence resource markets. If technological conditions and the demand for products necessitate extensive use of a resource (such as labor capable of operating a specific machine), firms will seek to hire many operators, which will raise wages. The higher wages will encourage more people to train and become operators. This principle operates similarly with land and capital. Firms also influence product markets by setting prices and hence consumption levels.

In brief, it is assumed that power is shared equally between households and firms. In a modern society, however, a global corporation has much more power than a corner grocery store or individual consumers.

Additions to and Losses from the Model: Leakages and Injections

The circular flow becomes more complex with additions (injections) to and withdrawals (leakages) from the circulatory flows (Figure 5-3, lines 5 and 6). The model is like a bathtub: Water runs in from a faucet (injection) and escapes from a drain (leakage). Leakages are the result of savings (S) and taxation (T). When people save and do not spend all their income, those who borrow from banks and spend more than their income are affected. Tax withdrawals from the money flow reduce private spending and aggregate demand; and so does buying from foreign businesses (Imp). Injections (additions) are investments (I), governmental spending (G), and exports (Exp).[24] The model's equilibrium is maintained when

$$\text{Leakages } (S + T + Imp) = \text{Injections } (I + G + Exp)$$

If the total leakages equal the total injections, the system remains balanced. That is, savings at full employment return to the circular activity through investment, and aggregate demand will be sufficient to buy all the goods and services that are produced. When aggregate demand is deficient, part of the income created by production does not return to producers in the form of spending, resulting in surpluses at current market prices and in employment levels. Producers respond to the surplus market situation by reducing production and income, causing people to lose their jobs (involuntary unemployment). On the other hand, the income (spending) stream will remain the same size only if the sum of the leakages (withdrawals) is exactly offset (equaled) by the sum of the injections (additions). When injections equal leakages, spending equals production values. Everything produced can be sold (the expenditure and income equation), and prosperity dominates. When this balance is not maintained, the economy will speed up or slow down. For more information, see R. H. Leftwich and A. M. Sharp, *Economics of Social Issues,* Fourth Edition (Dallas, TX: Business Publications, 1980), pp. 278–287, which provides explanations of unemployment and the material in this section.

Implications for Economic Stability:
Unemployment, Inflation, Recession, and Business Cycles

The model also explains mainstream economic functions, including employment, unemployment, inflation, and recession—the business cycles of the economy. Total output is determined by total spending, which supports the total level of economic activity, including employment and productivity (output per worker, per worker-hour, or per unit of capital and land). Thus the total amount of money received by the people who produce all this output equals the total amount being spent by all the buyers. If spending goes down, the total output goes down (recession). If spending increases, output increases until the economy reaches its full capacity; if spending increases further, there will be shortages and prices will rise (inflation). In other words, the total level of spending must be just right to have "full employment" and "stable prices."

In this view, overproduction is impossible; markets will always be sufficiently large to keep production forces employed. Classicists believe that production factors are employed in the production of capital goods and that savings are invested. But if savings become greater than investments, the interest rate at which entrepreneurs can borrow capital drops. This increases profits and encourages entrepreneurs to expand again. In this way, capital market mechanisms are reactivated and production always stays pressed against the ceiling of available productive factors.

UNEMPLOYMENT AND INFLATION

Involuntary Unemployment

Classical economists claimed that there can be no involuntary unemployment and thus provided no theoretical explanation of or solution to the unemployment of people and machines.[25] They believed that involuntary unemployment is prevented by two capitalist market defenses: the determination of demand by supply (Say's Law) and the existence of flexible real wage rates (because of competition).[26] They dismissed even protracted unemployment periods as frictional economic adjustments to changes in the product mix.[27]

Keynes[28] and his followers rejected both of these assumptions. They asserted that unemployment is inevitable in modern capitalist societies unless the government intervenes to correct the market. They believed that the economic system does not guarantee full employment, and that it is therefore the duty of governments to intervene within the market to enhance demand, promoting both consumption and investment and thus economic equilibrium at full employment. They explained that governmental intervention is required to restore full employment through fiscal and monetary policies designed to create aggregate demand levels that are sufficient to use fully the economy's production capacity.

Keynesian economists assert that the government must bolster free markets to prop up aggregate spending. Otherwise, the circulatory flow and its equivalence will not continue uninterrupted for very long. Investment, which is necessary to absorb savings, enlarges the capital stock and hence increases the economy's productive capacity, which in turn increases production and income in the next period. With higher incomes, however, there will be more savings, necessitating more investment, which must increase faster than income to continue to affect savings and permit firms to sell everything they produce. Since it becomes increasingly difficult to do so, only the government can step in when savings exceed investment. By borrowing excess savings, the government can spend them on socially useful projects.

The Keynesian approach to a managed economy provided the rationale for a welfare state. It promoted reforms for low-income classes without challenging the hegemony of private capital and without introducing socialist models.

Keynesians reject the inevitable mechanistic determination of the classical model and the belief that capitalism is a self-regulating economic system. There are no automatic mechanisms pushing the economy toward full employment. Hence, at times of high unemployment, they invariably prescribe governmental action to end the depression rather than rely on market forces (the adjustment of prices) to do so and secure full employment. Their economic formula: spend enough to offset the withdrawal of savings, cut taxes, or promote easy money (low interest rates). Without these Keynesian ideas, there is no solution to unemployment and depression because the market cannot recover by itself, as the monetarists believe.[29]

The balance required between leakages and injections also suggests that governmental interventions, including taxes and expenditures, are required to achieve equilibrium at full employment (see Figure 5-3). Unemployment falls when injections into the circular flow exceed leakages or when demand for aggregate output is greater than the output supplied at current prices and production levels. Employment falls when injections into the circular flow are less than leakages or when demand for aggregate output is less than the output supplied at current prices and production levels.

Trade-Off of Inflation and Unemployment (Phillips Curve)

Monetary and fiscal policies usually result in different mixes of unemployment and inflation. Unemployment wastes valuable human and material resources because it leads to poverty, crime, a reduced GNP, economic stagnation, increased welfare costs, social and political stress, individual psychological dysfunction, human degradation, and powerlessness. It is indefensible on both moral and purely macroeconomic grounds. Any policy that consciously sacrifices the economic well-being of millions of human beings is morally indefensible. Every 1 million unemployed workers cost the U.S. Treasury $30 billion in lost tax revenues, subsistence unemployment compensation, and welfare payments. Simultaneously, the private sector is deprived of $100 billion in goods and services not produced because of the lost purchasing power of these million unemployed workers.[30] This figure does not include the cost of treating those admitted to mental hospitals or of homicide, stress, and similar psychosocial problems that are usually long-range and expensive.

Inflation, on the other hand, robs most people of their savings; it increases prices of goods and services and the nation's average price level. It also intensifies class conflicts such as union-management discord, destroys the acceptability of money, and can cause the collapse of the market economic system. Those with more assets in the form of money and people on fixed incomes, as well as creditors and owners of banks, government bonds, mortgages, and life insurance policies, are hurt more by inflation. Inflation also affects the allocation of resources. It changes relative demand and supply, the relative prices of different goods and services, and the mix of resources used to produce them, thus reducing economic efficiency. It affects the national income output, changing the size of the economic pie itself.

Both unemployment and inflation have harmful effects. But unemployment dispro-portionately hurts those with less income while inflation hits harder on those with higher incomes and more assets because it is an erosion of the value of money. Thus, the economic establishment tends to combat inflation by trading it for unemploy-ment because it considers inflation to be the nation's worst economic malady. Yet this trade-off costs millions of workers their jobs.

The *Phillips curve* (developed in the 1950s by A. W. Phillips) illustrates the trade-offs between inflation and unemployment: the more unemployment, the less inflation, and vice versa. Governments can have a smaller unemployment rate only if they ac-cept a larger inflation rate; they usually would like to have minimal amounts of both.

The need to choose between inflation and unemployment is related to the economic market dilemma that total spending, which pushes up employment, out-put, and income, also pushes up prices. Whatever monetary or fiscal policy govern-ments implement to reduce unemployment is likely to increase inflation. As total spending speeds up, inflation accelerates before full employment is reached because inflationary and full employment spending levels overlap. As total spending slows down, unemployment increases even before all inflationary pressures cool down. This helps explain the claim of capitalism's critics that the free market system cannot pro-duce full employment and that it tends to generate unemployment because increased spending brings inflation before full employment is reached. Efforts to control infla-tion invariably prevent markets from reaching full employment.

Keynesian-Monetarist Debate

Much of macroeconomics is the Keynesian "demand-side" approach, focusing on aggregate demand.[31] The basic Keynesian idea for overcoming unemployment is to unbalance the governmental budget, reduce taxes, run the government at a deficit, create money to finance governmental expenditures, and thereby increase the spend-ing and income flow of the economy. As the government, firms, and people spend more, incomes and spending increase and prosperity results. By cutting taxes (in-stead of raising taxes to balance the budget and thus slow down the economy), the government stimulates the economy so that people and firms earn more income on which they pay higher taxes. The extra tax revenues are large enough to bring the budget into balance.

In the monetarist economic view, Keynesian approaches are unnecessary and wrong because macroeconomic conditions are determined mainly by the natural market forces of demand, supply, and price. Therefore, any governmental attempt to interfere is harmful. A 4% or 5% limit on the expansion of the money supply can deal with inflation, while automatic price adjustments and market forces will take care of unemployment and depression. Believing that the classical model reflects the real world, monetarists support a hands-off governmental policy.

Keynesians assert that appropriate governmental action can prevent depressed conditions and serious unemployment; they believe the monetarist "do-nothing" ap-proach is likely to generate high unemployment and depression. The policies of Presidents Bush and Reagan in the United States and of Prime Ministers Major and

Thatcher in the United Kingdom resulted in high unemployment rates, high interest rates, the bankruptcy of many businesses, and depression. Compared to Keynesians and liberals, monetarists, conservatives, supporters of Reaganomics, and supply-siders are more concerned about inflation than unemployment. Supply-siders, however, differ from monetarists in that they focus on generating a greater supply of products in the market rather than on a laissez-faire policy.

The Costs of Unemployment

The economic, social, and psychological costs of unemployment are crucial in the context of social policy planning. Unemployment's economic effects are related to its impact on the nation's GNP—idle human resources represent a waste and loss of real income. Differences between what may be produced at full employment and what is produced at lesser employment measure the total economic cost of unemployment (the gap between the actual and potential GNP). The productivity of labor and the economy's overall ability to produce in the future are also reduced during unemployment.

Unemployment's social effects are even more severe than its economic effects. Unemployment threatens individual freedom and the economic and social stability of families. In addition, psychological costs generate socioeconomic costs. Rises in unemployment rates are associated with increases in the rates of suicide, homicide, admission to mental hospitals, and welfare receipt. Each 1% increase in unemployment produces:

- a 5.7% rise in homicides
- a 4.1% increase in suicides
- a 4.0% increase in state prison admissions
- a 3.7% increase in admissions to mental hospitals
- a 1.9% increase in cardiovascular and renal disease mortality
- a 1.9% increase in the overall mortality rate.[32]

Studies of U.S. employment in the 1990s[33] reconfirm the effects of unemployment on health and social stress. They indicate that a 1% rise in the unemployment rate results in:

	Or an additional*
56.6% more deaths from heart attack	35,307 deaths
3.1% more deaths from stroke	2,771 deaths
6.7% more homicides	1,459 homicides
3.4% more violent crimes	62,607 crimes
2.4% more property crimes	223,550 crimes

*Estimated on the basis of the actual unemployment rates between 1990 and 1992 in the metropolitan areas of the study.

The same study estimates that the direct cost to imprison for one year 3% of those arrested for violent property crimes is approximately $45 million. This does not include the costs borne by the victims of these crimes. A policy of preventive investment makes more sense than building more prisons or allowing unemployment to increase as an anti-inflationary measure.

Unemployment strikes not only social classes and groups that are least capable of withstanding it (low-income minorities, women, and young adults), but also many who are not counted in official unemployment figures. During the worst post–World War II recession (September–October 1991), over 8 million workers in the United States were unemployed.[34] That "official" figure does not include several million who became discouraged and gave up looking for nonexistent jobs; it also leaves out part-time workers who would work full time if jobs were available. For far too long, the U.S. government has used unemployment as a means to slow inflation.

U.S. Employment Policy

Few doubt that full employment is fundamental to well-being. It gives people security, dignity, and income and eliminates the staggering waste of mass unemployment. However, full employment (even when set at less than 96%) is elusive in the United States. It is not even considered desirable if it means overheating the economy, increasing inflation, and threatening the interests of capital. Job security and full employment increase labor costs and thereby raise production costs, leading to lower profits for capitalists or increased inflation. The need to fight inflation results in increased unemployment (when price controls and economic planning are not used). Since classical economists believe that unemployment is necessary and desirable for the functioning of the capitalist economy, they treat it not as a social problem to be eliminated but as an economic tool to fight inflation. In their view, unemployment becomes a perennial problem only because social reformers and trade unions introduce minimum wages and unemployment compensation insurance, both of which distort the market's "natural" equilibrium.

The widespread resolve that public policy's goal is full employment was incorporated in the United Nations Charter. But in the Employment Act of 1946 the U.S. Congress subscribed not to full employment but to "maximum employment"—and only if it is consistent with economic needs. Historically, the United States has opted for less employment and more price stabilization, the creation of jobs being subordinate to inflation. The Full Employment and Balanced Growth Act of 1979 (the Humphrey-Hawkins bill) reflects the same rejection of full employment for balanced economic growth.

In the United States "full employment" reflects not a commitment to provide jobs for all but employment rates that are consistent with price stability. A 96% employment rate in a labor force of 86 million means that 3.4 million workers are involuntarily unemployed. A 1% rise in the unemployment rate condemns 860,000 more people to joblessness.

According to David Stockman, former President Reagan's director of the Office of Management and Budget, full employment is most critical for nearly 90% of America's poor. Stockman said that in 1982, 52.3% of the poor were 25–64-year-old adults, 32.8% were female heads of households, and 3.9% were 16–24-year-old single people, for a total of 89.1%. Social insurance (social security and Medicare), rather than full employment and job security, was critical for only 10.9% of the poor, those aged 65 and over.[35] Thus, involuntary unemployment is responsible for most poverty.

ECONOMIC STABILIZATION POLICIES

Regulating Business Cycles

Governments try to smooth out economic business cycles (market expansion and contraction), stabilize the economy, and reduce the effects of economic fluctuations by influencing total spending, income, output, and employment through monetary and fiscal policies. A stabilization policy, however, is controversial. Governments can use monetary and fiscal policy to increase total spending and create less unemployment if more inflation can be tolerated; or they can reduce inflation if more unemployment can be tolerated. It is total spending that controls both employment and the level of prices.

Monetary policy means governmental control of the size of the money supply and interest rates. Focusing on the availability and cost of credit, it aims to promote full employment, stable prices, and steady economic growth. The U.S. Federal Reserve Bank (Fed) has an arsenal of monetary control tools. It can lower or increase the discount rate (the interest rate the Fed charges a bank for borrowed reserves), making it easier or harder and more or less expensive to borrow. It can also open market operations (manipulate government securities that the public can purchase) and can change the reserve requirements (the amount in reserves to back up banks' demand deposits).[36] It is difficult to know when and how much to ease or tighten the money market.

Fiscal policy means adjusting taxes and governmental spending (the budget) to stabilize the economy. The budget is a powerful tool for raising or lowering aggregate demand levels, achieving stabilization, and stimulating economic development. To the extent that unemployment is the result of insufficient demand, it can be eliminated by increased governmental spending and transfer payments, reduced taxes, or a combination of the two.[37] The budget also reflects public revenues and expenditures that are required for governmental operations.[38] If governmental spending is increased, more money is injected into the total spending flow. This is a more direct approach, with more immediate effects, than making money easy through a monetary policy (particularly if nobody wants to borrow and buy bonds). Governments can increase their spending to hire all the unemployed people, which is the most direct way to solve involuntary unemployment. By building new schools, highways, and parks, they can create more jobs, income, and spending; the 1991 Transportation Act, passed by the U.S. Congress to stimulate the economy, is an example.

If governments reduce taxes on income and business profits, people can potentially spend more and businesses can invest more. This approach also puts more money (injections) into the total spending flow (like increased governmental spending).

These actions can speed up the economy and overcome a depression. To slow down an economic boom, a government can increase taxes on businesses and consumers, forcing businesses and consumers to decrease their spending. Or it can decrease governmental spending—or do both.[39]

Unbalanced Budgets and Debt Financing

When governments increase their spending and cut taxes, they unbalance their budgets, use deficit financing, and increase the national debt. To make up the difference in unbalanced budgets, the U.S. government, for example, sells bonds and treasury bills either to businesses and consumers or to the Fed (new money). This pulls money out of the economic system and returns it when the government spends the money.[40]

The federal government's debt under Presidents Reagan and Bush has increased to unprecedented levels. Although Reagan castigated President Carter for a $60 billion budget deficit, Reagan and Bush ran up deficits of more than $2 trillion by 1991.[41] While the public believes that a large national debt will bankrupt the economy (and shift the burden to future generations), economists are more concerned with how the national debt affects economic operations. A national deficit preempts the private sector's use of resources, regardless of whether the government finances its spending by borrowing or by taxing. It also causes inflation by forcing the Fed to monetize the debt or by forcing up interest rates and "crowding out" private investors.[42] A large national debt may redistribute income from low-income to high-income groups, reduce the national output and capital stock, and increase prices.

Governmental income, derived primarily from taxes (including income, payroll, and excise taxes), reduces the private sector's income for spending on goods and services or for saving. It affects social and tax policies, and influences justice and the distribution of income, wealth, and power. Tax policies that stimulate business investments tend to decrease governmental revenues. To the extent that tax incentives favor large corporations and high-income classes, they form a supply-side strategy, which shifts a heavier burden of financing public functions to the lower-income and middle classes.

Servicing the national debt redistributes income and therefore alters the distribution of the national output. Its impact depends upon the distribution of taxes and federal debt ownership. Federal taxes are less progressive than is federal debt ownership (more people pay taxes, and more rich people own federal securities).

Moreover, a large national debt may reduce productivity and output. When taxes increase to pay interest on the national debt, the economy becomes less efficient and produces less than it would without a national debt. Real output may also be reduced in the process of creating and servicing the debt; the government's competition for private savings reduces the formation of private capital and the accumulation of real capital assets.

Creation of Money

The U.S. government also finances its expenditures with dollar bills, which are another form of government bond (that never matures or pays interest) or another way of borrowing and taxing. However, creating money does not automatically open the necessary gap between the private sector's total income and spending. The creation of too much money may eventually increase prices and thereby have the same effect as taking away (taxing) people's money. Keynes warned that galloping inflation can cause recession because money no longer stores value.

Transfer Payments

Some governmental expenditures are direct payments for services received (such as public expenditures for military equipment). But others are direct payments to individuals for which no goods and services return to the government—that is, transfer payments.[43] Social welfare benefits, including veterans' benefits and services and public assistance, are transfer payments that do not involve the production of goods and services in the private sector (and are excluded from the GNP until they are spent for goods and services by the recipients).

DETERMINATION OF
EARNINGS, WAGES, AND INCOME

In the 1980s the salaries of chief executive officers (CEOs) of major corporations increased dramatically relative to those of workers. In 1987 alone, the average compensation of CEOs at 329 of the nation's largest publicly held corporations rose 48% to $1.8 million. The disparity in income between CEOs and workers rapidly accelerated during the Reagan years: from 29 times the income of average manufacturing workers in 1979 to 40 times in 1985 to 93 times in 1988.[44]

The debate over the determination of earnings is crucial not only in the context of the sources of economic inequality generated by the market, but also for understanding poverty, underemployment, the working poor, the social-class structure, and the need to democratize the economy. If one assumes (as do classical economists) that human labor is like other productive economic inputs, how is its price determined? By supply and demand, productivity and marketable skills, or by other institutional factors, including discrimination and the exploitation of labor? How and why do labor market outcomes such as wage rates, occupations, or the industry of employment differ between men and women, blacks and whites, or workers with more or less education?

The underlying issue is imputation: how to determine the share each production factor receives from the value of the final product. Assuming that each cooperating production factor (labor, capital, land, and entrepreneurship) helps create the output and its value, how is the product value to be imputed to each of the production factors? How is the value of a table to be broken down into the values of the cabinetmaker's work, the wood, and the capital needed? How much is each production factor responsible for the output?

Marginal Productivity Theory
(Theory of Labor Demand)

The theory of marginal productivity is based on classical economic principles.[45] It suggests that workers' wages are determined by workers' marginal productivities, employers being compelled by competition to pay wages that reflect what workers produce. The theory indicates that if one labor unit is added, the resulting increase in production is the marginal product of labor, which becomes increasingly smaller with successive additions of labor. As long as the marginal product of labor is greater than wages, it is profitable for employers to hire more workers. Therefore, workers are paid according to how much they contribute to increases in the marginal output. Although this is a theory of producers' profits, not an imputation principle, classicists and neoclassicists believe that if workers' income is too low, their productivity is too low, which implies that wages automatically increase when the productivity of workers increases.

Human Capital Theory

Human capital theory, a more contemporary version of marginal productivity, asserts that marketable knowledge and skills can be regarded as investments that increase productivity and therefore wages.[46] Wages are determined by marginal productivity and differential skills. If willing workers are unemployed, they lack skills or human capital for employment; if workers are employed and still poor, they lack factors that lead to higher output and increased marginal productivity. Education and training increase workers' marketable skills (their human capital), which in turn increase their productivity and result in higher earnings. Hence, individual behavior and productivity, rather than social institutional factors, determine earnings and income. Workers must produce more to increase their wages and the GNP.

While research in the 1950s focused on interindustry and interregional wage differentials (labor-demand side), in the 1960s it explored the supply side of wages and income discrimination, focusing on education, skills, training, health, mobility, and attitudes of the labor force.[47] Differences in individual income were attributed almost solely to individual differences in human capital (education, training, health, and mobility). The findings of this research provided a theoretical base for development strategies to increase the earnings of the poor.

Marginal productivity and human capital frameworks have been criticized because they are based only on casual observations (earnings increase with experience, for example). Furthermore, the human capital approach did not increase the income of the poor; it proved ineffective in ghetto labor markets, where educated and trained workers remained unemployed.[48] Other criticisms are that these approaches focus only on the labor market's supply side; that differences in income are caused by social institutions (not by poor people's failure to invest in themselves to improve their earning power or having inferior physical and intellectual abilities as the classicists suggest); that there is no direct cause-effect relation between an individual's human capital stock and productivity; and that education and training may lead to higher earnings, but not necessarily via increased productivity.[49] Although the education income correlation may be high for physicians versus janitors, the human capital implication for those who do not aspire to a college degree may be misleading.

Dual-Market Theory (Institutional Analysis)

The dual-market theory evolved from studies of particular labor markets showing that antipoverty programs did not perform as expected, which challenged the notion that better-educated and trained workers in inner cities get higher wages and experience less unemployment.[50] These studies also found that the determination and distribution of income cannot be fully explained by the theory of marginal productivity because substandard wages, the lack of work opportunities, and discrimination must also be considered. They concluded that institutional inequalities and discrimination practices produce a stratification of the labor market that is thoroughly resistant to competitive forces and individual decisions. They also emphasized that stratification persists because it supports labor market institutions.

The data challenged the concept of market continuity, which asserts that labor markets are not stratified, and suggested that labor market stratification exists and persists. Institutional inequalities and discriminatory practices produce cumulative stratification, and rigid market barriers are reinforced by educational stratification. Dual-market theorists point out that variations in people with similar human capital endowments are attributable to barriers to entry into industry. These barriers, created by employers or unions, relate to geographic mobility, lack of information about the labor market, and market discontinuity rather than to productivity.

Discontinuity refers to the existence of two markets resulting from class influences that affect educational attainment, quality, and attitudes. A "primary" (conventional) market provides high wages, low turnover, union security, relatively permanent employment, on-the-job training and upward mobility, and a "secondary" (nonconventional) market provides inadequate wages, no union protection, high turnover, no training or advancement, and transitory employment.

Dual-market theorists encourage primary firms to hire secondary workers, saying that secondary firms must become more like primary employers. They also suggest the legitimation of certain profitable activities such as numbers, racing, and prostitution, particularly those that are frequently combined with casual employment in secondary labor markets.

Opponents of this theory emphasize that it focuses only on primary and secondary markets and is therefore incomplete.

Social Stratification Theory

Neo-Marxists consider the effects of socialization and the cumulative impact of institutional inequalities and discriminatory practices that persistently stratify the labor market.[51] They believe that class-based influences affect educational equality and attainment as well as attitudes, resulting in both inadequate and hindered access to information on the labor market. Labor market barriers are reinforced by these educational stratifications and are thoroughly resistant to competitive forces and individual decisions. Class interests clash over the distribution of economic products.

In addition, they contend that public schools are state institutions controlled by capitalists (the ruling class). Thus, schools ensure that working-class children receive less and qualitatively different education than do rich children. They also suggest that there is an association between years of education and parents' income. Both work and schools are stratified to serve class interests. The perpetuation of the ruling class is the objective of salary determination, rather than the efficiency motive or the need for the division of labor. Specialization and the division of labor segment the working class, create the secondary market, and bias the selection of workers for promotion.

Radicals have little faith in educational programs and training because the "rules of the game" remain unchanged. Neither more general education nor the programs advocated by dual-market analysts will, by themselves, significantly alter relative income status. Instead, radicals opt for altering class relations.

Radical analysis is accused of being simplistic and of raising as many questions as it answers. For example, social-class analysis requires more empirical certification. Radicals fail to prove that alienation, inequality, racism, and sexism are found exclusively in the market system and that they are unique to capitalism rather than a product of industrialization.

SOCIALIST VIEWS OF THE CAPITALIST MARKET: CRITIQUE AND SOCIAL REFORM

Karl Marx (1818–1883) is the most systematic critic of capitalism and analyst of its instability, tensions, disorders, and eventual demise.[52] The intellectual roots of most socialist perspectives are directly related to Marx and his views regarding the dysfunction of capitalist markets.

Socialist reform emerged first as a reaction to certain shortcomings and negative social impacts of capitalist markets and later as proactive, reformist, economic models in applied socialism. Marx's penetrating analysis of capitalism's dynamics and his disagreement with Smith and Keynes established the epicenter of this historical movement.[53]

Capitalism in Marx's View

Karl Marx attempted to construct a theory of how capitalism works rather than a theory of how to manage a socialist economy. He considered capitalist profits the driving force of the economy and emphasized the instability of capitalism inherent in the market system. He also focused on the opposing demands of labor and capital.

In Marx's view, because profits fluctuate, the levels of investment activity and economic growth fluctuate as well. The ensuing business cycles may not be greatly disruptive at first, but they compound over time, with each downturn becoming more serious than the previous one. The steady progression of cycles builds to a crisis in which fundamental change must occur for profits to rise again and for growth to proceed. The instability increases until finally the system comes tumbling down. Unlike Adam Smith's smooth-growth model, Marx saw an intensification of the class struggle between a small group of capitalist magnates and a large mass of embittered workers and an inherent tendency of the capitalist system to generate crisis that undermines the economy. Marx's vision of capitalism is a continuously evolving system under tension.

Marx and his collaborator Friederich Engels developed the *historical materialism* approach as a theoretical base of scientific social analysis. This materialist analysis of history suggests that social, cultural, and political phenomena are determined by the mode of material production. Rather than using ideas as the main explanation of historical processes, Marx used the economy as causal priority in social analysis. This approach reflects Heraclitus's position that nothing is eternal or unchanging.

A crucial component of the broader historical materialism is *dialectical materialism,* associated with Marx and the philosophy of the former Soviet Union's

Communist party. Materialism suggests that all social phenomena are material. This opposes idealism, which offers interpretations of societal phenomena based on ideals such as religion.

Dialectical refers to the clash of contradictions leading to a new, more advanced synthesis.[54] It is a way of confronting and analyzing social problems to build theory based on three basic moments: thesis, antithesis, and synthesis. Thesis, antithesis, and synthesis (and dialectical materialism) imply transformation, the unity of opposites, and negation. For example, gradual quantitative changes give rise to revolutionary qualitative changes (transformation). The unity of concrete reality is the unity of opposites. In the clash of opposites one opposite negates another and is in turn negated by a higher level of historical development that preserves something of both negated terms (synthesis).

Dialectical materialism explains Marx's philosophy of society's development and historical events. The transmutation of economic and social forces throughout history is a change from certain kinds of productive modes and relations toward other, more progressive ones.[55] For example, historical development has changed the structure of society from primitive to communal to slave to feudal to capitalist and finally to socialist states.

In this context of historical materialism and dialectics, Marx's view of capitalism was different from Smith's. Smith saw a competitive but harmonious profit-seeking society and a self-regulating market mechanism. Through productivity it would enhance orderly material growth and the accumulation of capital and wealth. Marx's perception was just the opposite. For Marx, capitalist growth is dysfunctional and filled with continuing struggle among social classes that has been expressed in the contest between the ruling and the ruled over wages and profits.

Marx also admired capitalism. He was impressed by the energy with which capitalists revolutionized productivity and by their application of science in industry and other sectors of the economy. He admired the creation in just 100 years of more massive and colossal productive forces than all the preceding generations had mustered.[56]

As a critic and a pioneer of new, critical social thought, however, Marx also asserted that capitalism would be transcended by a still higher form of society: socialism. Under socialism workers would be the ruling class, the means of production would be collectively owned, and economic planning would guide production and distribution.

Marx stressed the instability and wavering, uncertain growth of capitalism. He asserted that the accumulation of wealth (one of the central capitalist goals) must overcome both uncertainty and the tension of the opposing demands of labor and capital. According to Marx, capital yields profits because the value of labor is less than the value of the commodities produced with the labor. If a worker works for seven hours but uses only five hours to produce the value of his wage, then the worker is exploited because he or she works two surplus hours for the capitalist.[57] The continuous difficulty in getting the production factors in the right price is the potential source of perpetual crises that may continue until the economic system fails.[58]

The lust for profits, not inherent human need, allocates and directs labor in capitalism, Marx believed. Anything that yields profits is undertaken in the market, including the most useless or socially harmful activities. For Marx, the fundamental evil of capitalism is that it systematically prevents most individuals from achieving their potential as human beings, diminishing their capacity to give and receive love and thwarting and preventing their potential development. While capitalism increases society's capacity to produce, it decreases the ability to meet some basic human needs because capitalism's purpose is to increase material profit. The accumulation of wealth at one end is simultaneously the accumulation of misery at the other.[59]

Marx believed that the social nature of work is central to developing the social potential of human beings. If production were a cooperative venture among social equals, it would develop bonds of affection and mutual affirmation among people. In capitalism, however, the production process has the exact opposite effect on workers because it separates and isolates the human conditions of work from price and production decisions (alienation). In Marx's view, alienation is rooted in social structures that deny people their essential human nature. Applied to the workplace, it describes laborers who are divorced from their work and fellow workers. In Marx's view, production and products are determined in the market by profit calculations, not by human needs or aspirations. The result is degradation and dehumanization of the working class.

As Erich Fromm and others have pointed out, alienation is almost total in modern society. It pervades the relationship of individuals to their work, to the things they consume, to the state, to their fellow citizens, and to themselves. The consumption-hungry forces that govern people and make them helpless appear more drastically in social phenomena, including economic depressions and wars, that are presented as natural catastrophes but are really caused by people.[60] Inherent in the structure of modern capitalist production is the alienation between citizens, which results in the loss of social bonds. People experience themselves as things to be employed successfully in the market. Their sense of self stems not from their activity as loving and thinking individuals but from their socioeconomic roles.

This concern is central to social work practice. The alienating and profoundly unsatisfactory character of work results in a deep-seated, often unconscious hostility toward work and everything and everybody connected with it. Alienated people usually have deep anxiety and cannot be healthy. They experience themselves as things or investments to be manipulated by themselves and others. If the modern age has been rightly called the age of anxiety, it is primarily because of this anxiety engendered by the lack of self that threatens the sense of security. Anxiety creates a craving for mindless conformity that in turn may produce a continuous but hidden sense of insecurity.[61]

Socialist Critique of the Market Paradigm

Socialist approaches reject certain dysfunctions of capitalist markets, including erratic business cycles that cause waste, inefficiency, unemployment, poverty, depression, and economic stagnation. They also reject the promotion of competitive human relations, alienation, greed, materialism, and inequity. They argue that the generation of monopolies undermines consumer freedom. Inherently, the market tends to respond almost exclusively to higher-income consumers and giant corporations rather than to those with lower incomes. Socialists also challenge the classical capitalist model of circulatory flows (Figure 5-3) as inaccurate and a distortion of the reality of capitalism.[62]

Nonmarket theorists disagree that the two main components of the capitalist model (households and business) are what they appear to be, interact the way capitalist theorists suggest, and are equal in power. Rather than a same-level, horizontal division of society, they suggest that the household unit consists of a vertical hierarchy of social classes in the form of a pyramid divided into a small upper class of owners and a larger lower class of workers, including the working poor and the unemployed (see Figure 5-4).

Household and business units are not on the same footing, homogeneous, or equal in power. Classicists ignore class and sectoral conflict, (viewing Rockefellers and sharecroppers as households with equal power), while socialists say that households of different social classes have unequal power. General Motors and the corner grocery store are unequal.

Capitalists treat consumers as sovereign (their choices determining all variables) and equal in all social classes. For socialists, consumer preferences have little or no effect on prices and income distribution. Owners have more economic power than do workers, the working poor, or the unemployed since they own industries and receive profits, while workers work for industries but receive wages. Workers consume but

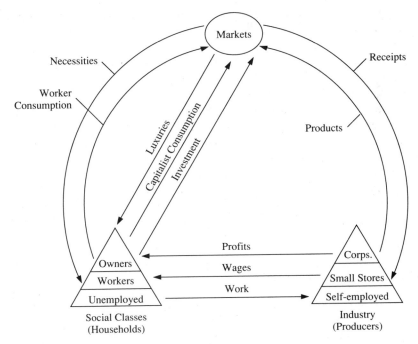

FIGURE 5-4 The socialist view of the market. From *Ideology in Social Science* by R. Blackburn (Ed.). Copyright © 1973 by Vintage Books.

rarely save. Owners consume and save in order to invest. Industry not only uses labor but also has access to resources such as land, mines, and so on. Total products are divided into "necessities," which are consumed by workers, "luxuries," which are consumed by the wealthy, and "new capital goods," which are installed in factories in return for investment payments.

In the socialist view wages are paid for work, but profits are not paid for anything. Since profit is not exchanged, there can be no equilibrium in the market model. While capitalists see consumers and firms (their interaction described by the model's equations), socialists are primarily interested in structure, in the patterns of dependence among established institutions, and in how the system holds together and works or fails to work. Rejecting that the distribution of wealth reflects technology or marginal productivity, socialists claim that ruling-class interests and the power of those who control the means of production determine prices and wages and therefore the distribution of income.

The issue, suggests socialists, is not where inflation originates, but how fast it proceeds in different markets.[63] The capitalist paradigm suggests that price increases in product markets are transmitted directly to factor markets and vice versa; unless costs and prices rise together, the circular flow cannot continue unimpeded. Socialists reject this paradigm. They believe that increases in costs and prices raise or lower profits in most cases. When wages rise faster than prices, there will be profit deflation; when prices rise faster than wages, profit inflation. Hence, inflation affects the distribution of income and thus aggregate demand and employment. Unequal inflation rates of wages and prices necessarily imply changes in the relative shares that go to capital and labor (Keynes). Inflation is partly a consequence of the ratio of demand to supply, but it also reflects relative market power. Here is where property confers advantages in setting prices and in bargaining for wages. How these advantages work is precisely the central question raised by socialists in their emphasis on distribution theory.

In the socialist view markets allocate scarce resources, income, and wealth not according to relative efficiency (the capitalist view) but according to economic power. This is why socialists exclude free markets from state control.

Socialist Socioeconomic Planning

Socialist planning is the socialist alternative to the free market in which the state and political decisions replace the market forces of supply, demand, and pricing.[64] The overall objectives of the plan are originally formulated by a state planning agency (JUCEPLAN in Cuba and GOSPLAN in the former Soviet Union).

The long-term overall plan is divided into one-year plans (specifying the output of major sectors of industry) and then is transmitted to various governmental ministries concerned with each sector of the economy for further analysis and recommendations. In Cuba, for example, the ministries include departments of sugar, transportation, and tobacco. This is the beginning of a complex planning process that in Cuba lasts one year and substitutes administration for the demand and supply forces of the free market.

The ministries refer the plans and their analyses further down the administrative line to their subdivisions in the provinces for further, more detailed analyses and recommendations. The downward process continues as the plan is submitted to large industrial plant units, enterprises, and their subunits. At each level and stage, the plan is broken down into its subsidiary components and subcomponents until finally the smallest production units are identified. Each enterprise thus has the demand objectives for the next year, specifying the output needed from the plant.[65]

Each plant, including health facilities, schools, and social service agencies, considers the various requirements of the plan. For example, they identify the labor force, space, tools, supplies, and equipment needed for achieving the demanded output. The process includes consultation with the representatives of workers, worker unions, and mass organizations in each plant. Then each plan transmits the supply requirements (and any changes in output) upward along the administrative hierarchy. Just as the demand is transmitted downward along the chain of command, the exigencies of supply flow upward, finally reaching the planning authority.

Based on the new information and recommendations, the planning agency reformulates the original output goals, makes plans for fulfilling the supply requirements, and adjusts its macroeconomic targets and policies. The entire plan is then approved by the government and is submitted for approval to the national assembly of the country to become law.[66]

The formulation, integration, and coordination of the overall plan is an exceedingly complicated task even when computer analysis techniques have simplified certain parts. The plan is a centralized, bureaucratic, inflexible, cumbersome, and mistake-prone undertaking that allows each local enterprise very little initiative or leeway. Each production unit must not only meet assigned production quotas but must overproduce. Bonuses, salaries, fringe benefits, and "profits" are tied directly to the overfulfillment of the plan. "Success indicators," including the number, weight, and length of the product to be produced, can easily be manipulated to distort the productive effort.[67]

Hence the idea of "profit" is introduced in countries of applied socialism: while prices (set by planners) cannot be manipulated by enterprises to create profits, each local enterprise can sell its output and buy its input rather than merely deliver or accept them. This way, enterprises are responsible to their consumers and consider their own needs when accepting supplies for production.

All profits belong to the state rather than to enterprises, individuals, or groups. But part of the profits can be allocated for bonuses, fringe benefits, and other rewards to the workers of the enterprise. This provides materialistic work incentives to increase efficiency and productivity. It is argued that this represents a combination of planning and market mechanisms, which does not undermine the socialist planning system.

Many of the motivating principles of the free market are increasingly being introduced in command economies not only to reduce excessively centralized social and political controls, but also to create some sense of freedom and choice and to increase efficiency, variety, productivity, and local autonomy in decision-making that command economies cannot provide. The effectiveness of such efforts is at best problematic as reflected in the recent collapse of the socialist economies in Central and Eastern Europe.

ECONOMIC DEMOCRATIZATION: IMPLICATIONS FOR THE WELFARE STATE AND SOCIAL WORK

The debate regarding the fairness of the capitalist market (and, by implication, the role of the state in guiding the market economy) characterizes early and modern forms of capitalism. In its unfettered form (without governmental intervention) the capitalist market generates unjust outcomes for citizens. Related to the issue of fairness is the problem of market dysfunction, such as inflation, unemployment, poverty, and recession, and the differential way these influence social classes. Economic markets may not be able to achieve continuous self-equilibrium and full employment without governmental intervention.

Dysfunction of an Unfettered Free Market

As a social institution, capitalism is inevitably connected both to the maximization of input and to democratic social and political forms. Relative to socialist economic planning, free markets tend to perform well in increasing output, but they can underperform in the just distribution of goods and services, in unemployment, and in poverty.

Advantages

The market system's fundamental advantage is that profitability guides the allocation of resources and labor. Profits under capitalism are not only a source of privileged income but an effective, versatile indicator of success for a system that aims to maximize its given input. Equally important, the market mechanism solves economic problems with a minimum of social and political control and central state bureaucracy. In contrast to central command socialist planning, free markets need no constant attention from central authorities: individual marketers can freely fulfill alone their public economic functions.

Problems

Free markets often fail in three major areas: common-interest services, including the welfare state and social services, that are excluded from their market concern; investments in human capital; macroeconomic ills (unemployment, inflation, poverty); and protecting the natural environment.

The market is an inefficient instrument for provisioning common-interest services such as education, public health, culture, welfare programs, and local governmental services to develop human resources. A market society buys such services by allocating a certain amount of taxes for these programs. Citizens tend to resent these taxes, in contrast with the items they voluntarily buy. A market society, therefore, can easily underallocate resources to common-interest services.

Another failing of the market system is its application of strictly economic, utilitarian logic to the satisfaction of human wants and needs. The market tends to serve the wealthy much more effectively than the poor. It creates the anomaly of a surplus of luxuries existing side by side with shortages of vital human needs. It pours energy and resources into the multiplication of luxuries for the wealthier classes while not meeting the more basic needs of the poor.

For example, the growing inequity of income and wealth among social classes in the United States has become a major issue in the past decade. While the per capita GNP in constant 1987 dollars expanded (more people entered the labor force) from $10,740 in 1980 to $12,287 in 1987, the weekly per-worker income was reduced from $366 in 1972 and $318 in 1980 to $312 in 1987.[68] While the poorest fifth of American households lost $2,834 in real income from 1972 to 1987 (almost two-thirds of this during the Reagan years), the income of the richest fifth expanded dramatically by more than $10,000 (over $8,000 of which occurred during the Reagan years).[69] Between 1977 and 1988 family income shifted similarly: The poorest decile had a net income loss of 14.8% while the top decile experienced a 16.5% gain (the top 1% experienced a 49.8% increase in income).[70]

The inequality of wealth (almost totally derived from the ownership of stocks, bonds, and capital goods) in the United States is even more lopsided than that of income (derived from jobs, rent, interest on savings, stock dividends, and transfer payments) alone: The top 1% of families own nearly one-fourth of all the net wealth, although they receive only 11% of all money income. The top 10% of families hold 70% of all the net wealth.[71] The number of very wealthy Americans also increased dramatically over the past decade (mainly in the Reagan years): from 600,000 millionaires in 1981 to 1.5 million in 1988; from 38,855 decamillionaires in 1982 to 100,000 in 1988; from 400 centimillionaires in 1982 to 1,200 in 1988; and from 13 billionaires in 1982 to 51 in 1988.[72]

In 1984, the Congressional Budget Office documented the impact of Reagan's tax and social policies. Families with incomes of less than $10,000 lost $390 a year. Tax cuts saved them $20, but reductions in social welfare programs cost them $410.[73] For wealthy families, those earning $80,000 or more, the Reagan-era policies were generous. As of 1984, they were saving $8,260 a year. Their tax bill decreased $8,390, whereas they lost $130 in social benefits.[74]

The third major category of market failures concerns the micro and macro ills that are consequences of its operations. Inflation, unemployment, poverty, and pollution are all mainly the products of the vital but careless, even dangerous, momentum that the market imparts to the social process.

To the extent that free markets promote amorality, triviality, commercialism, and social underdevelopment, they are both economic and moral failures. Without excessively centralized political and social controls, socialist economies tend to underperform free markets in ability to maximize input, but they can outperform free markets in common-interest services, investment in human resources, and more effective control of business cycles. While admired historically for maximization and productivity, the free market is also despised (even by its devoted supporters) for its aggression and its failure to distribute its abundance fairly. As Keynes noted in 1933:

> [Capitalism] is not a success. It is not intelligent, it is not beautiful, it is not just, it is not virtuous—and it does not deliver the goods. In short, we dislike it, and we are beginning to despise it. But when we wonder what to put in its place, we are extremely perplexed.[75]

Echoing a similar conviction, the National Conference of Catholic Bishops has called the level of poverty and unemployment in the United States a social and moral scandal and labeled the gaps between the incomes of the poor and rich morally unacceptable.[76]

Guiding the Free Economic Market

Although there is ideological debate regarding the nature and extent to which governmental intervention in the economic market is necessary or advisable, it is generally agreed that the state must provide social and merit (non-subsidized) goods to allow the market to function smoothly and to increase national well-being.[77] In providing public services, including education, welfare, justice, and defense, governments redistribute goods, services, and rights. The welfare state makes economic distributions fairer; for example, it raises the share of the national income that goes to the poor. If all income in a pure market economy were distributed according to each individual's output (or assets), several public services would atrophy and a large sector of the population, even entire regions, would become and remain destitute.

Conservative market theorists dispute the government's redistributive responsibility, prefer a minimal welfare state, and tax high-income families and corporate establishments only nominally. Liberal theorists advocate the opposite.

The debate also includes the sociopolitical implications of taxes, the government's choices between regressive and progressive taxes, and the burden placed upon the poor and the rich and on individuals, corporations, population groups, regions, and occupations. The selection of sources of taxation (family income tax, property tax, utility tax, sales tax, and turnpike tolls) and the priorities of taxation are also important issues in the debate.

Adherents of classical economic theory support little or no redistribution of market output, advise against taxing corporations and high-income groups, prefer regressive taxes (lower-income families paying proportionately more than higher-income families), advocate a minimal claim by the public sector on the private sector's output, and oppose public welfare transfers.

Not only must every citizen be self-sufficient, but the need for help is equated with personal failure rather than attributed to imperfections of the market. Classical economists tend, however, to object much less strenuously to state aid to banks and automobile makers or to subsidies to producers of certain goods if they are given to enhance market operations.

Liberals, on the other hand, support general taxes graduated according to means. Thus the rich should be taxed more progressively to offset economic imperfections from which they benefit most. They also support a more extensive welfare state and give top priority to the equitable distribution and redistribution of income and wealth as a right. Instead of from each according to ability, the motto becomes to each according to needs.

The government's responsibility to stabilize and guide the free market now becomes clearer. The economy experiences ups and downs that governments must stabilize through three budgetary approaches. Under full or nearly full employment and mostly stable prices, the economy can be stabilized by a balanced budget. In this case, the influence of fiscal operations on the aggregate demand level would be largely neutral. Under very high or full employment and inflation, the appropriate fiscal policy is a budgetary surplus. This will reduce the aggregate demand level and therefore will mitigate inflation. With low production and employment levels and a declining price level, a budgetary deficit is an appropriate fiscal policy to stimulate the economy. Keynesian economics are most effective under these conditions and strengthen the welfare state. The government's responsibility to stabilize the free market justifies its borrowing in recessions. Budgetary deficits would occur anyway, since tax collections automatically decline during recessions.

The maximization of input, common-interest services, the welfare state, and fairness are indispensable functions of modern governments.

A More Democratic and Fair Market: A Social Work View and Responsibility

Social workers increasingly appreciate that their interventions to improve individual behavior and societal conditions relate directly to the economy as a social institution and the expanded sociopolitical infrastructure that supports it. Social work's commitments to social justice, individual rights, empowerment of the powerless, and the elimination of poverty are also related to the marketplace. Even students who enter schools of social work with little knowledge of economics soon realize the direct, important connections between the economy and public social policy, between the economic market and the growth of the welfare state, and between the performance of the economy and the well-being of people, including their clients.

To bring about individual and social change, social workers must understand the interrelationship of economics and psychosocial function and dysfunction of economics and distributive justice, including freedom, human rights, and human and material resources; and of economics and sociopolitical orders in the context of social action. It is particularly important for social workers to note that because the economy consists fundamentally of people, its basic relationships are social. Since the interaction between households and businesses sets the economy's parameters, this classic economic model is essentially a social model of the economy.

The fundamental determinants of economic functions, progress, and justice are based on psychosocial relationships, including assumptions about what people are like, what they want, how they relate to each other, and how their aspirations are mobilized. Socioeconomic institutions shape relations between capitalists, workers, and other classes or groups of economic actors. Social relations define the role of the state in the economy and determine the modes of production.[78]

Although the democratization of economic institutions would yield enormous social dividends and would help prevent several psychosocial ills addressed in social work practice, social workers do not readily consider economic reform of the free market a vital component of their recommendations for reforming the institutions of society and the welfare state.

Reform of the economic market to serve human needs and social efficiency is a necessary and integral part of improving societal functions and the welfare state. Power relations—which are where the economic problems of poverty, deprivation, and injustice begin—are rooted in the economy and the goal of economic efficiency. Too often economic efficiency is used as an ideological weapon to defend the free market and its underlying values.

Basic social work values that serve human needs can guide the economic democratization of certain market imbalances. These principles include self-determination, self-government, fairness, participation of citizens in decisions that directly affect their lives, empowerment of the powerless, the provision of common-interest services for all people as a human right, the prevention of individual and social ills, and the actualization of every citizen's potential for growth and development.

The enormous waste of the free market system and the underdevelopment of people need not be. Now that the failure of right-wing economics is almost complete and President Clinton is developing more democratic policies, the present market system can be improved and democratized. It can become more responsive to human needs and less wasteful. Lowering taxes on the rich and businesses, attacking unions, and deregulating economic activities had the opposite effect. Not only did this not boost profits and investments but it increased this nation's social deficit and social underdevelopment.[79] The clearest example is in the areas of income distribution and poverty, where the gains that had been made in earlier decades were all but wiped out during the 1980s and early 1990s, reflecting the neoconservative vision of the economy.[80] President Clinton's administration includes a new awareness that the free market can be destructive as well as creative. There is a new awareness that poverty, health care, and environmental deterioration are problems and a new willingness to move the economy to serve human beings.

In contrast to an unfettered market, a more democratic and fair economy, based on a social work framework to serve human beings, can better guarantee the following to all citizens:

- Basic rights to an adequate economic livelihood and standard of living
- Effective participation of citizens in making economic decisions that affect their lives, discontinuing the economic dependence of workers on the whims of employers
- Adequate investment in human capital
- Fairness in the market between the economically powerful and powerless
- Significant reduction of micro and macro ills, including inflation, unemployment, recession, poverty, and environmental pollution.

Since we need to rely on economic regulation and income redistribution in a democratic market, the state and the welfare state are indispensable and crucial instruments. This should not lead to a blind faith in everything the government does. Like markets, governments often fail to achieve their desired results. Three areas seem central in any reform of the economic market:

- *Economic security.* In this area the fundamental policies for reform should include a real commitment to full employment, the right to a decent job, public jobs programs, higher minimum wages, family leave programs, lower interest rates, and a shorter standard workweek.
- *Democracy in the workplace.* Fundamental reform policies should also include a workers' bill of rights,[81] reform of the labor law to promote democratically functioning unions, plant-closing legislation, profit sharing, workers' cooperatives, and community enterprises.

• *Fairness in public priorities and services.* Reduced military spending and a national health insurance and services plan should also be included. Low-cost decent housing, expanded education for all, expanded public child care and community service centers, the equitable public allocation of resources, and increased tax rates on upper-income groups are also important ingredients of democratization.

Democracy that influences mainly the social and political domains and only marginally the economic market in free-market countries may be as dysfunctional as democracy that influences mainly economic markets and only marginally political domains and civil rights in countries of applied socialism. The democratization of the free market is a basic prerequisite for improving living standards and reforming the welfare state. Social workers' values and commitments and the welfare state should not be abandoned or compromised in the quest for economic revitalization. Rather, reform of the economic market is likely to advance fairness, democracy, common interests, and a better way of life.

Social workers should not assume that the democratization of the free market can be accomplished without strong and sustained reformist social movements. A new social consensus is needed to control uneven capitalist development and to bring about the necessary power-structure changes in the social, economic, and political institutions of society. The effort involves a distinct redistribution of power relations, particularly if the productive resources are to be owned by a wider range of people, if labor is to participate as a partner in production and in decisions of how to distribute profits, and if stability in the world economy is to be achieved via international cooperation rather than competition and antagonism.

Relatively few people at the top of the power pyramid are willing to lend a sympathetic ear to reformist pressures that center on the conflict over the shares of income and resources. Although the road ahead is not easy and the precise directions of change are still ambiguous, social workers should address the challenge of an economic policy that will secure basic material goods, freedom, and self-esteem for all citizens.

NOTES

1. D. Cohen, "Recession Forces States to Turn Budget Ax on Programs to Support Children, Families," *Education Week,* November 13, 1991, 1, 17.
2. L. Uchitelle, "Lots of Pressure to Fix the Economy, But Few Options," *New York Times,* November 24, 1991, sec. 4, 1.
3. *New York Times,* November 17, 1991, F15; and P. G. Gosselin, "As Economy Lags, Both Parties Split on Solutions," *Boston Globe,* November 21, 1991, 1.
4. Reuters, "Premier Says Lithuania Is Near Market Economy," *Boston Globe,* November 19, 1991, 10.
5. J. Fuerbringer, "Finland Startles Its Investors," *New York Times,* November 17, 1991, F15.
6. "Even Japan Is Slowing Down," *New York Times,* November 17, 1991, sec. 3, 1.
7. "British Standoffishness Softens," *New York Times,* November 17, 1991, sec. 3, 1.
8. Buenos Aires, "Argentina's Mr. Fix-It," *New York Times,* November 17, 1991, sec. 3, 12.
9. L. Uchitelle, "Trapped in the Impoverished Middle Class," *New York Times,* November 17, 1991, sec. 3, 1.

10. P. Passell, "Despite All the Talk of Tax Cuts, People Can Expect to Pay More," *New York Times,* November 17, 1991, 1.

11. M. Kranish, "From Bush Administration, Mixed Message on Economy," *Boston Globe,* November 18, 1991, 20.

12. M. F. Nolan, "Jerry Brown Lashes Out at Business," *Boston Globe,* November 26, 1991, 16.

13. "Bank Liability Limit is Fought in Senate," *Boston Globe,* November 19, 1991, 3.

14. P. B. Hernandes, "Domestic Violence on Rise in Mass.," *Boston Globe,* November 29, 1991, 1.

15. A. Etzioni, *The Moral Dimension: Toward a New Economics* (New York: The Free Press, 1988).

16. The *social* concept in social economy includes many other institutional relationships that transcend the boundaries of power and the state as political institutions.

17. Adam Smith, *The Wealth of Nations* (New York: Modern Library, 1947). Concepts of the beginning part of this section rely heavily on C. K. Wilber and K. P. Jameson, *Beyond Reaganomics* (Notre Dame, IN: University of Notre Dame Press, 1990), x, 10, 11.

18. Smith's concept of the division of labor describes the extreme separation of technical tasks in the production process through specialization. This occurs when production is broken up into a number of small specialized steps to increase workers' dexterity as they endlessly repeat one simple task, to reduce the time lost in shifting between tasks, and to simplify operations in a way that facilitates the introduction of machinery.

    In the social sciences the division of labor concept refers also to the social division of labor (differentiation in society as a whole) and to the sexual division of labor (social divisions between men and women). For Marx, the division of labor produced social conflict and was a primary cause of social-class inequity, private property, and alienation. Marx thought, however, that the technical division of labor was required in any industrial society (market or nonmarket). Supporters of Marx suggest that the extreme division of labor found in many firms serves only to increase the power of managers in the workplace. Comte and Durkeim thought that the division of labor in modern society has created a new social solidarity and a basis for social integration. Other commentators suggest that overspecialization may stunt the worker's personal development. See A. Comte, *The Positive Philosophy of Auguste Comte* (London: Bell, 1986); E. Durkeim, *The Division of Labor in Society* (Glencoe: Free Press, 1960).

19. The invisible-hand idea illustrates why the outcome of a market mechanism appears so orderly. After centuries of market experience, however, the scope and limitations of this doctrine are readily recognized: because of imperfect competition, instability, and other externalities, the market does not necessarily lead to the most efficient and equitable outcome for all.

20. The market mechanism thus imposes a discipline on its participants: Buyers must bid against other buyers and therefore cannot gang up against sellers; sellers must compete with other sellers and therefore cannot impose their will on buyers.

21. Historically, the continuous development of capitalism dates only from the 16th century and the growth of industrialization, although some of its commercial features were present in the preindustrial European economy. It came as a radical socioeconomic disruption that upset centuries-long routines of life and economic underdevelopment. One strategic external force that contributed to the breakup of medieval economic institutions was the increased volume of long-distance trade and the specialized industries that sprang up to serve it.

22. P. Lewis, in his article "Boom-and-Bust Theory Shines Like New," *New York Times,* October 17, 1982, E2, makes these points and questions whether the new industries, including microchips, biotechnology, and the development of new energy sources to replace oil,

will stimulate a fifth upturn. At the same time he notes that many policymakers dislike the Kondratieff theory because it implies that they have little ability to influence the future. See also N. Kondratieff, "The Long Waves in Economic Life," *Review of Economics and Statistics* 17:105–115 (1935); also reprinted in *Readings in Business Cycle Theory,* Philadelphia: Blakiston, 1944, 20–42); and G. Garvey, "Kondratieff's Theory of Long Cycles," *Review of Economics and Statistics* 25:204 (November, 1943).

23. The model in figure 5-3 is a modification and synthesis of diagrams that appear in textbooks of economics, including P. Samuelson and W. Nordhaus, *Economics,* 13th ed., (New York: McGraw-Hill, 1989); R. H. Leftwich and A. Sharp, *Economics of Social Issues,* 4th ed. (Dallas, TX: Business Publications, 1980); and E. V. Bowden, *Principles of Economics,* 4th ed. (Cincinnati: Southwestern Publishing, 1983). The elaboration of the model's concepts is also based on these sources.

24. Investments represent expenditures for domestic investment goods with money from savings (money not spent on consumption, taxes, or payments to foreigners for imported goods).

25. They believed that only insufficient demand would cause firms to curtail output, idle some machines, lay off workers, and not sell their total output.

26. Say claimed that because supply creates its own demand, there can be no unsold output (an insufficient demand to buy the entire output). If all output is sold, there can be no involuntary unemployment. Since people will spend their entire income, all output will be sold to consumers or investors. If temporary aberrations occur and savings exceed investment for a while, then competitive labor markets with flexible real wage rates will automatically restore equilibrium. When people are laid off, real wage rates decline until the demand and supply of labor equalize (unless they are prevented from doing so by the government, labor unions, or social reformers). For more on Jean Baptiste Say, see P. Samuelson and W. Nordhaus, *Economics,* 410–441 and E. V. Bowden, *Principles of Economics,* 176–177, 188.

27. *Frictional* unemployment is caused by the immobility of labor: the workers are not of the right sort or not in the right place. *Structural* unemployment in industries or localities is caused by a change of demand so great as to affect the main economic structure of the economy. *Cyclical* unemployment is caused by reductions in the aggregate demand for goods and services in the overall economy because of economic fluctuations.

28. Keynesian economics consist of the theories of macroeconomics initiated by John Maynard Keynes in the 1930s. Emphasis is on the determinants of total spending, especially the relationship between savings and investment and the importance of governmental withdrawals (taxes) and injections (expenditures). The propensity to consume, the income multiplier, and the effect of the marginal efficiency of capital and interest rates on investment decisions are all parts of Keynesian or "demand-side" economics. See P. Samuelson and W. Nordhaus, *Economics,* 47–48, 125–144; E. V. Bowden, *Principles of Economics,* 270–273; and R. Heilbroner and L. Thurow, *Economics Explained* (Englewood Cliffs, NJ: Prentice-Hall, 1982), 29–33.

29. Monetarists' views are rooted in classical tradition, that is, the body of economic thought that prevailed prior to the appearance in 1936 of J. M. Keynes' *General Theory of Employment, Interest, and Money* (New York: Harcourt Brace Jovanovich, 1965).

30. W. Winpisinger, "Growth and Employment," *Socialist Review* 75/76 (1984), 19–29.

31. Aggregate demand determines the speed of the economy, total production, and the quantity of production factors (labor, capital, land) that will be employed. Keynesian economics focuses on the rate of spending in the economy (understanding what motivates each sector to spend). Spending is what pulls forth the output and thus employment and income.

Therefore, public policies that change the level of spending in the economy will also change the level of employment, production, output, and income.

32. H. Brenner, who compared rates of employment and first-time admissions to mental hospitals over 127 years, documented how economic slumps and unemployment increase the incidence of murder, suicides, alcoholism, mental illness, infant mortality, and serious diseases. See M. H. Brenner, "Statement," *Cost of Unemployment Hearings before the Subcommittee on Domestic Monetary Policy of the Committee on Banking, Finance, and Urban Affairs, House of Representatives, 97th Congress, Second Session, August 12 and 17, 1982, Serial No. 97-85* (Washington, DC: U.S. Government Printing Office, 1982), 33–59. B. S. Brown, "The Impact of Political and Economic Changes upon Mental Health," *American Journal of Orthopsychiatry* 53 (October 1983), 583–592; M. Mahaffey, "Planning for Mental Health," *American Journal of Orthopsychiatry* 56 (January 1986), 4–13. See also the statement by H. Brenner in *Health and Other Effects of Unemployment,* Joint Hearing before the Committee on Labor and Human Resources, U.S. Senate, and the Subcommittee on Employment Opportunities of the Committee on Education and Labor, U.S. House of Representatives, 96th Congress, 2nd session, July 24, 1980 (Washington, DC: U.S. Government Printing Office, 1980); and H. Brenner, *Estimating the Social Costs of National Economic Policy* (Washington, DC: U.S. Government Printing Office, 1976).

33. M. Merva and R. Fowles, *Effects of Diminished Economic Opportunities on Social Stress: Heart Attacks, Strokes, and Crime* (Washington, DC: Economic Policy Institute, 1992).

34. Telephone interview with the Boston regional office of the U.S. Bureau of the Census, December 20, 1991, regarding unemployment data.

35. R. Pear, "Are There More of Those with Less?" *New York Times,* Nov. 27, 1983, E4.

36. Open market operations, the most frequently used tool, ease or tighten money in two different ways simultaneously: When the Fed buys bonds, it forces bond prices up and so pushes interest rates down. Simultaneously, new excess reserves are pushed into the banking system as the Fed pays for the bonds it bought. The opposite occurs when the Fed sells bonds.

37. When governmental expenditures exceed tax receipts, the government has three methods of financing: taxation, borrowing from the private sector, and creating money. These methods allow the public sector to borrow from the private sector.

38. Examples of governmental operations include the judicial system, national defense, police protection, education, health and welfare, and regulation of activities such as the generation and sale of electricity and natural gas, stock and bond sales, interstate transportation, and communications.

39. If all new governmental projects are delayed and selected ongoing projects are curtailed, the demand for labor and the other production factors will be reduced. Reduced governmental spending will release production factors so they can shift from the public to the private sector (relieving its shortages).

40. There are differences, however, between tax and debt financing. People have to pay taxes but do not have to buy government bonds. Tax financing pays for government bonds and services today, while debt financing pays over time. When the U.S. government uses deficit financing by selling bonds to the Fed, the money supply expands (possibly leading to inflation).

41. Editorial, "Bush Reads the Numbers . . . but Will He Create the Jobs?" *Boston Globe,* December 20, 1991, 22.

42. P. G. Roberts, "The Deficit: Coming to Terms with the Real Issues," *Business Week,* April 9, 1983, 13.

43. For more on transfer payments see, P. Samuelson and W. D. Nordhaus, *Economics,* 13th ed.; R. L. Heilbroner and L. C. Thurow, *Understanding Macroeconomics,* 5th ed. (Englewood Cliffs, NJ: Prentice-Hall, 1975).

44. K. Phillips, *The Politics of Rich and Poor* (New York: Random House, 1990), chap. 6.

45. For theories of income distribution, see H. Lyda, *The Structure of Earnings* (London: Oxford University Press, 1968); M. Reder, "A Partial Survey of the Theory of Income Size Distribution," in L. Sotow, ed., *Six Papers on the Size Distribution of Wealth and Income* (New York: National Bureau of Economic Research, 1969); J. Mincer, "The Distribution of Labor Incomes: A Survey," *Journal of Economic Literature,* 8:1 (March 1970), 1–26; and K. Bjerke, "Income and Wage Distributions: Part I: A Survey of the Literature," *Review of Income and Wealth* series 16, no. 3, (September 1970), 235–252. For theories of income determination, see J. T. Dunlop, "The Task of Contemporary Wage Theory," in Dunlop, ed., *The Theory of Wage Determination* (London: Macmillan, 1957); B. Fleisher, *Labor Economics: Theory and Evidence* (Englewood Cliffs, NJ: Prentice-Hall, 1970); and J. Hicks, *The Theory of Wages* (London: St. Martin's Press, 1964).

46. For human capital theory, see G. Becker, *The Economics of Discrimination* (Chicago: University of Chicago, 1957); G. Becker, *Human Capital* (New York: National Bureau of Economic Research, 1964); and G. Becker, *Human Capital and the Personal Distribution of Income* (Ann Arbor: University of Michigan Press, 1967).

47. G. S. Becker, "Crime and Punishment: An Economic Approach," *Journal of Political Economy* 76:2 (March/April 1968), 169–217; J. Mincer, "Labor Force Participation and Unemployment," in M.S. Gordon and R.A. Gordon, eds., *Prosperity and Unemployment* (New York: Wiley, 1966), 73–112; T.W. Schultz, *Human Capital: Policy Issues and Research Opportunities* (New York: National Bureau of Economic Research, 1979); "Investing in Poor People: An Economist's View," *American Economic Review,* 55(2) (May 1965); L. C. Thurow, *Investment in Human Capital* (Washington, DC: Brookings Institute, 1969); E. Denison, *The Sources of Economic Growth in the U.S. and the Alternatives Before Us* (New York: Committee for Economic Development, 1962).

48. For critiques of human capital theory, see P. Doeringer and M. J. Piore, *Internal Labor Markets and Manpower Analysis* (Lexington, MA: Heath, 1971); B. Harrison, "Education and Unemployment in an Urban Ghetto," in D. M. Gordon, ed., *Problems in Political Economy,* 2nd ed. (Lexington, MA: Heath, 1977), 252–263.

49. Educational attainment serves merely to identify preexisting differences in ability among individuals; ability is actually rewarded in markets. Education determines the best candidates for on-the-job training.

50. For dual-market theory, see M. J. Piore, "Public and Private Responsibility in On-the-job Training of Disadvantaged Workers," Working Paper (Cambridge, MA: Department of Economics, MIT, No. 23, June 1968); M. Piore, "On the Job Training in the Dual Labor Market," in A. Weber et al., *Public-private Manpower Policies* (Madison, WI: Industrial Research Association, 1969); D. M. Gordon, *Problems in Political Economy* (Lexington, MA: Heath, 1971); and B. Bluestone et al., *Low Wages and the Working Poor* (Ann Arbor: University of Michigan Press and Wayne State University Press, 1973).

51. For the neo-Marxist radical perspective, see R. C. Edwards et al., *The Capitalist System* (Englewood Cliffs, NJ: Prentice-Hall, 1978); R. J. Franklin and S. Resnik, *The Political Economy of Racism* (New York: Holt, Rinehart & Winston, 1974); D. M. Gordon, *Theories of Poverty and Underdevelopment* (Lexington, MA: Heath, 1972); and K. Stone, "The Origins of Job Structures in the Steel Industry," *Review of Radical Political Economics* (Summer, 1974), 117.

52. Other theorists have also contributed to the theory of capitalism, including Thomas R. Malthus (1766–1834), David Ricardo (1772–1823), John Stuart Mill (1806–1873), and Alfred Marshall (1842–1924), who is considered the founder of the neoclassical school of economic thought. The views of Max Weber (1864–1920) and their controversial political and social implications are also related to this debate. Weber emphasized the efficiency of industrial capitalism and its rational institutional and spiritual character. He believed that the acceptance of the Protestant ethic and the reinvestment rather than the consumption of capital eased the way to the organization of free labor (in contrast to medieval Catholicism, which presented obstacles to capitalist ideology and development and was hostile to material wealth) and provided justification for capitalism, making the capitalist system and inequality tolerable to the working class. See M. Weber, *Economy and Society* (New York: Bedminster Press, 1968) and M. Weber, *The Protestant Ethic and the Spirit of Capitalism* (London: Allen and Unwin, 1930). For Adam Smith, John Maynard Keynes, and Karl Marx, see E. V. Bowden, *Economic Evolution* (Cincinnati: Southwestern Publishing, 1985); R. Heilbroner and L. Thurow, *Economics Explained* (Englewood Cliffs, NJ: Prentice-Hall, 1982); and B. Caravan, *Economics for Beginners* (New York: Pantheon Books, 1983).

53. For Marx's analysis, including the complicated process through which surplus value is squeezed out of workers, see R. L. Heilbroner, *Marxism For and Against* (New York: Norton, 1980), and E. K. Hunt and H. J. Sherman, *Economics* (New York: Harper & Row, 1981).

54. First associated with G. Hegel and later developed by Engels, this doctrine later became part of the wider notion of historical materialism. Dialectics denotes the view that development depends on the clash of contradictions to create a new, more advanced synthesis. Marx used this concept to account for social and historical events, while Engels applied it also to natural domains.

55. For Marx's views see Rivs, *Marx for Beginners* (New York: Pantheon, 1976), and V. Adoratsky, ed., *Karl Marx: Selected Works* (London: Lawrence and Wishart Limited, 1943).

56. J. G. Gurley, *Challenges to Capitalism, 2nd ed.* (New York: Norton, 1979), 8.

57. For details, see E. K. Hunt and H. J. Sherman, *Economics*.

58. With each crisis, small firms go bankrupt and their assets are bought up by surviving firms; hence, the size of firms will steadily increase as the consequence of recurrent crises. In the process, the class struggle intensifies as a result of the proletarianization of the labor force, and the social structure is reduced to two classes: a small group of powerful capitalists, and a large mass of embittered workers.

59. K. Marx, *Capital* (Moscow: Foreign Language Publication House, 1961).

60. E. Fromm, *Marx's Concept of Man* (New York: Ungar, 1971).

61. Based on E. Fromm, *The Sane Society* (New York: Holt, Rinehart & Winston, 1955), chaps. 4 and 5.

62. This critique and several of the socialist arguments in this section are based on R. Blackburn, ed., *Ideology in Social Science: Readings in Critical Theory* (New York: Vintage Books, 1973), 76–95; R. Heilbroner and L. Thurow, *Economics Explained*, 23–29.

63. The standard approach is to distinguish demand-pull inflation (originating in final goods markets) from cost-push inflation (originating in factor markets).

64. For socialist central planning see M. Ellman, *Socialist Planning* (New York: Cambridge University Press, 1979).

65. See P. Brenner et al., eds., *Cuba Reader* (New York: Grove Press, 1989).

66. This section is based on the author's interviews with economic planners of JUCEPLAN in Havana, Cuba, completed during annual 15-day field work trips with his graduate students between 1975 and 1992. See D. Iatridis, *Cuba's Socioeconomic Developmental Model* (Chestnut Hill, MA: Boston College Graduate School of Social Work and Department

of University Audiovisual Services, 1987), videorecording; D. Iatridis, "Cuba's Health Care Policy: Prevention and Active Community Participation," *Social Work* 35:1 (1990), 29–35; D. Iatridis, *Health Care in Cuba* (Chestnut Hill, MA: Boston College Graduate School of Social Work, 1988), videorecording; and D. Iatridis, *China's Socialist Model* (Chestnut Hill, MA: Boston College Graduate School of Social Work and Department of University Audiovisual Services, 1988), videorecording.

67. J. M. del Aguila, *Cuba: Dilemmas of a Revolution* (London: Westview Press, 1988).
68. Phillips, *The Politics of Rich and Poor,* chap. 1.
69. D. Brown, *The Rich Get Richer* (Chicago: Nelson-Hall, 1991), 190–191.
70. Phillips, *The Politics of Rich and Poor,* 16–17.
71. Brown, *The Rich Get Richer,* 6–9.
72. Phillips, *The Politics of Rich and Poor,* table, 157.
73. "Reverse Robin Hood," *Boston Globe,* April 5, 1984.
74. Ibid.
75. J. M. Keynes, "National Self-Sufficiency," *The New Statesman and Nation,* July 8, 1933, 36–37, and July 15, 1933, 65–67, and *Yale Review* (Summer 1933); and F. Ackerman, *Hazardous to Our Health* (Boston: South End Press, 1984), 157. Today, the failure of communism in Eastern Europe and the self-destruction of the USSR make Keynes's bewilderment even more perplexing.
76. *Economic Justice for All: Pastoral Letter on Catholic Social Teaching and the U.S. Economy* (Washington, DC: National Conference of Catholic Bishops, 1986).
77. The debate focuses not only on the advisability of a hands-off state as a precondition for a healthy economy but equally on the social relations involved in modern capitalist production. Are inequities in income and wealth that are generated by the market just or unjust returns? Is it fair that the capitalist economy denies employees ownership and control of the instruments of economic productivity? Is it just that employees are subordinate to those who own and control these instruments?
78. These socioeconomic institutions that operate in a given economy are crucial forces that shape the long-term evolution of the economy. See S. Bowles, D. M. Gordon, and T. and E. Weisskopf, *After the Waste Land: A Democratic Economics for the Year 2000* (Armonk, NY: M. E. Sharp, 1990), 7, 8. These authors suggest that when these institutions (which they call the "Social Structure of Accumulation") operate smoothly and in a manner favorable to capital, capitalists will promote investments in the expansion of the economy. If, however, these social institutions make production less profitable, capitalists will slow down production and thus slow down economic growth. Thus they attribute the origin of the recent economic crisis to "the challenges to capitalist control."
79. D. Iatridis, "New Social Deficit: Neoconservatism's Policy of Social Underdevelopment," *Social Work* 33 (January/February 1988), 11–15.
80. C. K. Wilber and K. P. Jameson, *Beyond Reagonomics: A Further Inquiry into the Poverty of Economics* (Notre Dame, IN: University of Notre Dame Press, 1990).
81. Bowles, Gordon, and Weisskopf, in *After the Waste Land,* developed this theme in depth. This section reflects some of their recommendations.

CHAPTER 6

The Welfare State
in the Context of Social Economy

"As funds for welfare shrink, ideas flourish. Nobody likes welfare, and this year it shows. Across the country, officials are unveiling proposals to pay the poor less, work them more, and coerce or cajole them into families with fewer children and a father at home."[1]

"Cuomo seeks $1b cut in welfare, elimination of 6,200 state jobs."[2]

"Weld again to ask cuts in welfare, insurance."[3]

"New Jersey ends welfare aid for extra children."[4]

"President Bush . . . has denounced Lyndon B. Johnson's Great Society. . . . Bush, saying the Great Society backfired, wants a good society."[5]

"Justices to hear Pennsylvania abortion case."[6]

"Today, Kennedy is scheduled to move a second controversial bill—a measure designed to cap health care costs and extend medical insurance to 35 million uninsured U.S. workers—out of the Labor and Human Resources Committee, of which he is chairman."[7]

"Heart risk called greater for singles, poor."[8]

"Rights group calls on U.S. to relent on Haitians."[9]

"Bush to retool jobs program."[10]

"U.S. admits to improper waste disposal. At least several million pounds of radioactive wastes have been improperly shipped from federal nuclear weapon facilities to commercial waste treatment plants to be burned, the Energy Department acknowledged yesterday."[11]

"Papal encyclical urges capitalism to shed injustices. Human needs stressed. . . . 'The free market is the most efficient instrument for utilizing resources and effectively responding to needs,' the Pope said. 'But there are many human needs which find no place on the market . . . and many people without the purchasing power to meet their needs through the market.'"[12]

"A G.O.P. leader aims at 'welfare state' values. Representative Newt Gingrich of Georgia . . . has laid down a confrontational approach . . . by pledging to spend the year battling the 'welfare state'. . . . The Republican whip promised one specific legislative step: an effort to build more prisons."[13]

THE SOCIETAL
CONTEXT OF THE WELFARE STATE

Why the nationwide cuts in social welfare when the welfare state has been accepted and embedded in the social fabric of many nations? Why the attack on the welfare state, the poor, the homeless, and the disadvantaged? Why the increasing underinvestment in social development and human capital programs—health, education, jobs, training, housing, cities, safety, and security? Why does the new political right attack the Great Society and its civil rights components? Why do neoconservatives claim that the welfare state makes poor people dependent on government?

These issues are not driven only by current economic problems and limitations in economic resources. Certainly, welfare caseloads are up, coffers are nearly empty, and deficit-ridden state governments are looking for places to tinker and cut. But beyond the immediate budget-driven pressures, there is something more enduring under way in the welfare states of modern societies. What motivates a government simply to cut social welfare checks, add work requirements, and mix carrots and sticks to reform the poor and guide them into smaller and more stable families?

Answers to these and similar questions vary among contending ideologies and theoretical approaches with different fundamental views of the relationships among the welfare state, democratic institutions, and the structure of advanced capitalism.

THE WELFARE STATE
IN INDUSTRIAL COUNTRIES
An Expanding Role

The modern welfare state has emerged as a vital, central, and viable societal institution that regularly absorbs a significant part of the gross national product (GNP) of modern industrial nations. It represents an average of 20–25% of the GNP in countries of the industrial West, including Western Europe and North America, and represented 40–45% of the GNP in industrial countries of Central and Eastern Europe before the collapse of the state collectivist systems of welfare. Together, the industrial East and West have a total population of 1.06 billion. If the estimate of GNP invested in the welfare state is correct, the international annual investment in welfare states reached approximately $1.8 trillion in Western Europe and $1.4 trillion in Eastern Europe, or a total of $3.2 trillion in 1990.[14]

In the United States the total annual expenditure for public social welfare rose from 2.4% of the GNP in 1890 to 13% in 1967, to 20.2% in 1981, and to 18.6% in 1989.[15] Since 1975 governmental expenditures in social welfare represent more than half of government outlays (see Table 6-1).

TABLE 6-1   Public social welfare expenditures, 1970–1989

Year	Total (in billions of dollars)	% of GNP	% of government outlays
1970	146	14.7	46.5
1975	289	19.0	56.6
1980	492	18.4	57.1
1985	731	18.5	52.2
1987	833	18.8	53.4
1988	886	18.5	52.8
1989	956	18.6	53.0

SOURCE: U.S. Department of Commerce, Economics, and Statistics Administration, Bureau of the Census, *Statistical Abstract of the United States 1992, The National Data Book,* 112th ed. (Washington, DC: U.S. Government Printing Office, 1992), table 562, p. 356.

TABLE 6-2   Public social welfare expenditures, selected programs and fiscal years

	1980	1985	1989
Social insurance	8.6	9.4	9.1
Public aid	2.7	2.5	2.5
Health and medical programs	1.0	1.0	1.1
Veteran's programs	.8	.7	.6
Education	4.5	4.4	4.7
Other social welfare	.5	.3	.3
All health and medical care	3.8	4.3	4.7

SOURCE: *Social Security Bulletin,* 55:2 (Summer 1992), table 2, p. 65.

Total expenditures for social welfare amounted to $955.9 billion in fiscal year 1989 or 53.0% of total government outlays.

Social insurance programs accounted for about one-half of all social welfare expenditures, followed by the education and public aid categories. Public aid is almost four times less than social insurance (see Table 6-2).

Housing is included in Table 6-1 but not shown separately in Table 6-2. "All health and medical care" combines "health and medical programs" with medical services provided under the social insurance, public aid, veterans', and "other social welfare" categories.

The debate is no longer whether there will be a welfare state but what should be its nature, scope, structure, and cost. The debate, central and crucial to the future of the welfare state, involves unprecedented amounts of investment and concerns the well-being of over one billion people. The welfare state as an integral part of modern society's structure is a complex product of a wide range of society's institutions and value systems. The broader environment of a social economy restrains or maximizes the welfare state, including its antipoverty strategies and the expansion of state-provided social services (see Figure 6-1). Social workers recognize that the welfare state is a function of society's social, economic, and political arrangements and its institutional democratic base. Efforts to decrease or eliminate poverty and expand social

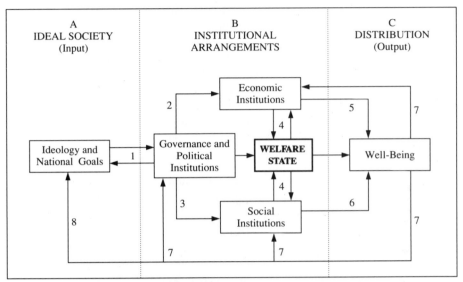

FIGURE 6-1   The welfare state in the social policy context

welfare provisions depend largely on the parameters of the social economy that shape the welfare state.[16]

In this context, a central policy issue is whether the welfare state is compatible with a healthy market-based economy and its ideology. Most of the current debate about poverty, health care, and social development centers on the relation between the market-based economy and the need for the welfare state.[17] President Clinton's effort to reform health care is systematically linked to the national deficit and the recovery of the economy.

Causal Societal Forces

Industrialization, Urbanization, and Nation-States

The emergence of the welfare state is associated with large-scale industrialization, the rapid growth of the population, and urbanization. It is also related to the expansion of nation-states, modernization, and the centralization of governmental power. The first two factors are associated with the welfare state because they generated the decline in agricultural employment and the rural population. They are related to the rapid increase of urbanization and the urban working class and the crises and dilemmas of involuntary unemployment. Population and urbanization relate to long-term economic growth, the changing patterns of family and community life, and the separation of home and workplace.

Most importantly, the rise of the welfare state is associated with the increasing prominence of certain population groups who are separated from the labor force and income. They include retirees, children, and the disabled. The excessive hardships inflicted by early industrialization on the working class, including women and children, also contributed to the growth of the welfare state. They provided a moral, humanitarian justification for its existence in capitalist markets.

Related to industrialization and urbanization is the growth of nation-states. This development centralized governmental powers and generated new governmental functions and structures, including responsibility for internal and social security and the creation of permanent civil services. The new governmental tasks included modernizing infrastructures, managing and coordinating industrial growth and commerce, and research for technological and communications growth. In this sense, some commentators view the welfare state as a product of the needs of the industrial capitalist society.[18]

Political Transformation

Some commentators see the extension of democratic movements, democratic institutions, and the democratic base of society as central to the emergence of the welfare state. They view the modern world as the product of a political revolution that included the rapid expansion of suffrage in the early 20th century, which transformed the population from subjects to citizens. The welfare state is the product of social and political mobilization emanating from mass democracies and expanding capitalist economies. This view associates the emergence of the welfare state with the institutionalization of social reform regarding civil, social, and political rights. It also relates the welfare state to the mobilization of the emergent working class and its effective incorporation into political life. Notably, in the context of an accommodation among competing social classes, this view emphasizes the role of the welfare state in implementing the social concessions made to the working class.

In brief, the welfare state is seen as a product of the expansion of legal citizenship, the extension of the franchise, the development of democratic institutions and political parties, and the accommodation of conflicts among social classes in a market economy.[19]

The Needs of the Free Market and Keynesian Macroeconomics

Other commentators associate the welfare state with the inherent characteristics of capitalist markets. They link the welfare state rationale with Keynesian economics and the need of the free market to be regulated by forces outside the economy. The failure of classical and neoclassical analyses to provide solutions opened the door to new economic views. The traditional belief that economic problems are best solved by benign governmental neglect was undermined by the Great Depression of the 1930s and the crucial problem of equality of opportunity.

Keynes proposed that since laissez-faire markets are inherently unstable, involuntary unemployment will occur unless the state initiates activist and interventionist economic policies. Convinced that the neoclassical belief in a self-regulating market that secures full employment is unfounded,[20] Keynes introduced a new macroeconomics concept: Economic equilibrium at full employment can be secured only outside the market by the state's management of macroeconomics. Appropriate governmental fiscal interventions, consisting primarily of public expenditures and taxation, could increase aggregate demand and overcome any unemployment caused by deficient aggregate demand.

Keynes observed that spending induces production, employment, and national income. *National income* includes the total of wages, salaries, profits, rents, commissions, royalties; it includes the net value of output, the flow of spending, and the volume of income. With this in mind, Keynes tried to explain why the flow of spending fluctuates. In the older framework of economic theory, market forces automatically kept the economy at full employment. But 16 depressions between 1870 and 1929, before the Great Depression, were an embarrassing discrepancy between classic theory and facts. In place of self-correcting, automatic adjustments to keep the economy at full employment, Keynes proposed a new theory of economics: Only forceful, vigilant governmental intervention could replace recurring depression and inflation with full employment and stable economic growth.

The Keynesian view of a managed economy provided a fundamental rationale for the emergence and growth of the welfare state without challenging the hegemony of private capital or the notion of a free economic market. Government expenditures for the welfare state stimulate production, augment the national income, and increase human capital investments. By spending money for the welfare state in a recession, governments can help the economy recover. Even if this governmental expenditure creates a budget deficit, the economic recovery will create budget surpluses that will offset the prior deficits. Thus, spending for the welfare state is beneficial rather than detrimental to the recessed economy. In this view, public expenditures for social welfare should increase rather than shrink at times of economic recession. This also makes sense because social welfare needs tend to increase at times of unemployment.

Thus, a wide range of social policies that were considered vices in classical and neoclassical economics suddenly became virtues in Keynesian economic and social welfare. The Keynesian view justifies and stimulates the expansion of social welfare income transfers to the poor and the redistribution of income, power, and services. It includes the expansion of social insurance and unemployment compensation, governmental creation of new jobs, and more adequate wages for workers. It also justifies in economic terms the compensation of those who suffer unduly from market dysfunctions. Keynesian philosophy, based on political control of economic life, justifies national strategies to fight poverty with a strong welfare state in the Western world.[21]

The origins of the welfare state, including the modern American, Danish, and Swedish welfare states, were, in part, responses to the Great Depression and Keynesian economics. In the United States the Social Security Act of 1935, the New Deal, the Employment Act of 1946, the New Frontier, and the Great Society policies and programs were applications of the Keynesian welfare state. The welfare state tries to correct the limitations inherent in the market economy. The 1946 Employment Act for example, committed the federal government to an activist economic policy and created a three-member Council of Economic Advisers to help the president achieve full employment and stable prices along with rapid economic growth and an equilibrium in the balance of payments.

But since 1975 Keynesian economics have been challenged.[22] Too often forecasts of macroeconomic models had failed, including those developed by the Federal Reserve, the Brookings Institution, the Massachusetts Institute of Technology (MIT), the University of Michigan, and the Wharton School of Finance. The goals of achieving full employment and of avoiding inflation dominated the political controversy, particularly in the 1970s. More importantly, Keynesian theory was attacked by Reaganomics in the 1970s and 1980s.

The dogma of the new political Right urged the return to classical capitalism, the reduction of government in economic matters, and the shrinking of the welfare state under the pretext of inflation and recession. Reaganomics could not be implemented, however, without first discrediting Keynesian economics. As a result, a lively controversy developed among economists and politicians on what model and economic approach best capture the nature of the economy and indicate what government should do to achieve real growth in the GNP, low unemployment, or low inflation.

Keynesian economists, including Nobel Prize winners James Tobin of Yale University and Paul Samuelson of MIT, have taken up the challenge and provided new insights regarding the Keynesian forecasting of economic behavior in the 1970s.[23]

THE CAPITALIST MARKET–WELFARE STATE LINK: OXYMORON OR SYMBIOSIS?

Symbiosis of the Market and the Welfare State

Some commentators believe that the welfare state is not only a necessary but also a harmonious component of developed capitalist economies. They argue that welfare state institutionalization in modern capitalist societies is caused by the needs inherent in the structure of the economic market in advanced industrialization, urbanization, and modernization. This harmony also represents the completion of the centuries-long reform movements for full and equal citizenship and for democratic institutions that encourage society to be fairer and more egalitarian. In brief, the welfare state is necessary because it tames the brute forces of industrialization, urbanization, and the free market while it enhances fairness and justice.[24]

The consensus that the welfare state is indispensable to a developed capitalist economy is associated with certain periods of the 20th century, most notably the reconstruction and economic development of Europe after World War II. At that time the economy and the welfare state expanded simultaneously, supported by strong public opinion. The distinct goal after World War II was to reconstruct society on social justice and equality. This also served as the justification of the unprecedented sacrifices and loss of life during World War II. The rapidly expanding economy immediately after the war created an environment of confidence that the market and the welfare state are complementary and symbiotic.

An Oxymoron

Some commentators, however, believe the welfare state to be incompatible with the principles and practices of any form of capitalism. They argue that the welfare state and its continuously increasing cost undermine the fundamental premises of liberal societies that were established in the 17th and 18th centuries. They contend that any further growth in the cost of the welfare state is not only unpopular but undermines the internationalization and deregulation of the modern world economy. Most important, they believe that the simultaneous expansion of the economy and the welfare state is almost impossible because economic growth can be restored and maintained only by draconian cuts in the Keynesian welfare state.[25]

Supporters of this view point out that with certain exceptions, notably after World War II, the history of capitalism reflects a long trend of thought that the capitalist economic organization is incompatible with the state provision of social welfare. Classical and neoclassical economists, including Smith, Senior, Malthus, Ricardo, Marx, and Friedman, and commentators on the new political Right argue that the harmonious existence of the welfare state in capitalist markets is an oxymoron.[26]

Symbiosis and Oxymoron

The relationship between the market economy and the welfare state is inherently both symbiotic and antithetical. Rather than being the product of a single force (the economic market), the expansion of the welfare state seems historically to be the combined outcome of several revolutionary changes that transformed traditional ways of life to their modern social, economic, technological, and political forms. These changes include the industrial and political revolutions of the 18th century, the extension of democracy in the late 19th and early 20th centuries, the Keynesian revolution of the mid-20th century, the ideology associated with the reconstruction after World War II, the end of the cold war, and the economic crisis of the 1970s, 1980s, and early 1990s.

Historically, for two centuries up to the early 1930s, economic activities and economic decisions were the exclusive province of individuals. Governmental intervention on the economic scene was practically unknown in "pure" capitalism. Governments confined themselves to the protection of property and the enforcement of contracts, except when industrialists demanded and got tariffs, special subsidies, or other benefits. Pragmatically, government moved onto the economic scene as monitor, decision-maker, and regulator in the 1930s. Recurrent economic instability, individual insecurity, and gross inequities, among other serious problems of "pure" capitalism, opened the door to the new roles of government.

In the United States the welfare state expanded during the Great Depression under the pioneering leadership of President F.D. Roosevelt. He asserted that government should administer the economy by making central decisions on economic matters of collective interest. The shift in the locus of economic power provoked businesses; but Democrats and Republicans in the United States, and Conservatives and Labourites in the United Kingdom, accepted the transition and the fundamental premise of the welfare state. In nearly every country of the West government and private enterprise learned to function together in peaceful symbiosis. Economic balance, economic justice, and economic growth became associated with the objectives of the welfare state.

The economic market, the government, and the welfare state worked in consonance to achieve development objectives for society and social progress. Political ideologies, democratic or anarchist, fascist or communist, supported this balance, justice, and growth as each one saw it. The deliberate attempt to deal with societal development problems through the use of public funds and the exercise of public regulation became one of the attributes of the welfare state. The affluence of the 1950s and the 1960s undoubtedly reinforced the positive perceptions of the welfare state. But in the 1970s, 1980s, and early 1990s the welfare state lost support as neoconservatism dominated the political agenda.

Historically, these developments include both symbiotic and antithetical elements in the relation between the economic market and the welfare state. When the blueprint of classical capitalism prevails, profits dictate economic decisions, and the government is supposed to stay out of economic affairs. The welfare state is likely to shrink under this ideology. In the liberal and radical tradition, government guides the economy toward the national goals of socioeconomic stability, justice, and growth. The welfare state is likely to expand under this ideology. Dominant political values determine conservative or progressive perceptions about the economic market. Conservative perceptions of the market and traditional value systems tend to emphasize the antithesis between the welfare state and the market. In contrast, liberal perceptions of the market and liberal value systems tend to emphasize the symbiosis between the two. Socialist perceptions tend to emphasize a strong government and a central welfare state to achieve humanitarian values.

THE CENTRALITY OF
VALUES AND POLITICAL IDEOLOGIES

The prevailing value system and political ideologies in society influence the specific relation between the economic market and the welfare state. At the epicenter are differential assumptions about the role of government and its relation to the individual. For example, conservative values have become largely an admonition to protect the status quo and make political changes slowly. Liberal values have become primarily a skeptical and wary attitude toward government. Socialist values have become essentially an effort to employ government to achieve egalitarian and humanitarian ideals. Values and ideologies form the base upon which the welfare state is built.

Classic conservatism assumes that individuals are basically evil, but their nature can be overcome by will. Individuals are responsible for their own success or failure to acquire material prosperity through hard work. By implication, the successful are "good" and the unsuccessful "bad." The conservative philosophy assumes that society's primary responsibility is the maintenance of law and order to enable prosperity. Failing or deviant individuals deserve not governmental help but only limited rehabilitation to spur self-help.

Liberal assumptions view individuals as fallible but having also the potential and ability to act with courage and unselfishness. Individuals can be hampered by external circumstances not under their own control. Liberal philosophy says that society and government can influence these environmental circumstances to improve both individuals and society.

The classic conservative position is the least likely to promote the welfare state. Individuals are viewed as totally responsible for their actions, although they can change if they have the will and moral character. Hence, social welfare becomes primarily a matter of providing rewards and punishments to induce the reform of the individual. In contrast, the liberal position accepts individual vulnerability and frees individuals from being totally responsible for their situations. It encourages society to provide some help to individuals, particularly in areas that involve external circumstances beyond individual control such as unemployment, childhood relations, health, and education. Thus social welfare also focuses on public policy issues of social organization.

The welfare state's concern with problems of individuals, public issues of social structure, and the interaction between the two is reinforced by the professionalization of the helping professions. Social workers, psychologists, and psychiatrists help individuals in the context of the social environment. The welfare state deals both with individual problems and public issues. Individual problems occur within the individual and his or her immediate relations with others. Values cherished by an individual are felt to be threatened. Public policy issues have to do with the institutional organization of society as a whole and its influence on individual behavior. Values cherished by the public and collectives are felt to be threatened. Social workers understand the linkages among a great variety of milieux, both of individual and public issues.

POLITICAL PERSPECTIVES
AND THE WELFARE STATE

Values and assumptions about the individual and society are embedded in political perspectives about the welfare state.

Traditional Conservative Views

Traditional thinking maintains that the chief threat to individual liberty is the government and its programs, including the welfare state. The surest road to progress, along with the best protection of liberty, is to rely on individual initiatives within the context of a free-market economy. Social welfare can best be secured, in this utilitarian view, by maximizing the sum of individual welfares, that is, by freeing individuals to pursue their own economic interests without external restraints by the state, including social welfare.

Governments have no responsibility to provide relief from destitution other than generalized welfare. Work and work incentives are crucial in healthy market economies. Therefore, to the extent that the welfare state reduces work incentives and creates poverty, it is both antithetical to the free market and a threat to individual liberty and to economic growth. Without the compulsion or the incentive to work (both of which are reduced by guaranteed social welfare), an efficient market economy is problematic. The traditional philosophy fears that with guaranteed social welfare, some individuals would enjoy idle living at the expense of the productive workers of society; the economy would in turn be undermined and in the long run society would be ruined.

Although not readily admitted or emphasized by supporters of this view, the poor are useful to the market economy; they foster economic growth. Poverty is a strong incentive to work in order to survive. It permits low or poverty-level wages through competition and unemployment. It increases the business profits because low wages reduce production costs. Poverty also helps the market to recover from recession because businesses expand when wages are low and hire more workers.

If the welfare state prevents or reduces poverty, it undermines the free market. Both Malthus and Ricardo noted the usefulness of poverty in capitalist markets, concluding that widespread poverty contributes to capitalist economic growth. Ricardo's Iron Law of Wages states that wages in free markets cannot rise above the subsistence level. He also formulated the Differential Rent theory, which explained why the market favors landowners. Both theories are pessimistic about the future welfare of most people. They view the economic deck as stacked in favor of capital owners and against everyone else.[27] Clearly, the welfare state upsets this status quo.

The New Political Right: Reaganomics

In this traditional context, modern neoconservatives see the government as an enemy of individual liberty. However, the threat to liberty from the power of large corporations does not arouse their concern. They believe that the corporate world can provide a healthy market and economic recovery. Neoconservatives view entrepreneurs as the heroes of modern capitalism, the social class that governments must support.[28]

Advocates of Reaganomics assert that complex economic problems, including stagflation (economic stagnation with inflation), arise from governmental intervention in the economy. Their solution is to remove government interference and return to unbridled individual freedom.[29] Using the traditional political slogan of austerity, Reaganomics in the 1980s and early 1990s proposed a simplistic solution to the problem of low growth and high unemployment: the supply-side effects of tax cuts to end inflation without lowering growth and employment.[30]

Neoconservatives in other parts of the world, including Thatcherists in the United Kingdom, followers of Friedrich Hayek, and former French Prime Minister Raymond Barre, argued along similar lines against the welfare state. Opponents of the Keynesian philosophy argued for the values of capitalism and against the ideology of the welfare state. Their view has been used to justify budgetary cuts and reductions in social welfare programs as a means to revitalize the economic market.

Neoconservative commentators in the United States, including George Gilder and Charles Murray, press for the reduction of the welfare state and for traditional conservative values. They refer to their views about the individual and the state as "Popular Wisdom;" they refer to the welfare state as "Elite Wisdom."[31] They say that Elite Wisdom promotes the concept that poverty is the fault of the system, not the individual, and that structural poverty should be overcome by welfare state programs. In contrast, Popular Wisdom calls for eliminating or reducing the welfare state because it conflicts with the development of the capitalist market.

Neoconservatives see the welfare state as immoral, unjust, and subversive of the market ethic. Poverty is the individual's fault, so the individual must overcome it. Governments should only provide a small dole and let the private sector aid the poor. Neoconservatives believe that in freeing the poor from responsibility for their own circumstances, the welfare state alters their lives for the worse. Welfare and social security encourage the very behavior that they try to eliminate. Thus, unemployment compensation promotes unemployment; Aid to Families with Dependent Children

(AFDC) makes more families dependent and fatherless; disability insurance encourages the promotion of small ills into temporary disabilities and partial disabilities into total permanent ones; and government "make-work" programs enhance dependence on the state without giving genuine work experience.[32]

Neoconservatives assert that the welfare state makes people lazy and makes it profitable for the poor to behave, in the short term, in ways that are destructive in the long term. Governmental aid to the poor masks the long-term losses and subsidizes irretrievable mistakes. The welfare state is not only useless but harmful to those it is supposed to help. It undermines productivity and the capitalist market. The only acceptable resources are the private job market, family members, friends, private philanthropy, and locally funded public services.

Gilder argued that 18th-century capitalist ideology, as articulated by Adam Smith, could revive ailing Western societies in the 1980s by restoring faith in the private entrepreneurial system. To this end, businesses and wealthy entrepreneurs must be given the latitude to serve society at their best through "rugged" competition, and their competition must not be constrained by governmental controls. If tax rates for the affluent are cut to the barest minimum and the welfare state is dismantled, investments will rise and cause higher productivity and full employment.[33]

Advocates of the Popular Wisdom ethic are hostile not only to the welfare state but to other egalitarian societal institutions. They are against lenient judicial decisions and judges because they encourage crime and disorder. They say that socially conscious schools are too busy busing children to teach them how to read. Affirmative action or equal opportunity programs ("favoritism" for blacks, women, and minorities) are unjust and undermine the free economic market. Simply put, these advocates contend that the government is meddling far too much in things that are none of its business.[34]

Supporters of Popular Wisdom also believe that the welfare state is inefficient in delivering services through the public sector and special-interest groups rather than through the private market. They point out that despite the huge state resources invested, the welfare state has failed to eliminate poverty; it provides work disincentives for labor and capital disincentives for investment. They call the welfare state despotic because it reflects the state's control of citizens and an arbitrary bureaucracy that regulates the people who need aid. Welfare is unproductive because it forces physical and human capital and resources out of the private economic sector; it is also undemocratic because the compulsory provision of services undermines consumers' freedom to choose among services and imposes heavy taxes on the public.

A Social Work Critique
of Popular Wisdom and Reaganomics

Despite its inherent contradictions, Reaganomics was effective in winning for former President Reagan eight years in the highest post in the United States and four years for President Bush. Social workers argue that the costs of this development and the price of taming inflation (the only economic success of the Reagan era) were high and in the long term counterproductive. We also argue that empirical findings contradict the fundamental assumptions of Popular Wisdom.

Social workers point out that the social price of Reaganomics included cutting aid to the poor and the morally and economically indefensible development of an underclass of poor people that includes a big section of the middle class. Children have become the largest group in poverty for the first time in the history of this country. They are trapped in the lowest wage sectors of the economy or outside the economy altogether, and they are frequently hungry and homeless. Overall poverty has increased. The use of involuntary unemployment as a weapon to fight inflation is indefensible, and the dangerously reduced investment in human capital has negative effects on the economy. At the same time destructively uneven development has widened the gap between the rich and the poor.[35]

In the economic domain, Reaganomics did not live up to its promises, except that of reducing inflation. Economic growth, productivity, and investment were lethargic. The recovery effort has been powered by consumer spending, not by the increased savings and investments that were supposed to result from the 1982 tax cut. The nation has been on a consumer binge, financed by liquidating national assets abroad and by gorging on a huge flow of imports. Businesses and bank failures climbed while governmental regulation took on a spectator's role. The tragic deferral of infrastructure maintenance created current and future economic problems. Deindustrialization increased with a consequent growth in the two-tier wage system. Most importantly, the country faces a skyrocketing national economic and social debt and a massive federal budget deficit. A substantial trade deficit has become the norm rather than the exception. In spite of large tax reductions for the rich to fuel an economic recovery, the country has faced a long recession. The Reagan and Bush legacy has been an illusive and haunted prosperity, the rediscovery of hunger and poverty, and the critical underdevelopment of human and physical capital.[36]

Does the welfare state increase poverty?   Murray and others have argued that poverty increased despite increasing welfare state expenditures since 1965. Did poverty rise while federal social spending increased? Did the welfare state increase poverty? Social workers do not think so.

In contrast to Murray's claims, social science studies demonstrated that the growth in pretransfer poverty coincides with rising unemployment as well as with the growth in social programs for the poor. As unemployment dropped between 1965 and 1969, pretransfer poverty declined. Since then, rates of unemployment and pretransfer poverty have risen. Throughout the 1970s, the poverty-increasing impact of rising unemployment was offset by rising transfers. When welfare transfers leveled off and unemployment continued to rise, the official poverty level rate rose. By 1983 it reached the level of the late 1960s.[37] Thus the economy, rather than the welfare state, increased poverty.

Moreover, statistical data suggest that even with the increase in poverty rates in the early 1980s, a significant percentage of poor families with children were removed from poverty by cash welfare benefits: 10.5% in 1983, 10.8% in 1984, and 11.6% in 1985. In 1979, before the Reagan welfare budgetary cuts, a much greater proportion, 18.9%, were removed from poverty.[38] Research by the Center on Budget and Policy Priorities also indicates that if the cash-benefit welfare programs were as well financed as they were in 1979, 545,000 more poor families with children would have been removed from poverty in 1983, 510,000 in 1984, and 458,000 in 1985.

Other studies have demonstrated that public welfare has clearly reduced poverty for the aged poor, the group with the largest increase in welfare transfers. Poverty, as officially measured among the aged, has been reduced by 30–50% since 1967.[39] A fairly steady decline in general poverty also occurred, from 22.4% in 1959 to 11.1% in 1973. Then poverty began to rise, reaching 13% in 1980 and 15.2% in 1983, before falling to 14.4% in 1984[40] and 13.1% in 1988 (31.9 million persons).[41] Progress in fighting poverty stopped in 1973 because that was the first year of a steady economy-wide decline in real earnings and family income as measured by the median income of whites.[42]

Median household income and earnings, rather than the welfare state, are the principal correlates of poverty. In spite of Murray's assertion, the per capita GNP is only moderately related to poverty. Several studies have shown that the per capita GNP can increase while poverty is increasing and family income is declining.[43] A decline in wage rates and an increase in the number of households cause poverty to rise even though the number of workers and the per capita GNP also increase. Murray excludes these and other data that contradict his conclusions.

Is the work ethic undermined?   Supporters of Popular Wisdom claim that crime, civil disorder, and other social pathologies exhibited by the poor have their roots in unemployment and family instability and in turn in the permissiveness of the welfare state. Hence, the key to reducing this "parasitism" is to rehabilitate the poor and their culture and force the poor to work.[44]

Contrary to these assertions, research has found that most welfare recipients either work or want to work, although their employment frequently does not allow them to overcome poverty. Income packages of welfare families often contain more income from labor than from welfare.[45] Compulsory experiments in workfare (forced work for welfare recipients) suggest that AFDC recipients believe they ought to work for their checks.[46]

According to social workers, the work-ethic argument becomes almost irrelevant for additional reasons. Children constitute 66% of AFDC recipients, with the remaining recipients being mothers (18%) and the aged (15%). Only 1% of all welfare recipients are able-bodied men.[47] Some scholars question the advisability of policies that force mothers of infants and young children to join the labor force, rather than focus on child rearing and family development, unless an emergency calls for it.

Does the welfare state create dependence?   The argument that the welfare state perpetuates dependence is not supported by research findings. Most AFDC recipients remain on welfare for a relatively short period: 25% of all AFDC cases are closed within six months, 33% within a year, and only 7.3% of all AFDC cases are on welfare for ten years or more.[48] Turnover is widespread, and persistent welfare is not common. Most of the poor do not even use public welfare. Two-thirds of the poor (22.1 million of the 32.5 million poor in 1985) received no money from AFDC.[49]

Problems of social and economic organization (mainly income inadequacy due to system dysfunction or lack of protection) cause most of the need for social welfare. Studies indicate that the most important causes for obtaining social welfare are divorce or separation (45%), an unmarried woman becoming a pregnant female household head (30%), and a drop in earnings of the female head of household (12%).[50] Social policies for prevention and reform should focus mainly on these issues rather than on the remote and unsubstantiated risk of dependence.

The Old and New Political Left

While classical liberals like Adam Smith and John Stuart Mill assumed that the chief threat to individual liberty was government, Karl Marx, neo-Marxists, and radicals disagree. They argue that the chief threats to individual liberty are large private power centers (particularly businesses) and the poverty and lack of opportunity that empty liberty of meaning.

The essence of Marx's view of the welfare state was that even if organized labor could achieve limited social reform, the securing of widespread state welfare for the majority of the population is inconsistent with the demands of capital accumulation. In the context of the class struggle and the belief that the free market optimizes individual welfare only for the capitalist minority as a class, Marx believed that the great majority of the exploited working class suffers from "diswelfare."

Neo-Marxists and the new political Left have incorporated some of these views in their analyses of the welfare state. They believe that a real and effective welfare state conflicts with the free market. They note that in the long run, economic markets coerce the welfare state to promote capital accumulation, the status quo, and powerful private economic centers. Thus the welfare state does not serve the real interests of the poor and powerless. Rather than support a coerced welfare state serving capitalist interests, they favor more radical societal reforms consistent with the welfare state.[51]

Modern commentators from social work and the other social sciences, including Piven and Cloward, have also noted that the upper classes in the United States believe in the economic, political, and social utility of maintaining poverty. They argue that welfare has been used as a device to control the poor to maintain social stability and to force them into the labor force.[52]

If poverty is defined as the exploitation of the poor by a ruling class, then it is reasonable for the old and new political Left to suggest that only a restructuring of society will solve the problems of poverty and of the welfare state. On the other hand, liberals who disagree, including right-wing modern neo-liberals, suggest that governments can curb the power of private economic centers, promote prosperity and opportunity, and fight poverty through the welfare state.

The responses of the new political Left to poverty and the welfare state vary significantly. But most commentators regard the welfare state as predominantly an instrument for the social control of the working class. The welfare state acts in favor of the long-run interests of capital accumulation. In this view, the logic of the capitalist market and its unequal distribution conflicts with the logic of the welfare state, social justice, individual rights, and fairness. At best, governmental interventions in the economic market promote mainly the long-term interests of the capitalist class rather than the needs of the working class. At the core of this argument is the assumption that the very goal of market efficiency is antithetical to the goal of serving human needs through the welfare state. The capitalist economic system tends to serve the capacity and requirements of the economic market rather than respond to real individual needs.

The feminist movement has developed its own critique of the welfare state that includes the power relations of patriarchy and those of capitalism. Feminist analyses look at the welfare state in terms of the socially structured relations between women and men, particularly in the context of women's oppression. In addition to exploiting women as cheap labor, feminists argue that the patriarchal welfare state also helps to reproduce destructive gender relations. By linking women's structural position in the family and in the reserve army of labor, they have exposed the distinct sexist ideology embedded in social policy and the welfare state. Women are over-represented among recipients of social welfare benefits and social work services and among welfare state workers.[53]

Commentators of the new political Left believe that social welfare should not distinguish between the "worthy" poor through Social Security and the "unworthy" poor through public assistance. Nor should its programs be fragmented, uncoordinated, temporary, residual, and punitive toward the poor.[54]

In brief, four broad areas attract major radical criticism in the United States.

The system's unresponsiveness to societal changes.   In the face of profound societal changes, the welfare state has been relatively unresponsive and immobile in the past few decades. Programs have simply failed to change significantly, leaving new needs and demands unanswered. The gap between social need and social provision has grown too large.

Social changes have produced a rising percentage of older people aged 65 and over—from 6% in 1935, to 8.1% in 1950, to 11% in 1980, to 12% in 1985. By 2030, 23% of the population will be over age 65, with fewer youths a result of declining birth and death rates.

Social changes have also given rise to different family forms and to changing patterns in the relationships between women and men. In the 1980s the model family of social welfare programs no longer had a wage-earning father and a homemaker mother. The reasons included greater female participation in the labor force and higher rates of divorce, separation, children born to unmarried mothers, people living alone, and families headed by females.[55]

The shift from manufacturing to today's service economy has increased demands on the welfare system. Technological changes have affected the organization of the labor force, the philosophy of management, unions, and conditions in the workplace. These dislocations have increased unemployment, poverty, and inequality. The displacement of labor has also increased: only a quarter of workers who lose their jobs find others that pay equally well.[56] Nearly a third of all new jobs created since 1980 have been part time.

The welfare state supplies low-wage labor.   Critics are also concerned with the welfare state's role in supplying the market with low-wage laborers. Because of its nature, the market requires low-wage workers that only a token welfare state can supply. The token U.S. welfare state forces the poor to enter the labor force as unskilled and therefore low-paid workers by regulating them and imposing various constraints on the receipt of welfare.[57] Workfare requirements for welfare eligibility and inadequate welfare benefits provide work incentives and an endless supply of low-wage workers. Only at times of economic prosperity does the market permit a limited version of the welfare state.

Subordination of social policy to the market.   The welfare state serves the economic market status quo. Social policy has emerged historically as a palliative or corrective instrument to cope with imminent social problems that were endangering the economic and political status quo. Social policy as a clearly circumscribed sector of governmental activity did not crystallize until the 17th and 18th centuries and only in countries where capitalism was beginning to appear.[58] Since then social policy and the welfare state in capitalist countries have remained subservient to market demands like employment, savings, and investments. They correct market injustice only when doing so does not affect the parameters of the economic market.

Inadequacies of social insurance.   Social insurance is not exempt from the radical critique; its financing is frequently questioned for numerous reasons. For example, income from all social insurance programs just barely matches outgoing benefits. Beneficiaries have steadily increased while contributions from wage earners are declining. Surpluses from trusts can distort budgetary deficits. Furthermore, calculations of social security benefits are based on the assumption of a steady work history lasting until normal retirement. This is a poor assumption for women who leave the work force for child rearing and whose subsequent employment is often substandard. The originally anticipated reserves that would earn interest to pay benefits did not materialize, and as premiums continue to rise, contributions will approach prohibitive levels.

In addition, the anticipated eventual phasing out of public welfare because of insurance schemes did not materialize. Instead public welfare increased. The maturation of social insurance failed to meet the income-support needs of all Americans, and many cannot qualify for it. Social insurance benefits are paid mostly to the nonpoor. The insurance tax is highly regressive, taking a much larger share of the income of the poor than of the rich. The average monthly benefits for a worker are insufficient to sustain acceptable minimum living standards. Without additional retirement or investment income, which is not available to most Americans, recipients would be in poverty, burdened further by the unmet need for national health insurance and health care services.[59]

MODELS OF WELFARE STATES

Recent developments and challenges to welfare states in Western Europe and North America raise the question of what types of welfare capitalism will evolve and be sustained in the decades to come. The collapse of state collectivist welfare (central command) in Central and Eastern Europe add weight to this question.[60] Since it is unlikely that there will be a market or centrally planned economy without some form of a welfare state, the critical issue is not to choose either a market or a bureaucratic welfare state. Rather, it is to decide how best to structure this relationship within the specific social values prevailing in a country.

Frameworks for Typologies

Commentators in the United States have provided general views about the types of the welfare state. For example, in the 1950s Wilensky and Lebeaux observed that the residual and institutional conceptions of social welfare were dominant in the United States. The residual view holds that the welfare state should come into play as an emergency function only when the normal structures of society, the family, and the market, break down. This conception dominated the field until the Great Depression but still represents a major viewpoint in the 1990s. The institutional view, in contrast, sees the welfare state as normal to meet the needs of modern industrial society.[61] The institutional perspective views the welfare state as a normal social institution in a complex, interdependent society, always necessary to help individuals and communities realize their full potential. This view rejects the notion that the welfare state is primarily a crisis service. The ideologies and policies of the New Deal, the New Frontier, and the Great Society reflect the institutional perspective.

C. Wright Mills also observed the dichotomy between residual and institutional perspectives of the welfare state. In delineating the distinction between the two, Mills observed the difference between personal problems and societal issues or between an individual who is unable to lead a productive life and the global dislocation that results from dysfunctional aspects of society that impinge on individual well-being.

Others include Peirce and his functional perspective of the welfare state, and Mencher, who dislikes the Protestant tradition of dealing with poverty. Peirce distinguished between the manifest function of the welfare state (provision of services and resources to those in need) and latent functions (social control and seeking to preserve the status quo). Mencher observed that the Elizabethan Poor Laws tradition of forced work requirements, means tests, limited eligibility, and inadequate benefits is no longer tenable in modern society.[62]

In Western Europe and North America several analysts, including Alber, Titmuss, Therborn, and Esping-Andersen, have attempted to identify more precise types of welfare capitalism. Despite their efforts, reflected in professional literature in the United States, there is no wide consensus regarding the appropriate criteria to be used for constructing such typologies.[63] Classifications based on variables like the scope, range, quality, financing, and type of benefits (Alber's model) are usually inconclusive in providing general or sharp definitions of welfare states according to ideological, political, social, geographic, or other crucial factors.

Titmuss suggested three models of social policy for the provision of social welfare. The *residual* welfare model asserts that social welfare institutions come into play only temporarily when the institutions of family and the private market fail. The industrial achievement-performance model says that social needs should be met on the basis of merit, work, and productivity. The institutional redistributive model calls for universal services to be provided outside the market and on the basis of need. Some commentators find this scheme rather limited because the characteristics of services used as criteria are usually present in most types of the welfare state.

Therborn used the level of social entitlements and the commitment to full employment as basic criteria for three major types of the welfare state. Strong interventionist welfare states provide extensive social policies; this category includes Austria,

Finland, Norway, and Sweden. Soft compensatory welfare states provide generous social entitlements; this includes Belgium, Denmark, Japan, and the Netherlands. Market-oriented welfare states provide limited social rights; this category includes Australia, Canada, New Zealand, the United Kingdom, and the United States.

Esping-Andersen suggested a three-category scheme based on ideal types of welfare states. The liberal welfare state is dominated by laissez-faire, private markets, efficiency at the expense of equality, strong work incentives at the expense of benefits, and means-tested approaches. This category includes Australia, Canada, and the United States. The conservative corporatist welfare state, which uses social policy to support the status quo and to stabilize social divisions only when the family and other traditional institutions do not provide benefits, describes Austria, France, Germany, and Italy. The social democratic welfare regime, which provides expanded benefits to the middle class based on equality, universalism, redistribution, and universal insurance systems describes Denmark, Norway, and Sweden.

Three basic elements characterize these classifications and analyses. First, they are based on a wide range of criteria rather than on one characteristic. They include, for example, the types and scope of welfare benefits, the characteristics of beneficiaries, the rationale of the welfare state, and the concern of social classes. Second, the reasons for selecting the criteria are not always clear. Third, regardless of the different approaches used, every scheme tends to group the same countries together. Thus, the Scandinavian countries are usually in one cluster, while Australia, Canada, the United Kingdom, and the United States are in another. Socialist countries are excluded.

There are several advantages to using one only criterion, rather than many. A single criterion provides clarity, simplicity, utility, and no need to rank criteria. Our analysis indicates that a central criterion is the relationship between the economic market and the government.

The Market-Government Relation: The Basic Criterion

In both the industrial West and the East, the relationship between government and market is a powerful element in understanding the structure of industrial welfare states. In the context of institutional analysis and this book's orientation, the government's role in the economy is crucial for social policies and the welfare state (see figure 6-1). The welfare state reflects the link between government, market, and social institutions based on a given ideology and value system.

The government-market relationship is central because it represents the fundamental concern about how societies determine use of their resources. Societies can often be classified by which of two mechanisms they emphasize in determining this allocation: market or government. The specific mix of the two allocating mechanisms is based on society's prevailing systems of social values. The structure of contemporary welfare states directly reflects the prevailing (or desired) relationship between market and government in the context of specific value choices—the degree to which the free market or the political will of governments dominates the allocation of resources. An effective base for a structural analysis of contemporary welfare states is provided by the pattern of allocating resources among competing uses.

The market component.   In a free economy, marked by wide extremes in the distribution of income and wealth, competition in the market means that some people are hungry and homeless while others use their buying power for luxuries. Without controls, the free market yields efficient economic results that leave some workers with no income (involuntary unemployment) and others working for poverty-level incomes. Some feel proud and successful, whereas others feel defeated, powerless, and inadequate. Depending upon the prevailing social values, free market outcomes may or may not be tolerated.

The government (or bureaucracy) component.   In a governmental control system, individual self-interest is again the motivating force, but it is limited because citizens accept societal constraints and prevailing social values.

Both mechanisms of allocating societal resources operate within the value system of a society and are influenced by it. In the context of social values, various outcomes—individual self-interest or collectivism, full employment or unemployment, uneven or even economic development, competition or cooperation, the burdens or privileges of social classes, investments in human or physical capital, the destruction or preservation of the environment, and education or illiteracy—can be limited or encouraged by a set of widely accepted moral values.

Outcomes produced by a different relationship between the market and government may not be tolerated because they deviate excessively from several other social values that help to determine the allocation of resources. The prevailing morality and value system may then cause the society to select a different way of allocating and distributing resources. For example, more governmental intervention in the market may be chosen.

Accordingly, different degrees of market control by government distinguish four models that describe this relationship. The scheme includes socialist countries. The numerical progression of the models (1 to 4) does not imply evolution or rank order. Rather, each model is associated with a different market-government mix that is based on different sets of prevailing social values.

Model 1: Laissez-faire. This model describes Australia, Canada, New Zealand, the United Kingdom, and the United States.
Model 2: Institutional. This model describes Belgium, France, Germany, and Japan.
Model 3: Interventionist. This model describes Sweden, Denmark, Norway, and Finland.
Model 4: Authoritative. This model describes Cuba, China, and the former USSR.

Even when a single characteristic, rather than several different criteria, is used, there is no apparent loss in the richness of this classification scheme, compared to other typologies. For example, approximately the same countries are included in each model.

Model 1 (Laissez-faire).   In this market-driven classical model, governments permit unfettered economic markets to control social policy and assume a posture of benign neglect toward social problems. In the prevailing laissez-faire attitude toward economic markets, private owners can negotiate prices and allocate resources without interference from the state or large private power blocs. The private free market acts as an automatic corrective mechanism, free of bureaucratic structure. The redistribution of income, wealth, and services is discouraged because market outcomes, based on assumptions of equality of opportunity, are considered fair and just. Wide inequalities in income and power are acceptable to promote economic efficiency.

Under these circumstances, laissez-faire welfare states are characterized by policies that provide temporary, emergency-oriented, means-tested, residual welfare benefits mainly to poor people, who are stigmatized for receiving them. Social policy, limited in scope, is designed to promote the status quo and to strengthen markets and families when they fail.

Exemplified by the welfare regime in the United States, this model also includes the somewhat different Labourite welfare state in the United Kingdom and the welfare regimes of the authoritarian populist dictators in Latin America.

Model 2 (Institutional).   This model is strongly market-oriented. Both the government and corporate groups (including the church and large private economic groups) contribute jointly to key economic, social, and political decisions regarding the allocation of resources. They leave underlying property relations intact while cooperatively formulating social policy. Corporate authority, including church authority, underpins social policy to standardize social divisions in society. Thus social policy, reflecting the coexistence of private, occupational, and state welfare approaches, constrains the redistribution of income in favor of market and corporate outcomes.

Under these circumstances, institutional welfare regimes are characterized by soft compensatory programs, negligible income redistribution, and the recognition of some social entitlements. Social programs based on merit, work, and productivity are focused on the traditional role of family in social care, and different forms of services are devised for different classes of society.

Exemplified by Belgium, France, and Germany, this model can also include the welfare system in Japan, characterized by strong paternalism in the workplace.

Model 3 (Interventionist).   In this model, governments establish extensive social policies by exercising political control to restrain, guide, and regulate the economic market. They have the main responsibility for ensuring equality and social welfare. Thus they prevent a certain amount of social dysfunction and redistribute market outcomes. The recognition of broad social rights for all citizens encourages extended social policies.

Exemplified by welfare regimes in Denmark, Finland, Norway, and Sweden, the interventionist types of welfare states provide universal services and social insurance. These services are provided outside the market on the basis of need. Social entitlement programs, redistributive to ameliorate inequalities, are extensive, effective, and include the middle class.

Model 4 (Authoritative).   In this model governments establish complete and authoritative control over the economic market, which is replaced by a central state bureaucracy. Centralism, statism, and totalitarianism in decision making permeate all aspects of organized life. A centrally determined and administered social policy

TABLE 6-3   Social value dimensions

Value Dimensions	Models			
	1	*2*	*3*	*4*
Social justice	Bentham's view (utilitarianism)	Nozick's view (market)	Rawls's view (rational)	Marx's view (classless, need-based)
Ownership	Private	Mixed	Balanced	Public
Locus of power	Individual (decentralized)	Groups (mixed)	Collectivist (balanced)	Statist (centralized)
Full employment	Optional	Desirable	A right	Legislatively guaranteed

framework provides few, if any, choices to recipients or flexibility to local communities. Designed to narrow the gap in the distribution of wages, income, and wealth, it provides extensive, universal welfare programs and services as a right of all citizens.[64]

Social Values and Choices

The relationship between government and market remains equally effective as a criterion even if more social values are included in the models. The addition of more criteria or social values reinforces the characteristics and homogeneity of each model. For example, key value dimensions of social justice, ownership, locus of power, and full employment enhance the structure of each model. In Table 6-3, the choices in each social value dimension (on a continuum from left to right) reinforce the character of each model (its vertical description).

Social justice.   At the core of social policy are views of distributive justice and equality. Horizontally, the choices of distributive justice range from utilitarianism (Model 1), to Nozick's and Friedman's views (Model 2), to Rawls's view (Model 3), to Marxist perspectives based on need, rather than on work (Model 4). The more work-related the views of justice, the more market-oriented becomes the model's rationale. In Models 1 and 2 market distributions of income are perceived as fair and objective, requiring no redistribution. At the same time, however, it is hard to justify major inequalities that arise.

The less work-related the notions of justice, the more need-oriented the model's logic becomes. Market distributions of income and wealth are then perceived as unjust with state redistribution to bridge the gap between poverty and wealth (Models 3 and 4). While work-related distributions raise questions of inequality, egalitarian distributions raise questions associated with the ethics of redistributing "earned" market income. The issue cannot be separated from concerns for efficiency. Closely related to social justice is the issue of citizenship, including social rights and equal entitlements of citizenship for all.

Ownership.   The rights of ownership are also a fundamental value in social policy. Ownership can be characterized as vested in a single individual, a group of individuals, a community, and the state. Each possibility has critical implications for the structure of the welfare state.

Locus of power.   The locus of power is where decisions are focused on a continuum ranging from the power of the individual to the power of society as a whole and consequently to central, regional, or local units of authority. The more decentralized the system of decision-making (Models 1 and 2), the greater the autonomy of local units, but also the greater the difficulty in ensuring even development among communities. Centralization favors equality (Models 3 and 4) at the expense of removing critical decisions further from the individual.

Full employment.   Although full employment is generally desired, certain governments place priority on a healthy market rather than on the full utilization of the labor force (Model 1). Other governments place priority on full employment only when it does not undermine economic goals (Model 2). Full employment can also be considered the right of every citizen (Models 3 and 4).

Each value dimension (horizontal axis) enhances the characteristics and cohesiveness of each model (vertical axis). For example, the laissez-faire model is vertically harmonious and cohesive in that its values are consistent with each other. The values of utilitarianism, private ownership of the means of production and of distribution, rugged individualism, decentralization of responsibility for welfare, and optional full employment are harmonious. They combine to construct a distinct homogeneous structure. The institutional model is also cohesive vertically. It consists of market justice, private ownership guided by corporatism, power vested in individuals and selected groups, and conditional full employment. The interventionist model is associated with the values of Rawlsian justice, balanced ownership, collectivist power, and full employment as a right. The authoritative model is associated with Marxist justice, public ownership, the centralization of power, and guaranteed full employment.

This analysis suggests that the restructuring of welfare states must be based on assumptions regarding the relationship of the government with the market economy in the context of specific value dimensions.

IMPLICATIONS FOR SOCIAL WORK

While the restructuring of welfare states affects the well-being and the quality of life of millions of people, it also has major, direct implications for social work practice. Underinvestment in human capital development and increased social deficits directly affect the well-being and functioning of clients. They also influence the prevention of psychosocial dysfunction and the empowerment of the disadvantaged. The distribution of power and the power structures are at the epicenter of the allocation and distribution of societal resources to citizens, groups, classes, and communities. They are crucial considerations in efforts to empower citizens and communities.

Power Frameworks

In the power context, what are the implications of differential welfare states for social work practice? What kind of welfare state is most appropriate? Which welfare models maximize the well-being of citizens in the social work context? Which combinations in the relationship between government and market maximize human development? Which optimize the most constructive aspects of individuals and communities? Which societal arrangements minimize the most destructive components of human environments?

Social work practitioners are directly concerned with social progress and the development of individuals and communities. Therefore, they are concerned with the social limits to economic growth and the economic limits to social development. The distribution of power translates to the struggle over uneven income, wealth, poverty, and power among social classes and geographic regions. In the context of doubts regarding continuous economic expansion, power relationships between governments and markets provide constructive insights.

Social workers approach this issue in the context of their own professional commitments, understanding, and experience. Social work values and goals and community norms, however, identify specific ranges of fundamental professional prerequisites in regard to the power role of governments and markets in the context of structuring welfare states.

For example, excessive concentration of power on economic markets (Model 1) or on governments (Model 4) is likely to be counterproductive to social work commitments and values. Social work practice is more likely to be enhanced by balanced sharing of power in the relationship between government and market (Models 2 and 3). Excessively powerful markets tend to overshadow central values of social justice and social conditions for the growth of individuals and communities. Moreover, they favor the uneven concentration of power in the hands of economically and socially advantaged citizens and groups. Consequently, social work and welfare-state efforts to empower disadvantaged and powerless citizens and communities become problematic.

A minimal role of the government in guiding the economy and unfettered economic markets is also associated with the structure of limited welfare states (Models 1 and 2). Such welfare states serve the disadvantaged only nominally. They tend to perpetuate ideologies and traditions that increase rather than prevent psychosocial dysfunction, including poverty, unemployment, and powerlessness. Limited rights of citizenship are also associated with unfettered markets that are driven by profit and excessive individualism.

Excessive concentration of power on government and the state (Model 4), on the other hand, provides for more even development of individuals and more adequate universal welfare benefits. But this is done at the expense of individual liberty, self-determination, and local community control. Experiences associated with the complete control of the market by the state present basic dilemmas. Social programs and services are a universal right in the context of egalitarian social policies designed to promote even human development. Yet, these societies are also characterized by statism, centralism, bureaucracy, paternalism, elitism, and the monopoly of power by one political party and hence totalitarianism. Such power structures conflict with basic social work values and commitments. They undermine individual liberty, the democratic participation of citizens in decisions that affect their lives, self-government, self-determination, and local community control.

The moral basis of society is fundamentally undercut by laissez-faire markets, which operate solely on individual self-interest and allocate resources to benefit the powerful. On the other hand, the moral basis of society is also undercut by centralized, totalitarian state power, which ignores the basic values of liberty, social accountability, and the participation of citizens in decisions regarding their own values, lifestyles, and choices.

If it is necessary to reintegrate the economy into the social system, there should be some degree of state management of the economy and some degree of market guidance of governmental decisions. From a social work perspective and values, the necessary ingredients in the distribution of power include the power and actions of communities (geographic, interest, gender, or lifestyle), self-determination, and self-government. Both Weberian state bureaucracies in the West and the statist apparatuses of socialist countries tend to provide for inadequate community power and control in decision-making. They also provide few opportunities for self-determination. Community power and action and community self-government are necessary ingredients to balance governmental and market relationships.

Poverty, a central concern of social work and social services, illustrates these concerns about power. It also highlights the cluster of value-dimensions (Table 6-3) that support specific power relationships important in welfare states and in social work practice. The focus of analysis will again be on the two ends of the spectrum.

Poverty

In market-oriented models poverty is recognized to have serious socioeconomic negative influences on societal progress and development. Yet perennial poverty is tolerated and frequently encouraged.

Few commentators would disagree that poverty is harmful to individuals, groups, communities, and society. Among other things, poverty weakens the nation's economy and depresses regions. It causes underdevelopment and severe social deficits. It arrests personal growth and development because of ill health, nutritional and educational deficiencies, learning disabilities, and inadequate socialization transmitted between generations. It generates inequality and social unjustice. It also causes social dysfunction, including work and consumption distortions and excessive credit and fraud. It undermines the social order.

Why, then, is poverty tolerated by governments in the context of laissez-faire markets? Is it just symptomatic that dominant causal paradigms of poverty in free economies tend to support the laissez-faire market structure, the existing distribution of power, and the ideology of the status quo? Is it relevant that prevailing values regarding social justice, the distribution of power, ownership, and full employment combine to form an institutional network that directly supports and enhances the power of the free economy rather than the eradication of poverty?

Even in the earlier days of laissez-faire ideology, theories of the causes of poverty held that poor people are responsible for their problems. Idleness, intemperance, gambling, hasty marriages, prostitution, migration, and extensive charity dampen individualism and individual initiative.[65] These interpretations relate directly to a traditional conviction that poor people are less deserving than are the nonpoor. This view reflects economic individualism and the philosophy of positivism, which, as an example of technical rationality, is associated with requirements to control societies. By the same token, this view rejects the assumption that poverty is an outcome of external circumstances that are beyond the control of individuals, such as involuntary unemployment or underemployment, inadequate wages, automation, discrimination, educational deficiencies, disability, ill health, or other dysfunctions of social organization.

The new political Right has adopted the laissez-faire view that poor people themselves are at fault for their condition. The doctrine of Reaganomics and Thatcherism, based on the desirability of unfettered markets, assumes that poverty is a deficiency in human capital. According to this view, the major causes of poverty are poor people's inferior culture and innate intellectual endowments. Since people are poor because they are inferior, society should focus on reforming or controlling their behavior rather than on reforming laissez-faire markets and other institutions. What is needed is not the welfare state, the Right believes. Rather, society needs unfettered markets, governmental inaction in the marketplace, the corrective punishment of the poor, and welfare requirements to force welfare recipients to work or forgo welfare benefits.

The ideology of a powerful, unfettered economic market also draws on two more contemporary and highly criticized social views about justice and power: the culture of poverty ("blaming the victim") and innate inferiority. Both support concepts of free market supremacy.

The culture of poverty view contends that the lifestyles of poor people are qualitatively different from those of nonpoor people. Poor people's lifestyles and their disengagement from major social institutions cause and perpetuate their poverty. In adapting to their cultural conditions of deprivation, they depend on and are gratified by their poverty conditions. Consequently, even if poverty were eliminated, the former poor would remain immoral and continue to exhibit the same behavior. As Banfield, among others, asserted:

> The poor have a culture of poverty that dooms them and their dependents to the lowest social class. This culture makes even the slums desirable to the slum dwellers. Although the poor have more "leisure" than almost anyone, the indifference or "apathy" of the lower-class person is such that he seldom makes even the simplest repairs to the place that he lives in. He is not troubled by dirt and dilapidation and he does not mind the inadequacy of public facilities such as schools, parks, hospitals, and libraries; indeed, where such things exist he may destroy them by carelessness or even by vandalism. Conditions that make the slum repellent to others are serviceable to them.[66]

The innate inferiority view contends that minorities, women, and poor people are less endowed mentally than are whites, men, and non-poor people. Although social Darwinism[67] has not been held in high esteem in the scientific community for nearly a century, it continues to provide a rationale for this view. It supports outcomes produced by free-market function and assumes that intelligence is largely inherited.

Jensen and Herrnstein suggest that the poor are in that condition because they do not measure up to the more well-to-do in the most fundamental way: intellectual endowment.[68] For Jensen there is a strong possibility that African Americans are less endowed mentally than are whites. He claims that approximately 80% of IQ is inherited, while the remaining 20% is attributable to the environment.[69] Since African Americans differ significantly from whites in their achievement on IQ tests and in school, Jensen believed it reasonable to hypothesize that the sources of these differences are mainly genetic and only marginally environmental.

Agreeing with this assumption, Herrnstein advocated that social stratification in market countries is based on inborn differences and occurs because mental ability is inherited. Success, prestige in jobs, and earnings in free markets depend on mental ability. Thus, a free-market meritocracy develops through the sorting process. This is another way of saying that in the context of free markets, the bright people are in the upper classes, and the dull dregs are at the bottom. Inequality in market economics is justified as it was years ago by social Darwinism.

The views of both the culture of poverty[70] and the innate inferiority[71] schools of thought have two major social consequences in the context of the power of free markets. First, they support value systems that maintain that inequality of income and wealth is unavoidable and desirable. They blame poor people for being inferior. They refuse to blame schools, culturally biased IQ tests, the social barriers of inequality (sexism, racism, and economic exploitation), or uneven power structures for causing poverty.

Second, they contend that poverty is inevitable and impossible to eradicate without reforming poor persons. This type of reasoning tends to justify the uneven and unfair outcomes of laissez-faire markets. It also frequently leads to national social policies that tolerate poverty, attack the moral behavior of poor people, enhance laissez-faire markets, and minimize the need for welfare states and social services.

These values dominate and coexist with laissez-faire environments. Views and values suggesting the need to fetter the market are dismissed or remain atrophic. In one such opposing view, conflict theorists focus on the benefits derived from the social functions of poverty, place the blame on laissez-faire markets, and maintain that poverty is due to the failure of free economics to provide enough jobs with adequate wages. In conceptualizing poverty, conflict theorists use class attributes like occupation, family income, education, and race to measure one's relative standing in the stratification system.[72] They join social workers in proposing that governments exercise greater control over markets to prevent market dysfunction. This will eliminate institutionalized market discrimination against minorities, women, the aged, and children. It will also redistribute the outcomes of the market to individuals and communities.

To the extent that poverty serves certain social functions in market economies, free markets tolerate poverty. Among other things, poverty stabilizes or reduces wages and increases the supply of unskilled workers. Poverty and unemployment favor employers in negotiating better terms with labor unions. They help the economy to rebound from depression to prosperity and secure the profitable turnover of employees. Poor people, including low-wage restaurant and hospital workers, servants, gardeners, and housekeepers, perform society's necessary but undesirable jobs. Most notably, poverty subsidizes various middle-class and upper-class economic activities. It creates jobs and clients for those in several occupations and professions that serve the poor or protect society from them. Included are social workers, penologists, police, numbers racketeers, and physicians and lawyers who cannot attract more affluent clients.

Conflict theorists also note that poverty increases the self-esteem and confidence of nonpoor people and provides an outlet for charity. Being powerless, the poor are also forced to absorb the costs of technological change, environmental pollution, and involuntary unemployment to fight inflation. First to be fired and last to be hired, the poor live in substandard neighborhoods that become dumping grounds of polluted waste.[73] In brief, this analysis suggests that the social utility of poverty in the context of unfettered markets promotes values of power structures that make poverty tolerable and necessary.

Social workers who work with poor people tend to relate poverty to unfettered market functions. They are aware that the working poor constitute a large part of the poor. Factors such as age, gender, disability, education, health, mobility, and unemployment influence the ability of the poor to work and in turn increase the propensity to live in poverty. Educational attainment is also related to poverty. Low levels of completed education and high rates of illiteracy among poor people have been observed for decades.

Different conceptions of poverty are associated with the excessive control of markets by the state (Model 4). Acquiring a societal cause rather than an etiology that blames mainly the individual, poverty is perceived in institutional rather than personal terms. Relative rather than absolute concepts and standards of poverty are practiced. According to absolute standards of poverty, poor people are those whose income falls below some absolute dollar amount that is necessary to sustain a minimal level of living (poverty line). Relative standards of poverty used in industrial countries of the West are based on measurements that compare the incomes of poor individuals or families to those of nonpoor individuals or families. There is no official poverty in nonmarket countries and consequently no measurement of poverty as such. Yet relative, comparative poverty takes the form of equality of income and wealth and equality in the free provision of basic services, including health care and education, to provide an adequate, egalitarian, common floor for development. Low living standards that may result from the country's low economic output are supposed to be shared equally by all citizens.

The nonmarket state guarantees employment for all and provides free minimum services designed to accelerate social development. Yet the emphasis on statism, totalitarianism, and central authority undercuts individual liberty, decentralized decision-making, self-determination, and community self-government. The concentration of power in state authority is also counterproductive to individual and community development as envisioned by social work practice.

There is certainty about the counterproductivity of poverty at the two ends of the spectrum of power in the relationship between the government and the market.

The problem of poverty, however, becomes more complex with regard to combinations and options available in other models—outside or within the proposed scheme. First, the potential for different combinations of power structures, social values, and welfare states is considerable. Second, the general consensus among social workers regarding professional values and priorities tends to be less cohesive when the differences are less pronounced in practice and the trade-off of options is more complex. In such cases, social workers have to rely more heavily on their experience and understanding of professional values. It is realistic to expect, however, that a considerable degree of emphasis and flexibility will have to be placed on promoting community control and action, a relatively new actor in contemporary power structures.

In the decades to come, new structures of welfare states will evolve in both the industrial West and the East. Social workers have the expertise to participate in this process and the responsibility to provide leadership and guidance.

NOTES

1. J. DeParle, "The Nation. As Funds for Welfare Shrink, Ideas Flourish," *New York Times*, May 12, 1991, E5.
2. Associated Press, "Cuomo Seeks $1b Cut in Welfare, Elimination of 6,200 State Jobs," *Boston Globe*, January 22, 1992, 10.
3. P. J. Howe, "Weld Again to Ask Cuts in Welfare, Insurance," *Boston Globe*, January 22, 1992, 1.
4. D. Treadwell, "New Jersey Ends Welfare Aid for Extra Children," *Boston Globe*, January 22, 1922, 3.
5. R. Pear, "Focusing on Welfare: Bush Plays Private Acts of Decency against the Government as a Helper," *New York Times*, May 11, 1991, 8.
6. K. Cullen, "Justices to Hear Pennsylvania Abortion Case," *Boston Globe*, January 22, 1992, 1.
7. J. A. Farrell, "Parties Spar on Education," *Boston Globe*, January 22, 1992, 3.
8. *Los Angeles Times*, "Heart Risk Called Greater for Singles, Poor," *Boston Globe*, January 22, 1992, 3.
9. Reuters, "Rights Group Calls on U.S. to Relent on Haitians," *Boston Globe*, January 22, 1992, 7.
10. Associated Press, "Bush to Retool Jobs Program," *Boston Globe*, January 22, 1992, 10.
11. "U.S. Admits to Improper Waste Disposal," *Boston Globe*, January 22, 1992, 11.
12. P. Steinfels, "Papal Encyclical Urges Capitalism to Shed Injustices," *New York Times*, May 3, 1991, 1.
13. A. Clymer, "A GOP Leader Aims at Welfare State Values," *New York Times*, January 5, 1992, 19.
14. In 1990, Central and Eastern Europe had a population of 428.2 million, compared to 634.8 million in Western Europe and North America, for a total of over 1 billion people. East and West produced a combined GNP of $13.1 trillion. The data were derived from M. S. Hoffman, ed., *The World Almanac and Book of Facts, 1991* (New York: Newspaper Enterprise Association, 1991).

15. P. Flora, *Growth to Limits,* vol. 1 (Berlin: De Gruyter, 1986), xxii; P. E. Weinberger, *Perspectives on Social Welfare: An Introductory Anthology,* 2nd ed. (New York: Macmillan, 1974), 19; and A. K. Bixby, "Public Social Welfare Expenditures, Fiscal Year 1989," *Social Security Bulletin* 55: 2 (Summer 1992).

16. In this study, the *welfare state* (an inexact concept) refers both to state measures for the provision of key welfare services (narrowly including health, education, housing, income maintenance, and social services) and to a distinctive form of state and polity: a country in which the state intervenes in the processes of economic production and distribution to reallocate resources and services between individuals and social classes. See C. Pierson, *Beyond the Welfare State?* (University Park: Pennsylvania State University Press, 1991), 6, 7.

17. See "Friction Between Economic and Social Goals" in chapter 1 of this book; T. H. Marshall, *Sociology at the Cross Roads and Other Essays* (London: Heinemann, 1963); W. I. Trattner, *From Poor Law to the Welfare State,* 4th ed. (New York: Free Press, 1989); E. Oyen, ed., *Comparing Welfare States and their Future* (Brookfield, VT: Gower, 1986); G. Room, *The Sociology of Welfare* (London: Martin Robertson, 1979); and Pierson, *Beyond The Welfare State?*

18. See P. Cutright, "Political Structure, Economic Development, and National Social Security Programs," *American Journal of Sociology* 70(5) (1965), 537–550; H. Wilensky, *The Welfare State and Equality: Structural and Ideological Roots of Public Expenditure* (Berkeley and Los Angeles: University of California Press, 1975); and H. Wilensky, *The 'New Corporatism,' Centralization, and the Welfare State* (London: Sage, 1976).

19. See W. Korpi, "Power, Politics, and State Autonomy in the Development of Social Citizenship: Social Rights during Sickness in Eighteen OECD Countries since 1930," *American Sociological Review* 54(1989), 309–328; G. Esping-Andersen, *Politics Against Markets* (Princeton, NJ: Princeton University Press, 1985); R. Erickson et al., eds., *The Scandinavian Model: Welfare States and Welfare Research* (Armonk, NY: Sharpe, 1987); M. Rein, G. Esping-Andersen, and M. Rainwater, eds., *Stagnation and Renewal* (New York: Sharp, 1987). See also papers of S. M. Miller, "Citizenship and the New Welfare State," and Z. Ferge, "From Subject to Citizen," presented at the international conference, "The Welfare State: Transition from Central Planning to Market Approaches," Budapest, Hungary, June 3–6, 1991, organized by the Boston College Graduate School of Social Work and the Institute of Sociology and Social Policy, Eotvos University, Budapest.

20. Neoclassical analysis, which began in the 1870s, turned from the classical concern with growth and poverty to the problem of efficient resource allocation.

21. D. Donnison, "Social Policy since Titmuss," *Journal of Social Policy* 8 (1979), 145–156.

22. R. Skidelsky, "The Decline of Keynesian Politics," in C. Crouch, ed., *State and Economy in Contemporary Capitalism* (London: Croom Helm, 1979), 55–87.

23. For neo-Keynesians, see "The Public Purse," *The Economist,* November 24, 1990, 77–78; N. G. Mankiw, "A Quick Refresher Course in Macroeconomics," *Journal of Economic Literature* 28 (December 1990), 1645–1660; and H. Kohler, *Macroeconomics* (Lexington, MA: Heath, 1992), 424–443.

24. For this view see G. Therborn, "Welfare State and Capitalist Markets," *Acta Sociologica* 30 (3/4) (1987), 237–254; P. Lassman, ed., *Politics and Social Theory* (London: Routledge & Kegan Paul, 1989); P. Flora, "History and Current Problems of the Welfare State," in S. N. Eisenstadt and O. Ahimer, eds., *The Welfare State and its Aftermath* (London: Croom Helm), 11–30; P. Flora and A. J. Heidenheimer, eds., *The Development of Welfare States in Europe and America* (London: Transaction Books, 1981); T. H. Marshall, *Social Policy in the Twentieth Century* (London: Hutchinson Education, 1975); M. Keynes, *The*

Central Theory of Employment, Interest, and Money (London: Macmillan, 1973); M. Weir, A. S. Orloff, and T. Skocpol, eds., *The Politics of Social Policy in the United States* (Princeton, NJ: Princeton University Press, 1988); C. Offe, *Contradictions of the Welfare State* (London: Hutchinson Education, 1984); C. Offe, "Democracy Against the Welfare State?" *Political Theory* 15 (1987), 501–537; D. Donnison, "Social Policy Since Titmuss"; W. Korpi, "Power, Politics, and State Autonomy in the Development of Social Citizenship"; W. Korpi, *The Working Class in Welfare Capitalism* (London: Routledge & Kegan Paul, 1979); G. Esping-Andersen, *The Three Worlds of Welfare Capitalism* (Cambridge: Polity, 1990); C. Pierson, "The 'Exceptional' United States: First New Nation or Last Welfare State?" *Social Policy and Administration* 24, (December, 1990), 186–198; and Pierson, *Beyond The Welfare State?*

25. For this view, see G. V. Rimingler, *Welfare Policy and Industrialization in Europe, America, and Russia* (New York: Wiley, 1974); I. Kristol, *Two Cheers for Capitalism* (New York: Basic Books, 1978); M. Friedman, *Capitalism and Freedom* (Chicago: University of Chicago Press, 1962); M. Friedman and R. Friedman, *Free to Choose* (London: Secker & Warburg, 1980); G. Gilder, *Wealth and Poverty* (London: Buchan & Enright, 1982); C. Murray, *Losing Ground: American Social Policy 1950–1980* (New York: Basic Books, 1984).

26. A. Smith, *The Wealth of Nations* (Oxford: Clarendon Press, 1976); N. A. Senior, *Historical and Political Essays* (London: Publisher unknown, 1865); T. R. Malthus, *An Essay on the Principle of Population* (London: Ward, Lock & Co, 1890); D. Ricardo, *Principles of Political Economy and Taxation* (London: J. M. Dent & Sons, 1912); K. Marx, *Capital* (Harmondsworth, England: Penguin, 1973); and Friedman, *Capitalism and Freedom*.

27. See Ricardo, *Principles of Political Economy and Taxation.* 1912.

28. See C. K. Wilber and K. P. Jameson, *Beyond Reaganomics: A Further Inquiry into the Poverty of Economics* (Notre Dame, IN: University of Notre Dame Press, 1990); and H. Johnson, *Sleepwalking through History* (New York: Norton, 1991).

29. See Friedman and Friedman, *Free to Choose.*

30. Supply-side economists include M. Boskin, Chairman of President Bush's first Council of Economic Advisers; L. Kemp, President Bush's Secretary of Housing and Urban Development; and A. Laffer and P. Roberts of the Reagan years.

31. Gilder, *Wealth and Poverty;* and Murray, *Losing Ground.* For Gilder's arguments, see D. Iatridis, "Neoconservatism Reviewed," *Social Work* 28 (March/April 1983), 101–107; and D. Iatridis, "Iatridis Replies," *Social Work* 28 (November/December 1983), 492–493.

32. Gilder, *Wealth and Poverty,* 111.

33. Friedman, *Capitalism and Freedom;* and Friedman and Friedman, *Free to Choose.* For a summary and analysis of Gilder's position, see Iatridis, "Neoconservatism Reviewed."

34. Murray, *Losing Ground,* 146.

35. Wilber and Jameson, in *Beyond Reaganomics,* 92–121, provide quantitative data for the observations made in this section. See also J. L. Brown, "Hunger in the U.S.," *Scientific American,* February 1987; H. Johnson, *Sleepwalking through History* (New York: Norton, 1991); S. Shames, *Outside the Dream: Child Poverty in America* (New York: Aperture and Washington, DC: Children's Defense Fund, 1991); *The State of America's Children, 1991* (Washington, DC: Children's Defense Fund, 1991); and *A Children's Defense Budget* (Washington, DC: Children's Defense Fund, 1990).

36. See Wilber and Jameson, *Beyond Reaganomics;* and Johnson, *Sleepwalking through History.*

37. S. Danziger and P. Gottschalk, "Social Programs: A Partial Solution to but not a Cause of Poverty: An Alternative to Charles Murray's View," in *Losing Ground: A Critique* (IRP

Special Report No. 38; Madison: Institute for Research on Poverty, University of Wisconsin, 1985), 78.

38. Press release (Washington, DC: Center on Budget and Policy Priorities, November 25, 1986).

39. Danziger and Gottschalk, "Social Programs," 79.

40. *Focus* 8(3) (Institute for Research on Poverty, University of Wisconsin-Madison, 1985), 4.

41. *Current Population Reports* (U.S. Department of Commerce, Bureau of the Census, 1989).

42. G. Cain, "Comments on Murray's Analysis of the Impact of the War on Poverty on the Labor Market Behavior of the Poor," *Losing Ground: A Critique,* 10.

43. Ibid., 14.

44. See F. F. Piven and R. A. Cloward, *Poor People's Movements: Why They Succeed, How They Fail* (New York: Vintage Books, 1977), 336–337; and D. P. Moynihan, *The Politics of Guaranteed Income* (New York: Random House, 1973).

45. Duncan and Hoffman, *Welfare Dynamics and Welfare Policy.* Unpublished manuscript, Institute for Social Research, University of Michigan, Ann Arbor, 1987.

46. M. Harrington, *Who Are the Poor?* (Washington, DC: Justice for All, 1987), 21; H. Karger and D. Stoesz, *American Social Welfare Policy* (New York: Longman, 1990), 184.

47. See *The State of America's Children;* and Karger and Stoesz, *American Social Welfare Policy,* 182.

48. Harrington, *Who are the Poor?* 20.

49. Ibid., 20.

50. Duncan and Hoffman, *Welfare Dynamics and Welfare Policy.*

51. For neo-Marxist views, see A. Gramsci, *The Prison Notebooks* (London: Lawrence & Wishart, 1971); R. Miliband, *The State in Capitalist Society* (London: Weidenfeld & Nicholson, 1969); N. Poulantzas, *Political Power and Social Classes* (London: Verso, 1973); and N. Poulantzas, *State, Power, Socialism* (London: Verso, 1978).

52. F. F. Piven and R. A. Cloward, *Regulating the Poor: The Functions of Public Welfare* (New York: Random House, 1971); and Piven and Cloward, *Poor People's Movements: Why They Succeed, How They Fail.*

53. M. McIntosh, "Feminism and Social Policy," *Critical Social Policy* 1(1)(1981).

54. N. Kohlert, "Welfare Reform: A Historic Consensus," *Social Work* 34 (1989), 303–306.

55. This view is developed by J. Axxin and M. Stern, *Dependency and Poverty* (Lexington, MA: Lexington Books, 1988), 9–26.

56. *U.S. Department of Labor News,* October 14, 1986.

57. See Piven and Cloward, *Regulating the Poor* (1971).

58. Z. Ferge, *A Society in the Making* (White Plains, NY: Sharpe, 1979).

59. U.S. Department of Commerce, Bureau of the Census, *Statistical Abstract of the U.S.,* (1992), Table 516, 318.

60. For social policy developments in Eastern Europe see B. Deacon et al., *Eastern Europe in the 1990s: Past Developments and Future Prospects for Social Policy* (London: Sage, 1992); B. Deacon, ed., *Social Policy, Social Justice, and Citizenship in Eastern Europe* (Brookfield: Avebury, 1992).

61. H. L. Wilensky and C. N. Lebeaux, *Industrial Society and Social Welfare* (New York: Russell Sage Foundation, 1958); and P. E. Weinberger, *Perspectives on Social Welfare,* 2nd ed. (New York: Macmillan, 1974).

62. F. J. Peirce, "A Functional Perspective of Social Welfare," *Social Work Education Reporter,* 18: 1 (March 1970), 36; and S. Mencher, "Newburgh: The Recurrent Crisis of Public Assistance," *Social Work* 7: 1 (January 1962), 3–11.

63. See J. Alber, "Continuities and Changes in the Idea of the Welfare State," *Politics and Society,* 16(4), 1988, 451–207; R. M. Titmuss, *Social Policy* (London: Allen & Unwin,

1974); G. Therborn, *"Welfare State and Capitalist Markets,"* Acta Sociologica, 30(3/4), 1987, 237–254; Esping-Andersen, *The Three Worlds of Welfare Capitalism* (Cambridge: Polity).

64. For more information, see Rutkevich et al., eds., *Transformations of Social Structure in the USSR and Poland* (Moscow-Warsaw: 1974).

65. S. E. Zimbalist, *Historical Themes and Landmarks in Social Welfare Research* (New York: Harper & Row, 1977), 35–41.

66. E. D. Banfield, *The Unheavenly City Revisited* (Boston: Little, Brown, 1974), 12.

67. R. Hofstadter, *Social Darwinism in American Thought* (Boston: Beacon, 1955).

68. See A. R. Jensen, "How Much Can We Boost IQ and Scholastic Achievement?" *Harvard Education Review* 39 (Winter 1969), 1–123. (Subsequent issues of this journal included numerous replies to Jensen's article.) R. J. Herrnstein, "IQ," *Atlantic Monthly* 228 (September 1971), 43–68; and R. J. Herrnstein, *IQ in the Meritocracy* (Boston: Little, Brown, 1971).

69. Jensen used data from studies of identical twins, conducted in the 1940s and 1950s, by British psychologist Sir Cyril Burt. These studies have since come under suspicion. See "An Epitaph for Sir Cyril?" *Newsweek* (December 20, 1976), 76; "Basic Study on IQ Pattern Challenged," *Christian Science Monitor* (November 30, 1976), 15. In brief, Burt was accused of fraud and of reporting tests that were never done.

70. W. Ryan, "Is Banfield Serious?" *Social Policy* (November-December, 1970), 76; "Postscript: "A Call to Action," *Social Policy* (May-June, 1972), 54; W. Ryan, *Blaming the Victim* (New York: Pantheon, 1971); E. B. Leacock, ed., *The Culture of Poverty: A Critique* (New York: Simon & Schuster, 1971); and S. Scarr-Salapat and R. Weinberg, "When Black Children Grow Up in White Homes," *Psychology Today* 9 (December 1975), 80–82.

71. N. Chomsky, "The Fallacy of Rischard Herrnstein's IQ," *Social Policy* 3 (May-June 1972), 19–25; K. W. Deutsch and T. Edsall, "The Meritocracy Scare," *Society* 9 (September-October, 1972), 71–79; A. S. Goldberger, *Mysteries of the Meritocracy* (Madison: University of Wisconsin, Institute on Research on Poverty, October 1974); J. Ryan, "IQ—The Illusion of Objectivity," in *Race and Intelligence,* K. Richardson and D. Spears, eds. (Baltimore, MD: Penguin Books, 1972).

72. S. M. Miller and P. A. Roby, *The Future of Inequality* (New York: Basic Books, 1970); M. Rein, "Problems in the Definition and Measurement of Poverty," in L. A. Ferman et al., eds., *Poverty in America* (Ann Arbor, MI: University of Michigan, 1969).

73. This view relies heavily on H. Gans, *The uses of poverty,* in *Poverty in America,* 20–24; and H. Gans, *More Equality* (New York: Pantheon, 1973).

CHAPTER 7

Well-Being in the
Context of Social Change

"Anguish in Adaptation:[1]

"Is democracy working, or does it have serious problems?"

	Hungary	Poland	Czechoslovakia
Working	18%	15%	8%
Serious problems	69%	60%	83%
Don't know	13%	25%	10%

"Thinking about your own economic situation, is it better, worse, or about the same as under the Communists?"

Better	4%	12%	6%
Worse	72%	41%	58%
Same	23%	44%	35%

"Do you think things in your country will be better, worse, or the same five years from now?"

Better	49%	59%	70%
Worse	27%	8%	6%
Same	13%	8%	8%

"How Arkansas ranks:"[2]

	Teachers' salaries	Spending per pupil	Income	AFDC caseload
U.S.	$31,600	$4,980	$18,691	+21.0%
Ark.	22,000	3,272	14,188	+9.2%
Rank	49	48	47	47

"Few statistics about the United States are more startling than the growth of the prison population during the quarter-century since Americans abandoned the war on poverty. . . . The U.S. is pulling away from second-place South Africa as champion incarcerator of the world."[3]

"Infant mortality:"[4]

District of Columbia	23.2%
Detroit	21.0%
Baltimore	18.0%
Memphis	17.6%
Philadelphia	17.5%
Boston	13.9%
San Jose	7.8%

THE SOCIETAL CONTEXT OF WELL-BEING

How do these social statistics relate to well-being? What do they signify about social change or the achievement of societal goals? The well-being of all citizens, individually and collectively, is the crucial goal of society and the ultimate objective of social policies. But how should we understand and measure well-being in efforts to prevent or eliminate problems and to maximize opportunities for development?

Answers to these and similar questions depend on various conceptions of the well-being of society, on perceptions of the nature of social change, and on different strategies of social development. They also depend on the different types of social indicators available to measure social change and social progress. Much of the literature on well-being and social indicators has focused on these concerns. There is no consensus, however, on the nature of well-being, the social indicators that should be used, and the distribution of well-being in society. Nor is there consensus about how to measure well-being, social development, and healthy social functioning.

APPROACHES TO WELL-BEING
AND SOCIAL INDICATORS

Central to social policy are the nature of well-being, its measurement, and its distribution. In a pragmatic context, social policy aims to increase and distribute well-being in just and fair ways (see Figure 1-2). Social workers recognize that in practice they have to select specific concepts of well-being to guide their interventions. The choice of theory is not easy, but it is crucial. In deciding which are the optimal frameworks for structuring well-being and formulating social policy, social workers rely on their own knowledge, experience, and skills and on available literature and research.

Three major approaches to well-being and its measurement stand out in the limited and controversial literature on the subject. The first two study the satisfaction (or dissatisfaction) of basic human needs of individuals and of society and development strategies. The third pragmatically considers the relation between goals desired and results achieved.

Basic Individual Needs

Human beings need particular things to survive and to realize their capabilities and potential. Most concepts of human potential relate directly to the satisfaction of human needs.

The human-needs framework is valuable in outlining the inadequacies of current social conditions, in orienting social priorities, and in creating visions of a desirable society. By moving from market criteria, the idea of basic needs can place human beings at the center of the stage. Moreover, the simplicity of the concept is appealing: If a realistically small number of basic needs can be identified, including nutrition, health, and literacy, the likelihood of eliciting general agreement will increase.

But the concept of basic needs itself is controversial. Although there is some agreement about the fundamental material prerequisites for physical survival, including the adequate per capita daily caloric intake developed by the World Health Organization, there has been far less agreement about nonmaterial prerequisites and other structural variables such as poverty, inequality, or access to employment opportunities. Psychologists have constructed lists of needs to explain human behavior. For example, Maslow formulated this hierarchy of basic human needs: physiological, safety, belongingness and love, esteem, and self-actualization. Allardt, who studied Scandinavian countries, organized needs in three groups: living (having material resources), interpersonal relationships (loving), and relations with the wider society (being: control over one's fate and lack of alienation).[5]

Brodsky suggested that well-being is more than the mere absence of maladjustment or an equilibrium between discomfort and comfort. He saw well-being as a subjective emotional state of positive affect (for example, happiness, pleasure, enjoyment, joy, and fun), relatively low negative affect (for example, unhappiness, depression, anger, frustration, or anxiety), and general life satisfaction. In this view, well-being is subjective and emotional, it is a temporary state, it is the product of personal goals and purposes, and it is more than the absence of negative affect and personal conflicts.[6]

Erikson emphasized life stages and the continuity of life from birth to death; he concluded that psychosocial strength depends on a total process that regulates individual life cycles, the sequence of generations, and the structure of society simultaneously, for all three have evolved together. From the cycle of life, Erikson maintained, such dispositions as faith, willpower, purpose, efficiency, devotion, affection, responsibility, and sagacity flow into the life of institutions. Without them, institutions wilt.[7] On the basis of Freud's model of the structure of personality and its components (the id, ego, and superego) Murray and Levinson stressed the division of a personality and the ego ideal in connection with personal growth and motivation.[8] Commentators such as Jahoda have suggested several empirical indicators for positive mental health: attitude toward the self; growth, development, and self-actualization; integration; autonomy; perception of reality; and environmental mastery.[9] Although these and other lists of needs offer several choices, there is no consensus on their usefulness in social policy planning.

Given this wide range of basic individual needs (for security, welfare, freedom of access to resources, freedom from surveillance and incarceration, identity, and ecological balance, to mention a few), how can their satisfaction be prioritized and optimized? Are physical and mental health, the prospect of survival, and the mental capacity to choose or to learn basic human needs?[10] There is no consensus about the selection of single social indicators or an overall index. The formidable problem of comparing and weighting each social indicator remains to be resolved.[11]

Basic Needs of Society

Communities and society as a whole also have collective needs. Their satisfaction enhances or constricts the society's human environment. Therefore, it is important to identify and measure a set of societal needs that are essential for a community to survive and meet its members' needs.

What collective needs are critical in organizing community life, social relations, and political authority? What societal arrangements encourage or discourage the satisfaction of individual needs and social development? What social preconditions optimize societal development for individual growth? Is there a hierarchy to rank physical safety, public health, autonomy, material production and distribution, reproduction and infant care, education, the welfare state, communication, conflict, and cooperation? Without such societal preconditions, individual and social needs are unlikely to be met. What theories of social structure and organization or social change are most suitable?

Parsons's conceptualization of the "human action system" includes the organism, the personality, the social system, and the cultural system. The primary social subsystems, according to Parsons, are the societal community (the core structure of society), characterized by influence; the economy, characterized by money; the polity, characterized by power; and the cultural community, characterized by value commitments and pattern maintenance.[12] Parsons suggested that the unit of interpretation between a personality and a social system is not the individual but a role or set of roles. Social systems can be regarded as information or input-output systems. The primary desired output of social systems is to the personalities of their members.[13] Rewards, for example, are output from the social system to personalities; personalities input contributions to the social system. The parts of a system are linked by media of exchange such as language, money, influence, or commitments.

Theories that attribute social change to evolution (including those of Comte, Spencer, and Durkheim) contend that change occurs by the progression of society from rural to agrarian forms to more complex industrial, urban patterns. Other theories claim that social change is brought about by revolution and action (including those of Marx, Parsons, Dahrendorf, and Etzioni and Etzioni); class conflict or consensus and political struggle are the principal mechanisms of change. Both types of theories are frameworks for structuring and measuring well-being.[14]

Developmental Approaches and Social Functioning

Economic and human development frameworks combine both the satisfaction of individual needs and societal prerequisites. Economic development strategies provide traditional structures and measurement of well-being in the form of economic reports, including the GNP and other economic indicators of production and consumption.

Conventional models of development emphasize macroeconomic growth based on high levels of industrialization and on welfare economics, which is concerned not with the welfare system but with the efficient allocation of resources in a perfectly competitive economy. Welfare economics constitutes a normative analysis of the economy's functioning to determine how best to organize economic activity, distribute income, and structure tax policy. Economic technical tools, including Pareto's efficiency or optimum (a condition that cannot be altered to the advantage of one participant without at least some disadvantage to some other person) attempt to measure the losses that arise from misplaced governmental interference with a competitive equilibrium.[15] Neoclassical welfare economics reduces well-being to material affluence or an accumulation of commodities and thus represents welfare in terms of money values and equates national well-being with the per capita GNP or other economic statistics.

Concepts of human development use a broader societal development framework that focuses on the dynamic processes of social life—the relationships between individuals and the social structure.[16] This concept of development implies not merely the possession of material resources but a process that makes human well-being the goal of economic, social, and political change.

Concepts of human development are also reflected in approaches to well-being that emphasize social functioning—the competence with which societal institutions perform social and cultural roles. Enhancing appropriate individual, group, and community behavior is a central concept in social work practice.[17] Social workers have direct experience with developmental concepts, healthy and unhealthy functioning, and approaches that define health as a state of complete physical, mental, and social well-being—not merely the absence of disease or infirmity.[18] Can this perspective be used to evaluate societal well-being and to define it not merely as the absence of undesirable social conditions but rather as a developmental state of competent psychosocial and economic functioning?

Goal-Achievement Approaches: Input-Output Strategies

Needs-oriented approaches (individual and societal) have resulted in several frameworks for studying well-being. They lack, however, consensus regarding the nature and ranking of needs. In contrast, some commentators argue that goal-and-achievement approaches can be more effective. The relationship between goals desired and results achieved provides less controversial and more pragmatic strategies to structure and improve well-being.

Several theoretical and technical perspectives are crucial in the debate about the nature of well-being. At the core of the challenge is the extent to which the major goals of a society have been achieved. The establishment of effective national, state, and local social policy depends largely on knowing where we want to be as a society, where we are, and how to achieve desired goals (see Chapter 1). Concepts of well-being and quality of life are measures of welfare; they measure the social health of a society and describe the condition of the society's major concerns. Analysis of change and development of policies and actions necessary to improve well-being depend on these aggregate perspectives and measures.

In the context of social policy, these approaches examine how well a society has achieved its major goals. The status of well-being (the end or outcome of the social policy process) is related to the societal goals (the beginning input of the policy process). The feedback between input and output forms a basic framework for the distribution of well-being in relation to desired goals.

Measures of output are distinguished from those of input to avoid duplicating essentially identical information. In education, for example, this distinction is apparent: the quantity and quality of education can be assessed by the level of achievement on tests and years of schooling.

Societal goals for citizens, communities, and society converge and interact to guide the structuring and measurement of well-being and the quality of life. Ideological, political, economic, and social goals reflect where society wants to be. They also suggest that well-being is a multidimensional, multidisciplinary, and interactional (between the individual and society) concept. Thus national well-being should be measured by multidimensional concerns. However, in the United States, for example, it is not: the president is required by law to report annually on only the economic health of the nation. Is it not equally important to report on the country's social health?

Egalitarian concerns, including the distribution of power, discrimination, citizenship, health, education, crime, wealth, and income, should determine the methods of measuring the status of achieved outcomes. If the development of laissez-faire markets is a major societal goal, the status of the free economy and the degree of governmental intervention in market functions should guide the assessment of societal well-being and its components. If the elimination of poverty is a societal goal, the status of poor people should influence the approaches to well-being and the assessment of society's achievements. To the extent that political, economic, and social democracy constitutes a major goal of society, the status of democratic practice should be incorporated into the quality-of-life index.

Problems arise when society's major goals are not clear. In the context of social policy, it is frequently difficult to distinguish the stated and actual priorities of the country, particularly if they are not clearly articulated or widely publicized. Pluralistic societies tend to have several goals, some more explicit than others and some in conflict with each other. For example, economic growth frequently conflicts with protecting or improving the physical environment; full employment conflicts with reducing inflation; and eliminating poverty conflicts with maintaining laissez-faire markets. Similarly, maximizing individual, family, and community well-being does not necessarily suggest complementary priorities. In social policy practice, the ranking of goals and outcomes to establish priorities is a frequent and crucial decision.

In the context of social work values, goals, commitments, knowledge, and skills, social workers must choose among alternatives to structure and measure well-being.[19] Innovative, alternative approaches to well-being require effective syntheses of theories of normal individual and societal development and healthy functioning with theories of maladaptation and dysfunction; of market and government responsibility; of power, social justice, equality, and fairness; of dynamic decision-making processes that secure democratic participation; and of democracy in the polity, the economic market, and sociocultural relations.

The Social Indicators Movement and the Quality of Life

In the 1960s, social indicators were proclaimed to be tools that could dramatically enhance the design and implementation of social policy planning to improve well-being. Despite the wide use of the term *social indicator,* however, there is still no agreement on its definition. For some writers, any social statistic is a social indicator. For others, a social indicator is a statistical measure that monitors levels and changes in a fundamental area of concern to social policy planners.[20]

Social indicators came into common usage in the mid-1960s in the United States.[21] Durkheim, Thorndike, and others used different indicators for a "general goodness" index.[22] In 1966, Bauer edited *Social Indicators* for the National Aeronautics and Space Administration, focusing on the economic benefits of its operations.[23] By the late 1960s emphasis moved to examination of potential social indicators and systems of social indicators in the context of governmental social policy.[24] The War on Poverty, increased economic prosperity, the crisis in the cities, and environmental pollution directed interest toward social indicators and a quality-of-life index to measure and assess the basic functions of the American society in the context of planning.[25]

The social indicators movement arose in the 1960s in an attempt to bring new methods to bear on the persistent problems of Western societies. Social indicators were proposed to monitor unpredictable patterns of national development and provide data to simplify decisions about complex issues of social change. Soon social indicators were seen as equally applicable to the severe problems of poorer countries. Keynesian economic development policies, economic growth regulations, and planning for social welfare intensified the need for indicators. Just as econometrics and economic indicators had transformed economic policy-making, social indicators were seen as integral to the planning system of modern society. Since economic growth was secured, it was thought, the state's main challenge would now be to improve the quality of life. Already people were talking about the "social indicators movement."

Interest was also generated outside the United States and was reflected in publications inspired by social indicators thinking, including Britain's annual *Social Trends*. In 1974 France's Ministry of the Environment was renamed the Ministry for the Quality of Life. The United Nations promoted the use of social indicators in efficient planning to improve the living standards of Third World countries. Although the U.N. Research Institute for Social Development (UNRISD) began to publish the results of its research on social indicators in the late 1960s, a U.N. report on defining and measuring levels of living for developmental planning was published as early as 1954. Levels of living were defined in terms of social indicators of health, education, and nutritional levels rather than in terms of material living standards, with emphasis on the influence of levels of living on economic growth.[26] The U.N.'s work on levels of living, or "Social Minimum Level of Living," was designed as a strategic tool to guide policy-making and the assessment of well-being.[27]

Social indicators were soon designed to determine the extent of poverty and to evaluate antipoverty programs. Attention shifted from problems of economic inefficiency or the underutilization of human resources toward the structural determinants of poverty and the ways in which inequalities are created and reproduced. A World Bank study found that conventional development strategies tend to worsen economic inequalities in the poorest countries.[28] This confirms UNRISD's conclusions that such inequalities might mean that growth would not benefit the mass of the population. As a result of concern for the human consequences of development strategies and in recognition that economic development does not necessarily improve well-being, the Organization for Economic Cooperation and Development (OECD) established a program to develop social indicators to measure social change and the distribution of well-being in its member countries.[29] These social indicators could enable policies to provide immediate benefits for the poorest in society and weaken the vicious circles in which they are often trapped. The United Nations Education and Scientific Organization

(UNESCO), for instance, moved its focus from human resources indicators to the linkage of social and economic indicators that are relevant to measuring trends and disparities within countries.

Several diverse lists of indicators, based on various assumptions about well-being and methods of measurement, were constructed at that time.[30] A list of social indicators presented to the U.S. Congress represents the then-dominant strategy:[31]

1. Infant mortality (per 1,000 live births).
2. Maternal mortality (per 100,000 live births).
3. Family planning services for low-income women aged 15 to 44.
4. Deaths from accidents (per 100,000 population).
5. Number of persons in state mental hospitals.
6. Expectancy of a healthy life.
7. Percentage of 3- to 5-year-olds in school or preschool.
8. Percentage of people aged 25 and older who graduated from high school.
9. Percentage of people aged 25 and older who graduated from college.
10. Number of people in the learning force.
11. Percentage of major cities with public community colleges.
12. Number of first-year students in medical schools.
13. Percentage of handicapped people rehabilitated.
14. Average weekly hours of work in manufacturing.
15. Labor force participation rate for women aged 35 to 64.
16. Average annual paid vacation in manufacturing.
17. Percentage of housing units with bathtubs or showers.
18. Percentage of the population that is illiterate.
19. Voters as a percentage of the voting-age population.
20. Private philanthropy as a percentage of the GNP.
21. Public and private expenditures for health, education, and welfare as a percentage of the GNP.
22. Percentage of the population in poverty.
23. Income of the lowest fifth of the population.
24. Percentage of people who work during the year.
25. Life expectancy.

Quality of life became an all-inclusive catchword, and several governmental agencies, including the U.S. Environmental Protection Agency, researched quality-of-life indicators.[32] Publications addressing the issue of Minimum Living Standards proliferated in the United States and abroad. Social reports portraying major aspects of social change in terms of social statistics were published regularly by official statistical agencies in most Western countries. The World Bank provides data for assessing human welfare in more than 170 countries.[33]

In the 1980s and 1990s, there was a backlash against social indicators; governments opted less for social engineering and social reform and more for repressive solutions and toleration of high social costs (including those associated with increased unemployment). When Reaganomics and Thatcherism identified governmental interventions and social reform as a cause rather than a cure of social problems and refused to take responsibility for social welfare, activities to promote social indicators came under threat. The monetarist concern with limiting governmental expenditures and the view of the new political Right that the welfare state produces poverty (rather than helping to ameliorate the degrading effects of unregulated market activities) deflated the interest in social indicators.

Although improved social data can lead to a more sensitive understanding of the interrelations between economic development and other social phenomena, the administrations of Presidents Nixon, Reagan, and Bush curtailed developmental work on social indicators. Thus, at the end of 1983 the U.S. Center for Coordination of Research on Social Indicators was closed, and its newsletter suspended publication.[34] Since 1983 relatively little progress in this area has been made in the United States; research and publications on the subject have been reduced and major efforts to define and measure well-being have been severely curtailed or discontinued.

What Can Social Indicators Do?

Can social indicators improve the design and implementation of social policy? Although the social indicators movement has enhanced social policy planning by improving the measurement and evaluation of well-being and social change, it has not lived up to all of its original promises. Social indicators can be used to set targets for social development, monitor the consequences of social policies or programs, forecast the effects of different interventions, and compare and evaluate social policies. However, some other claims that were made early in the movement proved unrealistic. For example, the idea that social indicators can help automatically identify priorities and thus establish social policy goals has been replaced by the idea that the definition of overall social goals determines which social indicators are relevant. Thus, social indicators will not by themselves define well-being or show the important features of social change or human development. Rather, the construction and selection of social indicators depend on theories about the well-being of society, social change, and human development.

Social policy planners put different social indicators to different uses. Some indicators explain social change; others determine which changes are under way, how the changes are interrelated, and what their impact will be on people. Social indicators also ascertain the degree to which social goals are being achieved.

Social indicators are thus instruments that use social data to represent social change and the realization of social goals; they indicate how a social concern is structured or is changing, guide human concern (such as how well people are fed, housed, or educated), and are surrogates for concepts and theories.

In another sense, social indicators compare, aggregate, and analyze social statistics. Quantification has its pitfalls, and quantitative information is certainly not necessarily superior to qualitative information. But in the context of social policy planning, it is often useful to show how and where conditions are getting better or worse. Hence, social indicators can show not only that specific concerns are improving or deteriorating, but also that this is occurring at different rates or places and among various social groups. Statistical analysis can relate social indicators to test explanations of social change and to build models of change for analysis or forecasting.

Different concepts of social change and the status quo lead to various explanations of social progress and social concerns—and to different social indicators. The important concerns of society and the features of well-being or social change are controversial and operationally unclear. The choice of social indicators varies according to the prevailing theory of reality (see the discussion of Heraclitean and Parmenidean theories in Chapter 1) and to different strategies for social change and views about human development. In the Keynesian theory of economic development, in which the demand side of the economy is important, social indicators relate to aggregate demand, while in Reaganomics or supply-side economic theories of development, social indicators relate to aggregate supply. If the absence of disease is central to a definition of health, well-being, and human development, social indicators should measure illness. But if the total behavior and competent functioning of an individual are criteria of health, social indicators should measure the competence with which a person performs roles in society.

Major Types of Indicators

The distinctions between different types of social indicators are related to their intended uses. In social policy practice it is important to know why social indicators are constructed before one considers the possible application of the indicators to other purposes. The major types of social indicators include direct, indirect, input and output, objective, subjective, system, and aggregated social indicators.[35]

Direct social indicators (such as special household surveys) are specifically designed to measure social conditions, while *indirect* social indicators (including data on employment, education, health, income, or demography) are based on administrative accounting statistics.

Input-output social indicators report actual results achieved in social policy planning. Statistics that are used to discuss the welfare state and its programs reflect the resources deployed in coping with particular problems but do not provide evidence of the seriousness of the actual problems or the results of programs. A genuine commitment to a social goal requires more than appropriating funds; it also includes monitoring the effectiveness of the expenditures. Hence, one of the main uses of input-output social indicators is to evaluate policies.[36] However, in social policy analysis it is rarely easy to trace the links between input and output or between changes in a policy and changes in social conditions.

It has been argued that in the context of well-being or the quality of life, the most important output must be an individual's experience. This experience is a *subjective* output social indicator that reflects a person's summary assessment of a social condition—how satisfactory the person's state of health or happiness is. An *objective* output social indicator is a physician's judgment of a person's health (based on a physical examination, laboratory tests, and other medical criteria. Most social indicators are objective measures that involve environmental conditions or physiological attributes recorded similarly by any reliable observer. In contrast, subjective measures are based on individual reports of attitudes, evaluations, emotional states, aspirations, or intentions.

Subjective social indicators are concerned with how people feel about their lives. Personal views relate to the satisfaction of a broad spectrum of needs that are usually associated with the ends individuals choose. Objective social indicators assess social conditions and the satisfaction of general human needs.

People may achieve enough economic security to liberate them from obsessive concern with income and the accumulation of material objects but still be dissatisfied with their lives or their government. Economic and material values have not disappeared, nor are they likely to, but today more and more people in this country are concerned with other values and nonmaterial needs—the need for sensitive and responsive relationships, for creative work, for empowerment, for the respect and approval of friends, for identification with the community, and for a stimulating and fulfilling life. In this context, numerous projects examine well-being in various specific areas of people's lives and measure happiness and satisfaction.[37] The boundaries between objective and subjective measures are imprecise. Rather than reflect the true value of the data, subjective and objective social indicators distinguish between private experiences and public phenomena.

Attempts to assess the quality of life from subjective social indicators have typically asked survey respondents to rate their feelings.[38] Feelings, beliefs, and satisfaction may, however, be the product of personal expectations and aspirations (or other diverse forces that make up an individual's inner life) rather than of objective circumstances. Since ideological orientations tend to condition responses to questions about social institutions, some commentators dislike the use of subjective quality-of-life measures as the prime indicators of well-being. But such measures are useful in several other functions, including interpreting the significance of social changes or social processes.

Many *aggregated* (individual) social indicators are simple totals (for example, levels of marriage and divorce), averages (such as average household income), rates (such as the age-adjusted mortality rate), or distributions (such as the inequality of land ownership). *System* (global) indicators, on the other hand, refer to some property of a human collectivity that is not derived from statistics about individuals (such as governmental expenditures, rates of deforestation, and the gross national product).

Social Accounting and Social Reports

Social accounting is still in its infancy, and efforts to design social accounts have been experimental. Social accounting approaches, complex and technically complicated, attempt to relate trends and structures in an explicit, consistent way. Social accounting frameworks are patterned on methods of economic accounting; they organize data into compact structures that represent flows of resources among various institutions or the application of resources to various activities. The aim is to trace and assess the implications of change in one institution or the resources needed by a social phenomenon for the whole society.

Unlike economic accounts, social accounting is expressed in nonmonetary terms and therefore has been limited to a narrow range of social phenomena. A particularly comprehensive demography-based social accounting system (the System of Social and Demographic Statistics) was developed by the United Nations Statistical Office on the assumption that human life can be described in terms of states and transitions between states. It is an accounting framework for recording people's changing positions rather than an explanatory model.[39]

While social accounting aims to capture interrelationships among social activities, *social reports* detail the relevance of institutions and their output to well-being, welfare, or national goals. Social reports are familiar figures in the statistical apparatus of many countries and are among the most successful initial objectives of the social indicators movement.

The first recognizable social reports were the series of volumes edited by Ogburn in the United States after World War I and during the Great Depression.[40] Several studies and efforts to structure national social reports have been published since, particularly in the 1960s and 1970s. The studies of Sheldon and Moore and of Gross were early attempts to demonstrate what a social report might look like; Campbell and Converse focused on subjective social indicators; and the report of the U.S. Department of Health, Education, and Welfare is an example of social reporting.[41]

Both the United Nations and the Organization for Economic Cooperation and Development (OECD) have worked on ideal sets of social indicators for national reporting. Although they differ in their choice of specific indicators and in the number and range of indicators, the reports tend to include similar broad categories. Typically, data are organized into groups of indexes that deal with concerns of different governmental departments: demography, environment, science and technology, education, the arts and culture, employment, income, inequality and stratification, production and consumption, welfare services, health, family patterns, housing, social participation, political activities, leisure, the media, crime and law, and intergroup relations (discrimination).

Like economic reports, social reports are a compendium of social indicators describing a country, a region, or a major social concern. Although they are used for several divergent purposes, social reports usually set out to provide an overview of social change and the quality of life. In a broad sense, they are a quality-of-life index; they reflect a theoretical framework that recognizes individual impacts of and interrelationships among various factors and enables meaningful trade-offs among them. Social reports imply a set of guidelines with which to interpret social, economic, political, and ideological phenomena and trends in a country.

Quality-of-life indicators are most useful in social policy when they are aggregated in a single index capable of summing the indicators to a broader context. However, this task has often proved elusive.

THE NORMATIVE BASE OF
WELL-BEING AND SOCIAL INDICATORS

Insurmountable difficulties are posed by the search for a single, composite measure of well-being, welfare, or quality of life. The apparent simplicity or the technical sophistication of such measures is appealing but often misleading. Typically, social indicators tend to treat major social concerns, including inequality and the distribution of power, as irrelevant to well-being; and it is rare to find the rationale for these judgments explicated.

Social interests, ideology, and concepts of social power, distributive justice, and equality enter into social indicators and social reports. Rather than being neutral, social indicators or social reports are representations of social reality and conflict and are framed in terms of implicit or explicit theories. A social statistic becomes a social indicator or a social report (a system of social indicators) only when the statistic is related to other information in a conceptual system of some sort: a theory of well-being or human development. Hence, social reports are based on theoretical frameworks structured by the concepts that interrelate data about society's goals or social processes.

Although there is no consensus on whether indicators must be normative, the very process of developing indicators is value-laden. Fundamentally, indicators have direction with one pole regarded as "good" and the other regarded as "bad." What is thought of as good in the perspective of some may be considered bad in the view of others. A high unemployment rate in a region is distressing to residents (an indicator of privation) but is encouraging to an industry that is seeking a large pool of low-wage workers (an indicator of economic opportunity).

In the normative context, indicators reflect, exclude, or obscure major values, including power, discrimination, fairness, and societal costs. The GNP measures economic growth but excludes costs related to pollution, psychosocial dysfunction, or reductions in the quality of life.[42] Industrial production may pollute the physical environment, reduce forests, increase stress and psychological problems, and produce traffic congestion in cities. Should these effects be measured and included in the GNP indicator? Should "net economic welfare" (GNP minus costs) be calculated by adjusting GNP numbers to such problems?[43]

The selection and structure of the official poverty line reflects its normative nature. For example, the United States selected an absolute definition of poverty: individuals or families whose income falls below some absolute dollar amount that is necessary to sustain a minimal level of living. The European Community or other industrialized countries chose a relative definition of poverty: people who earn incomes that are too far below others in the country. Usually the poverty line is set at half the median national family income. In contrast to absolute definitions, which use an absolute dollar standard, relative approaches to poverty focus on the distance separating economic classes, on social stratification, and on the distribution of power.

Is it symptomatic that absolute definitions of poverty understate the number of poor and the level of poverty? Does the selection of absolute indicators of poverty reflect the dominant views about poverty and the welfare state? The absolute definition of poverty prevailing in the United States (and other countries represented by Models 1 and 2 of welfare states) reflects laissez-faire principles, utilitarian or market perspectives of distributive justice, and a strong emphasis on private property and individual failure and provides only subsistence levels of benefits for brief emergencies. In contrast, relative definitions of poverty (associated with Models 3 and 4) reflect Rawlsian concepts of distributive justice, equality, and citizenship, the need for governmental interventions in the economic market and commitments to full employment. (See Tables 6-1 and 6-2.)

In brief, social indicators and social or economic reports are value-laden. While they appear to be technical, neutral tools to define and measure poverty or other major concerns of society, they tend to obscure their normative base.[44]

WELL-BEING AND SOCIAL POLICY:
A CHALLENGE TO SOCIAL WORK

Social reports are valuable collections of social indicators that are required to understand and guide social change and social policies for development. Those that have been published to date have played an important role in the social policy debate and in the design and evaluation of social policy. By bringing together material on a wide range of social phenomena related to well-being, they provide a ready source of information with which to contrast and supplement the more accessible collection of economic statistics. Basic changes in energy, the consumption of goods, demography, food, shelter, health, clothing, employment, the work force, education, welfare, crime, and housing are elaborated in the social indicators literature, at least with regard to their distribution and the circumstances of specific groups, including the poor. Although most social indicators focus on consumption and on other economic indicators, some social indicators go beyond actual consumption to consider the potential possession of commodities: for example, the amount of work that women in various Asian countries would have to do to afford a number of different commodities; or how higher state expenditures for public welfare and education contribute to individual and family well-being.[45]

Existing social reports are not detailed enough to be central to measuring well-being or to overall development strategies. Many publications and collections of data are not so much social reports or tools for social policy practitioners as data sources for researchers. Furthermore, most literature on social indicators concerns individual consumption and possession of various commodities but neglects the structure and function of social institutions and the distribution of power, the control and allocation of resources, social classes, empowerment of the powerless, discrimination, the ecosystem, and distributive justice.

In spite of certain common dimensions in most social reports, the widely divergent views on well-being and the selection of indicators to measure it are at the epicenter of the debate on social indicators.[46] What are the most powerful frameworks or theories of behavior to guide social change and the improvement of society? Should we measure well-being of individuals, of major social institutions, or of both? Since few proposals include subjective indicators, should such indicators be excluded from measuring well-being? Should social stratification and social mobility be included or excluded? Although work and employment are typical dimensions of efforts to define and measure societal well-being, should control of the labor force (the relations between workers and owners) or democracy in the workplace receive less attention?

Most proposals rely on data and social indicators from governmental agencies, but should the organization of social problems and concerns be defined by governmental agencies? Should these institutions decide what questions of societal organization and structure, social class interest groups, and discrimination should be included or excluded? Why are data about controversial issues, including elitism, the concentration of power, the lack of empowerment, and inequality, either unavailable or deemed unworthy for social reporting? The class system (except occupational categories) and gender issues (except demography, health, and education)—two areas in which lines of power are hard to trace in social reports—are typically neglected in accounts of well-being. The very poor receive little attention, but the very rich receive none.

Although a plethora of social statistics is systematically collected by governmental agencies, there is a striking lack of informed debate about the rationale or the concepts of well-being on which they are based. Usually there is no explanation of the absence of certain data, including data on power in society and the control of social conditions.

NOTES

1. From "Anguish in Adaptation" by J. Kaufman. In the *Boston Globe,* February 23, 1992, 1, 8. Copyright © 1992 by Globe Newspaper Co. Reprinted by permission of Globe Newspaper Co. Affiliated Publications.
2. From "Clinton's Record: Fodders for Friends, Foes Alike" by A. Pertman. In the *Boston Globe,* February 23, 1992, 1, 16. Copyright © 1992 by Globe Newspaper Co. Reprinted by permission of Globe Newspaper Co. Affiliated Publications.
3. "Lock-'em-Up Leader of the World," editorial, *Boston Globe,* February 22, 1992, 10.
4. From "Dimensions: Infant Mortality, 1988." In *Education Week,* September 4, 1991, 3. Copyright © Editorial Projects in Education. Reprinted by permission of Editorial Projects in Education.
5. A. H. Maslow, *Motivation and Personality,* 2nd ed. (New York: Harper, 1970); E. Allardt, "A Welfare Model for Selecting Indicators of National Development," *Policy Sciences* 4(1), (1973), 63–74. See also C. Towle, *Common Human Needs,* rev. ed. (Silver Spring, MD: National Association of Social Workers, 1987); J. McHale and M. C. McHale, *Basic Human Needs: A Framework for Action: A Report to the United Nations Environmental Programme, April 1977* (New Brunswick, NJ: Transaction Books, 1978).
6. S. L. Brodsky, *The Psychology of Adjustment and Well-Being* (New York: Holt, Rinehart & Winston, 1988).
7. E. H. Erikson, "Life Cycle," in *International Encyclopedia of the Social Sciences,* vol. 9 (New York: Free Press, 1968), 288–292.
8. H. A. Murray, "Personality: Contemporary Viewpoints, II. Components of an Evolving Personological System," in *International Encyclopedia of the Social Sciences,* vol. 12 (New York: Free Press, 1968), 7; H. Levinson, *The Exceptional Executive: A Psychological Conception* (Cambridge, MA: Harvard University Press, 1968).
9. M. Jahoda, *Current Concepts of Positive Mental Health* (New York: Basic Books, 1958).
10. L. Doyal and I. Gough, "A Theory of Human Needs," *Critical Social Policy* 10 (1984), 6–38; and L. Doyal and I. Gough, *A Theory of Human Need* (New York: Guilford Press, 1991).
11. Although factor analysis provides one mathematical approach to the resolution of the weighting problem, the issue has several problematic aspects.
12. T. Parsons, "Systems Analysis: Social Systems," in *International Encyclopedia of Social Sciences,* vol. 15 (New York: Free Press, 1968), 461–469.
13. Ibid., 469.
14. A. Comte, *The Positive Philosophy of August Comte* (London: Bell, 1938); H. Spencer, *Principles of Sociology* (New York: Appleton, 1896); E. Durkheim, *On Institutional Analysis* (Chicago: Chicago University Press, 1978); P. Worsley, *Marx and Marxism* (London: Tavistock Publications, 1982); T. Parsons et al., *Working Papers in the Theory of Action* (New York: Free Press, 1953); R. Dahrendorf, *The New Liberty* (London: Routledge

& Kegan Paul, 1975); A. Etzioni and E. Etzioni, *Social Change: Sources, Patterns, and Consequences* (New York: Basic Books, 1964).

15. See P. Samuelson and W. Nordhaus, *Economics* (New York: McGraw-Hill, 1989), 748–750, 827, 984.

16. See I. Miles, *Social Indicators for Human Development* (New York: St. Martin's Press, 1985), 11. In this view, human development refers to the development of human beings in all life stages and consists of a harmonious relationship among people, society, and nature, ensuring the fullest flowering of human potential without degrading or destroying society or nature. See also K. C. Land and S. Spilerman, *Social Indicator Models* (New York: Russell Sage Foundation, 1975).

17. For a social functioning model applied to health care and human services, see R. M. Butler, *Well-Being* (Littleton, MA: Copley, 1989); R. M. Butler, *Social Functioning Framework: An Approach to the Human Behavior and Social Environment Sequence* (New York: Council of Social Work Education, 1970).

18. World Health Organization, *Basic Documents,* 37th ed. (Geneva, Switzerland: World Health Organization, 1988), 1.

19. J. E. Tropman, *American Values and Social Welfare: Cultural Contradictions in the Welfare State* (Englewood Cliffs, NJ: Prentice-Hall, 1989).

20. See Organization for Economic Cooperation and Development, *Measuring Social Well-Being: A Progress Report on the Development of Social Indicators* (Paris, France: Organization for Economic Cooperation and Development, 1976), 14.

21. B. Russett's *World Handbook of Political and Social Indicators* (New Haven, CT: Yale University Press, 1964) was probably the first book to use the term *social indicator* in its title.

22. E. Durkheim, *Suicide* (New York: Free Press, 1951); and E. Thorndike, *Your City* (New York: Arno Press, 1976).

23. R. A. Bauer, ed., *Social Indicators* (Cambridge, MA: MIT Press, 1966).

24. For psychological viewpoints and "subjective" approaches, see F. M. Andrews et al., *Social Indicators of Well-Being: America's Perception of Life Quality* (New York: Plenum Press, 1981); N. M. Bradburg, *The Structure of Psychological Well-being* (Chicago: Aldine, 1969); A. Campbell and P. Converse, *The Human Meaning of Social Change* (New York: Russell Sage Foundation, 1992); A. Campbell, P. Converse, and W. Roger, *The Quality of American Life* (New York: Russell Sage Foundation, 1976); B. Strumpel, "Economic Life Styles, Values and Subjective Welfare: An Empirical Approach," in E. B. Sheldon, ed., *Family Income Behavior* (Philadelphia: Lippincott, 1973); B. Strumpel, ed., *Subjective Elements of Well-being* (Paris: Organization for Economic Cooperation and Development, 1974).

25. M. Carley, *Social Measurement and Social Indicators: Issues of Policy and Theory* (Boston: Allen & Unwin, 1981); D. MacRae, *Policy Indicators: Links Between Social Science and Public Debate* (Chapel Hill: University of North Carolina Press, 1985); P. A. Corning, *An Index for the Quality of Life,* paper presented at the 138th meeting of the American Association of Science, December 1971; N. C. Dalkey, *Quality of Life* (Santa Monica, CA: Rand Corporation, 1968); *Report of the National Goals Research Staff: Toward Balanced Growth: Quantity and Quality* (Washington, DC: U.S. Government Printing Office 1970); N. M. Kamrany and A. Christakis, *Social Indicators in Perspective* (Santa Monica, CA: System Development Corporation, 1969); Stanford Research Institute, *Toward Master Social Indicators* (Washington, DC: Department of Health, Education, and Welfare, U.S. Office of Education, Bureau of Research, February 1969); R. J. Estes, *Trends in World Social Development: The Social Progress of Nations* (New York: Praeger, 1988).

26. W. Scott, *Measurement and Analysis of Progress at the Local Level,* Report No. 1 (Geneva, Switzerland: United Nations Research Institute for Social Development, 1978).

27. J. Drewnowski and W. Scott, *The Level of Living Index,* Report No. 4 (Geneva, Switzerland: United Nations Research Institute for Social Development, 1966). See also *United Nations Conference of European Ministers Responsible for Social Welfare* (New York: United Nations, 1972).

28. H. B. Chenery et al., eds., *Redistribution with Growth: Policies to Improve Income Distribution in Developing Countries in the Context of Economic Growth: A Joint StudyCommissioned by The World Bank's Development Research Center and the Institute of Development Studies, University of Essex* (London: Oxford University Press, 1974).

29. Organization for Economic Cooperation and Development, *Measuring Social Well-Being* (Paris, France: OECD Social Indicator Programme, 1976).

30. For essays on the quality of life (nature, scope, and trends), see T. M. Smeeding et al., eds., *Poverty, Inequality, and Income Distribution in a Comparative Perspective: The Luxemburg Income Study (LIS)* (Washington, DC: Urban Institute Press, 1990); ABC-CLIO, *World Quality of Life Indicators* (Santa Barbara, CA: American Bibliographic Center-CLIO, 1989); Commission on Critical Choices for Americans, *Qualities of Life: Critical Choices for Americans* (3 vols.) (Lexington, MA: Heath, 1967); A. Mitchell, T. J. Loqotheti, and R. E. Kantor, *An Approach to Measuring Quality of Life* (Menlo Park, CA: Stanford Research Institute, September 1971); E. R. Morse, *Report on the Social Indicators Conference* (held at George Washington University, sponsored by the National Science Foundation, November 5–6, 1971); and U.S. Environmental Protection Agency, *Quality of Life Indicators* (Washington, DC: Office of Research, Environmental Studies Division, December 1972).

31. Presented to Congress by Secretary Wilbur Cohen. See "Full Opportunity Act—Hearings before the Special Subcommittee on Evaluation and Planning of Social Programs of the Committee on Labor and Public Welfare, U.S. Senate, 91st Congress, 1972," in Environmental Protection Agency, *Quality of Life Indicators* (Washington, DC: U.S. Government Printing Office, 1972).

32. U.S. Environmental Protection Agency, *Quality of Life Indicators* (Washington, DC: Environmental Studies Division, Office of Research and Monitoring, Environmental Protection Agency, December 1972); D. W. Katzner, *Choice and The Quality of Life* (Beverly Hills, CA: Sage, 1979); R. J. Rossi and K. J. Gilmartin, *The Handbook of Social Indicators: Sources, Characteristics, and Analysis* (New York: Garland STPM Press, 1980).

33. The International Bank for Reconstruction and Development, *Social Indicators of Development 1990* (Baltimore, MD: Johns Hopkins University Press and the World Bank, 1991).

34. See the special issue of *Items* on the center's program in *Social Indicators Newsletter* 19 (December 1983).

35. This section reflects ideas in Miles, *Social Indicators for Human Development.*

36. See J. I. de Neufville, *Social Indicators and Public Policy* (New York: Elsevier, 1975); I. L. Horowitz and J. E. Katz, *Social Science and Public Policy in the United States* (New York: Praeger, 1975).

37. G. Gurin, J. Veroff, and S. Feld, *Americans View Their Mental Health* (New York: Arno Press, 1980); and A. Campbell, *The Sense of Well-Being in America: Recent Patterns and Trends* (New York: McGraw-Hill, 1981).

38. See the pioneering cross-national study by H. Cantril, *The Pattern of Human Concerns* (New Brunswick, NJ: Rutgers University Press, 1965); F. M. Andrews and J. B. Withey, *Social Indicators of Well-Being* (New York: Plenum Press, 1976); and research at the Survey Research Center, Institute of Social Research, University of Michigan, particularly the

surveys of A. Campbell et al., *The Quality of American Life* (Ann Arbor: Institute of Social Research, University of Michigan, 1975); A. Campbell et al., *The Quality of American Life: Perceptions, Evaluations, and Satisfactions* (New York: Russell Sage Foundation, 1976); A. Campbell and P. E. Converse, *The Quality of American Life* (Ann Arbor, MI: Inter-University Consortium for Political and Social Research, 1980); A. Campbell, *The Sense of Well-Being in America: Recent Patterns and Trends;* F. M. Andrews, ed., *Research on the Quality of Life* (Ann Arbor: Survey Research Center, Institute for Social Research, University of Michigan, 1986).

39. United Nations Statistical Office, *Toward a System of Social and Demographic Statistics* (New York: United Nations, Statistical Office, 1975).

40. The first volume was W. F. Ogburn, ed., *Recent Social Changes in the United States since the War and Particularly in 1927* (Chicago: University of Chicago Press, 1929).

41. E. B. Sheldon and W. E. Moore, eds., *Indicators of Social Change* (New York: Russell Sage Foundation, 1968); B. M. Gross, ed., *Social Intelligence for America's Future* (Boston: Allyn & Bacon, 1969); A. Campbell and P. E. Converse, eds., *The Human Meaning of Social Change* (New York: Russell Sage Foundation, 1972); U.S. Department of Health, Education, and Welfare, *Toward a Social Report* (Washington, DC: U.S. Government Printing Office, 1969).

42. A. A. Berle, "What GNP Doesn't Tell Us," *Saturday Review,* August 31, 1969.

43. For this notion see Samuelson and Nordhaus, *Economics;* M. Moss, ed., *The Measurement of Economic and Social Performance* (New York: National Bureau of Economic Research, 1973); and W. Nordhaus and J. Tobin, "Is Growth Obsolete?" in *Fiftieth Anniversary Colloquium V,* National Bureau of Economic Research (New York: Columbia University Press, 1972).

44. For measuring poverty in the ideological context, see D. M. Gordon, "Trends in Poverty," in *Problems in Political Economy,* 295–300; R. H. Ropers, *Persistent Poverty* (New York: Plenum Press, Insight Books, 1991); H. R. Rodgers, Jr., and G. Weiher, *Rural Poverty: Special Causes and Policy Reforms* (New York: Greenwood Press, 1989); G. Room, *New Poverty in the European Community* (New York: St. Martin's Press, 1990); B. Williamson et al., *Strategies Against Poverty in America* (New York: Wiley, 1975); D. K. Applebaum, "The Level of the Poverty Line: A Historical Essay," *Social Service Review* 51 (September 1977), 514–523; P. Townsend, "The Measuring of Poverty," *British Journal of Sociology* 13 (1962), 210–227; T. Smeeding, *Cost of Living Differentials at Low Income Levels,* discussion paper 170–174 (Madison: Institute for Research on Poverty, University of Wisconsin, 1974); M. Orshansky, "How Poverty is Measured," *Monthly Labor Review* 92 (February, 1969), 37–41; H. V. Watts, "The Iso-Prop Index: An Approach to the Determination of Differential Poverty Income Thresholds," *Journal of Human Resources* 2 (Winter 1967), 3–18; S. Mancher, "The Problem of Measuring Poverty," in Roach and Roach, eds., *Poverty* (Baltimore: Penguin Books, 1972), and *Boston Globe,* March 15, 1979; M. Sherraden, *Assets and the Poor: A New American Welfare Policy* (Armonk, NY: Sharp, 1991); E. Weisband, ed., *Poverty Amidst Plenty* (San Francisco: Westview Press, 1989); H. R. Rodgers, Jr., ed., *Beyond Welfare* (Armonk, NY: Sharp, 1988); S. A. Hewlett, *When the Bough Breaks* (New York: Basic Books, 1991).

45. S. L. Zimmerman, "State-Local Public Policy as a Predictor of Individual and Family Well-Being," *Women and Health* 12(3–4) (1989), 161–188.

46. J. Griffin, *Well-Being: Its Meaning, Measurement, and Moral Importance* (New York: Clarendon Press, 1987); R. J. Wheeler, *General Well-Being Questionnaire Manual* (St. Louis: Health Line, 1985); P. Marris and M. Rein, *Dilemmas of Social Reform* (New York: Atherton Press, 1967); D. J. Jones, *Prescriptions and Policies: The Social Well-Being of African Americans in the 1990s* (New Brunswick, NJ: Transaction Publishers, 1991).

Choices Are the Challenge

"Is This the Best America Can Do?

Every 12 seconds of the school day, an American child drops out (380,000 a year).

Every 13 seconds, an American child is reported abused or neglected (2.7 million a year).

Every 26 seconds, an American child runs away from home (1.2 million a year).

About every minute, an American teenager has a baby.

Every 9 minutes, an American child is arrested for a drug offense.

Every 40 minutes, an American child is arrested for drunken driving.

Every 53 minutes in our rich land, an American child dies from poverty.

Every 3 hours, a child is murdered."[1]

Modern society and social workers face a great challenge: to choose social policies that foster the growth and development of all citizens, groups, and communities. What kind of society do we really want?

The choices concern social policy in the context of broader societal concerns: a society's goals, how it should organize its institutional structure to implement these goals, and how it should distribute its achievements. Social workers believe that some types of societal organization are better suited to satisfying human needs than others. The choice of optimal organizational patterns and social policies that increase well-being is crucial. This book has presented issues and alternatives for readers to weigh critically and ultimately to select as most beneficial for their clients and for the society in which they live.

The quality of life of all citizens is increasingly a fundamental public and professional concern. Inescapably, social workers have to make critical professional and personal choices about social change. The election of Ronald Reagan and George Bush to the presidency set the tone for a radical departure from the responsive philosophy, societal organization, and social policies of the 1960s and 1970s. Before these policies could effect the transition to greater self-determination by the needy and powerless, the new political Right moved vigorously to reduce federal spending in many categories of social support and to shift the primary responsibility for the poor and disadvantaged to states and localities. This shift in public policy was designed to increase allocations for defense, to cut social programs, and to cut taxes to benefit the rich. Inequality of income and wealth, poverty, and powerlessness increased while investments in the growth of human capital decreased.

Choices have to be made between responsive social policy and policies based on the new political Right's assumptions that government's fiscal burdens are too heavy, that the beleaguered American taxpayer should not be expected to bear the cost of social change, that citizens should become more vigilant about fiscal decision-making, and that power should be concentrated in the elite. These policies implicitly reject the social transformation ideology, democracy, and citizenship rights of advanced welfare states.

Choices must also be made about the role of government in modern society. Did the government's power lessen in the 1980s or did it increase? Did federal defense spending continue to escalate? Did the federal government bail out troubled banks, did states bail out troubled localities, and did states and localities invent or extend user fees and public enterprises and consolidate their operations in lieu of raising property taxes? If well-being has a strict priority over other political goals, then all people have the right to optimal need satisfaction based on the best available knowledge. Social workers stress the importance of individuals being able to explore their physical, emotional, and intellectual capabilities in optimal ways. To do so, they must have the right to maximum self-determination (provided that it does not violate the basic needs of others). This means that the private domain must be regulated in some way by democratic public authority through a democratic social contract. The welfare state can provide a variety of public resources to give citizens access to welfare entitlements based on citizenship rights that conform to social work commitments and Rawls's principles of justice. Does any institutional body other than the state have the power and resources to do so? Is any further extension of the power of the state an anathema, as asserted by those who criticize the traditional welfare state's ability to optimize well-being? Social workers need to choose and define the responsibility of the state and explain why it is so crucial to social work's vision of the necessary conditions for human liberation.

Has our emphasis on personal autonomy generated a strong form of individualism that denies the role of the social and its place in promoting well-being? Social workers must choose which societal preconditions must be met for institutions to survive over long periods, thus ensuring an environment within which individuality can evolve. What are the social dimensions of individual autonomy and self-determination?

The conceptualization and implementation of social policy should not be left exclusively to the powerful in society—to the elite, who want to preserve the status quo and profit from the market, and to governmental bureaucrats. Social workers have the knowledge and skills to understand the development of individuals and communities. They should guide the definition and evaluation of social policy and through citizen participation engage in social action for social change.

A decade of unrestrained capitalism has demonstrated that the economic market will not solve society's problems of justice and fairness. Some believe the market causes these problems, including poverty and unemployment, an antiquated health care system, a polluted environment, lackluster schools, homelessness, insufficient and overpriced housing, crime, and drug addiction. Clearly, alternatives must be critically reviewed and new choices must be made. Likewise, now that decades of communism in Central and Eastern European countries have demonstrated that statism, centralization, and dictatorship will not solve society's problems, alternatives to communism must be reviewed and new choices made.

Now more than ever, new choices for social policy and societal change are especially crucial for human development. Social workers have a professional responsibility to make such choices and to participate in the broader societal debate to resolve issues of social change.

NOTE

1. From Children's Defense Fund, *The State of America's Children, 1992* (Washington, DC: 1992), x.

Index

TO THE OWNER OF THIS BOOK:

We hope that you have found *Social Policy: Institutional Context of Social Develoment and Human Services* useful. So that this book can be improved in a future edition, would you take the time to complete this sheet and return it? Thank you.

School and address: _____

Department: _____

Instructor's name: _____

1. What I like most about this book is: _____

_____

2. What I like least about this book is: _____

_____

3. My general reaction to this book is: _____

_____

4. The name of the course in which I used this book is: _____

_____

5. Were all of the chapters of the book assigned for you to read? _____

If not, which ones weren't? _____

_____

6. In the space below, or on a separate sheet of paper, please write specific suggestions for improving this book and anything else you'd care to share about your experience in using the book.

_____

_____

_____

_____

_____

_____

Optional:

Your name: _____ Date: _____

May Brooks/Cole quote you either in promotion for *Social Policy: Institutional Context of Social Development and Human Services* or in future publishing ventures?

Yes: _____ No: _____

Sincerely,

Demetrius Iatridis

Brooks/Cole is dedicated to publishing quality publications for education in the human services fields. If you are interested in learning more about our publications, please fill in your name and address and request our latest catalogue, using this prepaid mailer.

Name: _____

Street Address: _____

City, State, and Zip: _____

FOLD HERE

FOLD HERE